MW00580681

"This is my horse."

NIGEL TUFNEL: Now this is special, too, it's a . . . look, see, still got the ol' tag on it. See, never even played it.

MOVIE DIRECTOR MARTY DiBERGI: You just bought it and . . .

TUFNEL: Don't touch it! Don't touch it! No one, no one, no! Don't touch it!

DiBERGI: Well, I wasn't, uh, I wasn't gonna touch it. I was just pointing at it.

TUFNEL: Well, don't point, even.

DiBERGI: Don't even point?

TUFNEL: No. It can't be played . . . never.

DiBERGI: Can I look at it?

TUFNEL: No.

—This Is Spinal Tap

"All the Americans will wish they could play on this guitar! At least it's got tone, you can hear the chords like you can on the piano. Don't talk to me any more about their tinpot guitars! Listen to this, it speaks like a cathedral!"

—DJANGO REINHARDT

"Right after I'd seen Steve Winwood playing his white Strat, I was in Nashville, and I went into this shop called Sho-Bud where they had stacks of Strats going for virtually nothing because they were so unfashionable and so unwanted. I bought a big pile of them all for a song—they were really cheap, like $300 or $400 each—and I took them home and gave them out. . . . I made Blackie out of a group of them: I took the pickups out of one, the scratchplate off another, and the neck off another and I made my own guitar— a hybrid guitar that had all the best bits from all these Strats. . . . What makes Blackie unique for me is the fact that I made it! It was one of the last guitars that I actually built myself, really. Therefore it felt like it was invested with some kind of soul, you know."

—ERIC CLAPTON

"It doesn't have any dead spots or any high spots—which is very, very strange. It makes it fun to play lead, because you don't have to worry where you're at. It's not much of a solo instrument, but I can't really play by myself worth a darn, so it doesn't make much of a difference."

—DAVE RAWLINGS

"I used to play a place called Twist, Arkansas, on weekends, mostly at the beginning of my career. It got quite cold in Twist, so they would take a big garbage can, half-fill it with kerosene, and light that fuel for heat. One night in 1949 two guys got to fighting, and one of them knocked the other over on that container and it spilled on the floor. It looked like a river of fire. Everybody started running for the front door, including B. B. King. But when I got outside, I realized that I left my guitar, a Gibson acoustic, and I went back for it. When I did, the building started to collapse around me. I almost lost my life trying to save my guitar. The next morning we found out that the two guys had been fighting about a lady. I never did meet her, but I learned her name was Lucille. So I named my guitar—and every guitar I had since then—Lucille, to remind me never to do a thing like that again."

—B. B. KING

"There's no reason for my guitar being called Micawber, apart from the fact that it's such an unlikely name. There's no one around me called Micawber, so when I scream for Micawber, everyone knows what I'm talking about."

—KEITH RICHARDS

"I joke that I should just have a collection of Jazzmasters and Jaguars. I can do pretty much anything, get any sound from my Jazzmasters and I don't need another guitar."

—NELS CLINE

"She's a '59 Stratocaster. I've always called her my first wife. And she don't talk back to me, she talks for me. She don't scream at me, she screams for me."

—STEVIE RAY VAUGHAN

ULTIMATE

THE GUITARS

EXPANDED EDITION

STAR GUITARS
THAT ROCKED THE WORLD

DAVE HUNTER

chartwell
books

Quarto

For Jess, Freddie, and Flo. Thanks for putting up with all the noise.

Acquiring Editor: Dennis Pernu
Project Manager: Madeleine Vasaly
Art Director: James Kegley

Cover Designer: James Kegley
Layout: Simon Larkin

On the frontispiece: Brian Setzer and one of his Gretsch 6120s. *Robert Knight Archive/ Redferns/Getty Images*

Printed in China

CONTENTS

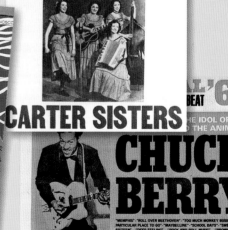

ACKNOWLEDGMENTS

OUR THANKS TO Mary Katherine Aldin; Rob Alford; Jim Altieri; Jean-Marc Anglès; Alain Antonietto; Lee Bolton; Travis Bone; Brian Blauser; Peter Cardoso; Jaime Cervantes; Steph Chernikowski; Barry Cleveland at *Guitar Player* magazine; Nels Cline; Bobby Cochran; Bonnie Gallup Creef; Stacy Curtis and Mile 44; Dick Dale and Matt Marshall; Michael DeKay; Dan Erlewine; Kevin Estrada; Jon Flannery and Powerhouse Factories; Bob Frank; Thomas Gage; Billy F Gibbons; Robert Gordon; Steve Gorospe; Rick Gould; Justin Hampton; Jim Heath; Annie Heller-Gutwillig; Peter Hince; Jefferson Holland; Justice Howard; Bruce Iglauer at Alligator Records; Takeshi Imura at P-Vine Records; Rob Jones; Les Kippel and Relix International; Chris Kro; Gary Kroman; John Lackey; Jenny Lens; Benjamin Levin at TMMI; Ben Marcus; Robert Matheu; Ward Meeker at *Vintage Guitar* magazine; Jay Michael; Scotty Moore; Philip Morris; Nigel Osborne; Les Paul; David Perry; Steve Pitkin; Bonnie Raitt (along with Common Ground Relief, New Orleans Habitat for Humanity, and the New Orleans Musicians' Assistance Fund); Arlen Roth; Jay Allen Sanford at Revolutionary Comics; John Seman at EMP; Rob Servo; Todd Slater; A. Micah Smith; Tiffany Steffens at Monotone Inc.; John "Four-Oh Ford" Sticha; Jason Verlinde and the crew at *The Fretboard Journal*; Patrice Verrier at Le Musée de la Musique; "TV" Tom Vickers; Jack White; Chris Williams; and Richie Wiseman.

INTRODUCTION

WELCOME TO THE MOST COMPREHENSIVE COMPENDIUM OF REAL-WORLD WORKHORSE GUITARS you're likely to lay your mitts on. If you're looking for museum pieces, you've come to the wrong place, although I'm convinced you'll find the subjects within these pages far more exciting than any glass-cased collector's item ever could be. *Ultimate Star Guitars* is about guitars in action, instruments bent by the greatest practitioners to that rare alchemy that turns this world, for three to five minutes at a time, into a place of utter beauty and wonder.

Most guitarists are fascinated by the charms of vintage and collectible guitars, but put those guitars in the hands of the leading players of the past ninety years and our interest intensifies to an entirely new dimension. The stories of those enduring partnerships—of how the magic struck and the pairs bonded, guitarist to guitar—are told in intimate detail within these pages. These are the stories of the guitars that many of the leading rock, blues, jazz, folk, country, and alternative guitarists have used to ply their trade, and as such

(although many have inevitably ended up in the hands of collectors) they are the very antithesis of "collection pieces." They are tools that have been used, and used hard, day in and day out, to create groundbreaking and crowd-pleasing music.

In celebrating these guitars, *Ultimate Star Guitars*, which adds thirty-five new profiles to my original *Star Guitars* of 2010, is unusual and unique among guitar books. This isn't a list of "best guitarists," nor is it a compilation of "best guitars." You'll find plenty of both here, certainly, and the two cross paths on many occasions. All of the instruments here have made the cut, however, by virtue of that special bond between *player* and *playee*: bring to mind any of the artists featured here, and a very specific guitar or model of guitar (or in some cases, a few of them) is likely to come to mind right along with them. However valuable any collectible guitar might have become, its intrinsic value is really very little when separated from its ability to make music. This book puts the craftsmen and their tools back together

and applauds them as a unit. It explores, wherever possible, how these guitars were acquired, what drew the artists to them, how and why they have been modified, and the intricacies of the specific sounds they have brought to the music—all to the end of better understanding how that partnership works.

These instruments might be beat up, modified, or simply not that impressive when viewed out of the context in which we find them here, but they have been *played*, and played like hell, in the course of forging much of the most exciting work in popular culture. Sure, there are plenty of great guitarists who have jumped between instruments without forging a noteworthy bond with any particular guitar and who have made incredible music in the process. That's all well and good—but they're not included here.

Many of the guitars in this book would be valuable vintage pieces in their own right: the Les Pauls played by Michael Bloomfield, Peter Green, and Billy F Gibbons; the Stratocasters played by Hank Marvin and Mark Knopfler; Eric Clapton's ES-335; Brian Setzer's Gretsch 6120; Roy Buchanan's Fender Telecaster; Elvis Presley's Martin D-18; and

many others would all be highly collectible t if their associated artists had never laid hand them. Others, quite frankly, would not be, bu Cobain's modified Fender Mustang, Reverend Heat's Japanese-made reissue Gretsch 6120, E Van Halen's cobbled-together "Frankenstrat," White's Airline Res-O-Glas, and Prince's Hoh HG490—these artists' use of these guitars ma fascinating instruments to consider. And still from Neil Young's 1953 Les Paul to Lonnie Ma 1958 Flying V, Thurston Moore's and Lee Ran assorted Jazzmasters, and Gatemouth Brown's '60s Firebird—show the lengths to which gifte players will go to tweak their beloved guitars sonic and ergonomic perfection, even while d them as "collector items" in anyone else's han

Sure, the mint-condition museum piece i a wonder to behold, but give me a hard-loved, played workhorse any day. After years of mak music, the beauty of these beasts runs far mor just skin deep: their battle scars and playing v reveal the heart and soul of the most moving a in all of popular culture.

The Duane Allman 1959 Cherry Sunburst Les Paul, as issued by the Gibson Custom Shop in 2013. *Gibson Musical Instruments*

DURING HIS TRAGICALLY BRIEF LIFE and career, Duane Allman bought, borrowed, and swapped so many guitars that it has often been difficult to document which model appears on what studio recording. What is beyond a doubt, however, is how the best-remembered examples of his touch and tone are classic Les Paul—and that's the guitar with which he will always be most closely associated. As part of a project conducted for Gibson (documented alongside the release of the Custom Shop Duane Allman Cherry Sunburst '59 Les Paul in 2013), guitarist and Country Songwriter Hall of Fame inductee Lee Roy Parnell wove together the threads of a scattered, myth-riddled story to give credit to what he concluded was Allman's most-recorded guitar.

Duane and 'burst perform with the Allman Brothers at Spartanburg, South Carolina, October 1970. *Michael Ochs Archives/Getty Images*

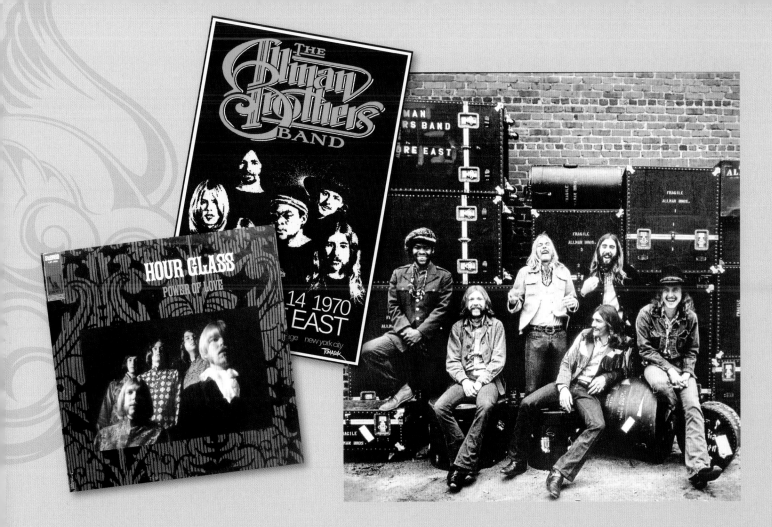

"We believe that this particular guitar [the '59 Cherry Sunburst Les Paul] was the one that Duane had used most often to record and perform live," Parnell told Gibson. "However, because Duane's life and career were so short, much of his fame was coming just as he passed away. There are a lot of pictures of Duane over a short period of time, which made it difficult to determine which guitar he was playing on any given recording." For some, Allman is most associated with the tobacco-sunburst Les Paul that makes an appearance in a great many of those pictures, but the current thinking—from Parnell, and other corners—is that the majority of Allman's most notable recordings were done on the cherry 'burst, a guitar he owned during a period of heavy studio activity (brief though it might have been), before acquiring the tobacco-burst LP. Allman also frequently played a goldtop 1957 Les Paul early in his career with the band, which he swapped to guitarist Rick Stine of the band Stone Balloon for the '59 with cherry sunburst, just a week before the latter made its Allman Brothers debut at the Fillmore East in New York City on September 23, 1970.

Whatever the history, and whichever guitar was used when and where, the sound of Allman's playing has long been held up as a prime example of superlative Les Paul tone. Listen to any of Allman's most notable recordings—live or in the studio—and tracks like "Whipping Post," "Melissa," "Midnight Rider," and "One Way Out"—or Derek & the Dominoes' "Layla," for that matter—exhibit iconic old-school Les Paul tone. Duane's touch, dynamics, and unbridled musicianship resulted in a tone that was never particularly heavy or overdistorted but always brimming with character. Of course, he had a little help from a 50-watt Marshall head or a 100-watt Fender Showman (and sometimes both), plus the glass Coricidin medicine bottle that he used for slide—and a certain lead-guitar partner by the name of Dickey Betts. Allman also liked to "top wrap" his strings around the Les Paul's stopbar tailpiece, enabling the bar to be adjusted down tight to the guitar's top—a practice still used today by guitarists who feel it enhances resonance and sustain. Duane Allman died in a motorcycle crash in Macon, Georgia, on October 28, 1971. ★

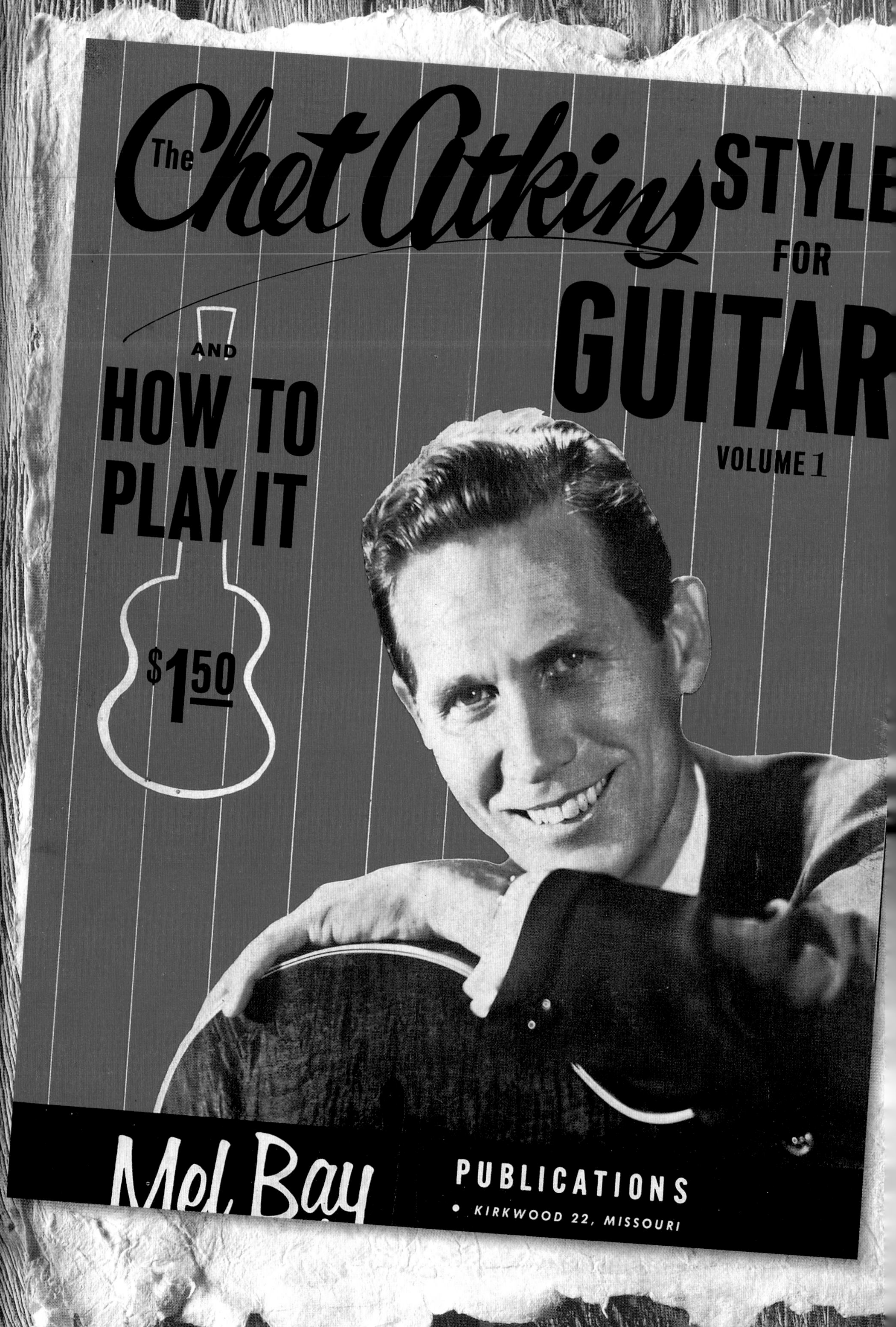

The **Chet Atkins** STYLE
FOR
GUITAR

VOLUME 1

AND
HOW TO
PLAY IT

$1.50

Mel Bay

PUBLICATIONS
• KIRKWOOD 22, MISSOURI

ARTIST SIGNATURE MODELS are pretty routine today, but an added dose of respect and awe is owed to the few artists who *originated* legendary electric guitars, not only by putting their names on them, but by collaborating in the design efforts too. In this respect, Chet Atkins is right up there toward the top, arguably exceeded only by Les Paul and the Gibson that bears his name.

Gretsch got an early foothold in the rock 'n' roll business—even before the term, or the music it defined, was in wide circulation—with its "solid-body" (actually semi-solid) Duo Jet of 1953 and its flash-colored siblings of 1954: the Silver Jet and Jet Firebird, and the Cadillac Green Country Club model of the same year. But the New York–based guitar maker wanted a hip young guitar star to rival Gibson's star endorsee, so it wooed Atkins, then a Nashville ace.

Chet Atkins's 1955 Gretsch Model 6120. This is one of several guitars sent to Mr. Guitar by Gretsch and kept throughout his life. An early example of the 6120, it featured a different control setup and six-saddle bridge. *Courtesy Nigel Osborne/Jawbone Press*

A 1957 Gretsch ad featuring Mr. Guitar playing the Chet Atkins solid-body version of the Model 6120, soon to become the Model 6122 Round Up.

CHET ATKINS AT HOME

RCA VICTOR
LPM-1544

HUM and **STRUM** along with **CHET ATKINS**

LPM-2025

RCA VICTOR

Gretsch originally sought Atkins's name to capitalize on his popularity in the country and western market, and the original 6120 Chet Atkins Hollow Body of 1954 carried the cowboy-junk "G" brand, steer's head inlay, and Southwestern-themed fingerboard inlay engravings that the company hoped would help it achieve this. None of these were to the star's liking, although the Bigsby tailpiece and general dimensions were all arrived at with his consultation. Atkins, nevertheless, promoted the guitar as offered, although the Western-kitsch decorative touches disappeared from the 6120 over the next couple of years. Which is just as well: Although born wearing the name of a major country star, the 6120 Chet Atkins Hollow Body was becoming a prime mover in the rock 'n' roll boom. While the bright yet meaty DeArmond pickups suited Atkins's fluid, virtuosic picking well enough, they suited biting, snarly rock 'n' roll even better, particularly when the amp was cranked up a little further.

Atkins's personal taste in guitars evolved, but the single-cutaway 6120 of the mid- to late '50s remained fixed in stone as a rock 'n' roll icon. Rather like Les Paul over at rival Gibson, Atkins couldn't resist tinkering with the foundations of the original design. Also like Paul, Atkins's tastes didn't always converge with those of the guitar-buying public. His desire for a smoother, quieter pickup with less magnetic pull on the strings spawned the Filter'Tron humbucker from the bench of tech/inventor Ray Butts and proved to be a significant development. And while his suggestions of thinning the guitar's body, giving it twin cutaways, and eliminating the f-holes to help reduce feedback proved popular with many players, later contraptions such as the Super Chet of 1972 and the Chet Atkins Super Axe of 1977 (with onboard effects circuitry) were considered abominations by many guitarists and certainly as odd as Les Paul's beloved low-impedance Artist, Personal, and Recording models over at Gibson.

Regardless of what it and its namesake spawned down the years though, the original 6120 Chet Atkins Hollow Body lives on as a classic of rock 'n' roll *and* country. ★

1959 FENDER STRATOCASTER "THE LEGEND" RANDY BACHMAN

Bachman and "The Legend" take care of business, circa 1975.
Chris Walter/WireImage/Getty Images

6167 025
Stereo
mercury

BACHMANN TURNER OVERDRIV

You Ain't Seen Nothin' Yet
Free Wheelin'

CANNED WHEAT

PACKED BY

THE GUESS WHO

ANOTHER PROUD PRAIRIE PRODUCT

THERE'S A SAYING AMONG HOT RODDERS that anyone can build a hot rod, but it takes a real man to cut one up. This old adage refers, of course, to the act of taking torch and hacksaw to rare, vintage tin with the intention modifying it to do things that Henry Ford never intended.

When it comes to guitars, Randy Bachman is a first-class hot rodder.

Though he often has been seen taking care of business with a Gibson Les Paul and is known as one of the world's foremost collectors of Gretsch instruments, Bachman is also closely associated with the Fender Stratocaster, thanks to a guitar known as "the Legend." Bachman, founder of Canadian rock giants The Guess Who and Bachman-Turner Overdrive, obtained The Legend in the late 1960s. It had already been modified a bit by a previous owner, but Bachman was fearless when it came to laying the thing down on his workbench and applying chisel, saw, and sundry other tools, all in an effort to make the guitar do what he wanted it to do—things Leo never intended. As Bachman told photographer Rick Gould:

Originally a black '59 Strat, the Legend was stripped to bare wood. The upper horn had my name in rub-on decals as well as a round metal Titano accordion logo. The guitar had been modded to be a nine-string and had extra tuners on it, which I took off, leaving three extra holes in the headstock. Also, the big curved part on the headstock had broken off when I threw the guitar into a speaker cabinet à la Pete Townshend. I also broke off the wang bar and had to redrill the tremolo block to accommodate a bigger screw-in arm that I had made by a blacksmith. It was a "T" with an arm to grab over the pickups and a big one that went out back past the strap attachment. This allowed for extreme Hendrixian wang-bar tactics with feedback.

In the back, I chiseled out a long channel, thinking I could create my own B-bender by cutting out the B saddle, stabilizing the trem block, and keeping just one spring on the cutout B saddle. Then I found out I couldn't hacksaw the trem block so I just left it.

When the nut broke to pieces, I didn't have a replacement so I used my mother's metal knitting needle. It didn't have grooves and it was cool how the strings slid around for low bending. I sanded and steel-wooled the back of the neck like a violin neck with no finish, which made playing such an ease.

I reversed the innie jack to be an outie, which I thought Fender always should have done anyway because it allows bigger jacks and L jacks to be easily used.

If it seems like all this gouging and soldering made the Legend a Stratocaster in name only, you ain't seen nothin' yet. Reportedly, the guitar also featured a swapped-in rounder-profile Fender Jazzmaster neck and three on-off pots in place of the usual three-position selector, allowing Bachman to combine any two pickups, including the bridge and neck units.

Bachman: "My bridge pickup was a '50s Tele that was held to the pickguard with clear bathtub caulking, which prevented feedback and squeal. I had a Rickenbacker pickup at the neck for a while and then a '59 Humbucker. The last mod was three off/on pickup switches that allowed for an amazing combination of pickups—neck and bridge, all three, bridge and middle, neck and middle, et cetera. Problem? Yes. I was too wild onstage and would hit them all. Of course the guitar would have no sound because all the pickups had been switched off."

"There's something about the Strat sound that just rings out," Bachman wrote in his book, *Vinyl Tap Stories.* "If you take that same guitar and run it through a small tweed Fender amp cranked right up, you get a really great bluesy sound."

As for The Legend, sadly it went the way of many other hard-touring rock 'n' roll axes: Bachman reports that it was stolen. "It would be the thrill of a lifetime to get the guitar back, but it was just a wreck, so unless someone knows what it is . . .," he said. "But what a sound and monster it was." ★

—*Dennis Pernu*

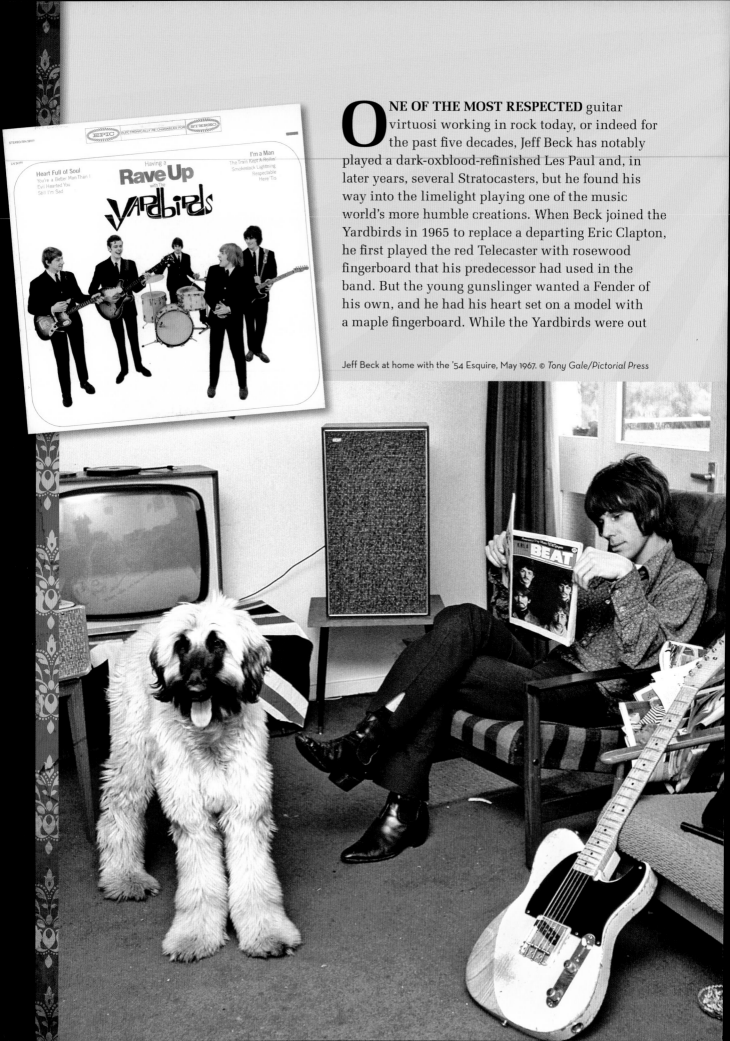

I'm a Man
The Train Kept A-Rollin'
Smokestack Lightning
Respectable
Here 'Tis

Heart Full of Soul
You're a Better Man Than I
Evil Hearted You
Still I'm Sad

Having a
Rave Up
with The
yardbirds

ONE OF THE MOST RESPECTED guitar virtuosi working in rock today, or indeed for the past five decades, Jeff Beck has notably played a dark-oxblood-refinished Les Paul and, in later years, several Stratocasters, but he found his way into the limelight playing one of the music world's more humble creations. When Beck joined the Yardbirds in 1965 to replace a departing Eric Clapton, he first played the red Telecaster with rosewood fingerboard that his predecessor had used in the band. But the young gunslinger wanted a Fender of his own, and he had his heart set on a model with a maple fingerboard. While the Yardbirds were out

Jeff Beck at home with the '54 Esquire, May 1967. © Tony Gale/Pictorial Press

on tour with the Walker Brothers, Beck talked John Walker (real name John Maus) into selling him his own '54 Esquire, and over the course of the following year he applied this simple tool to some of the most groundbreaking playing the rock and pop worlds had yet witnessed, in the process making it one of the most recognizable electric guitars in history.

The guitar forever after referred to as "Jeff Beck's Esquire"—although it was in his possession for a relatively short time—is known for its deep forearm and ribcage contours, heavily scarred finish, and black pickguard. Maus himself sanded these contours in the guitar's body to give it more of the playing comfort of a Stratocaster, which was built with such contours at the factory, although the Yardbirds' heavy touring and recording schedule across the US and the UK from 1965 to early 1966 certainly contributed further wear to the body. This Esquire was actually an early whiteguard model, as seen in photos and film footage of Beck playing with the Yardbirds shortly after acquiring it, but the artist replaced the white plastic pickguard with a blackguard to give it the look of an earlier model.

As simple an instrument as this one-pickup Fender is, Jeff Beck bent it to a dizzying range of innovative performances. His creative use of the Esquire's volume and tone controls helped to craft ear-catching guitar parts on songs such as "Train Kept A Rollin'." He ran it through a Sola Sound Tone Bender fuzz pedal on "Heart Full of Soul" and just *thranged* it for all it was worth on "I'm a Man." Like so many great players, however, Beck only ever regarded the Esquire, or any of his other significant guitars, as a tool for making music, and he clearly held little sentimental regard for this legendary instrument. In 1966 he acquired a Gibson Les Paul and largely retired the Esquire for the short time he had left with the Yardbirds. In the mid-'70s, likely returning the favor of a Telecaster that Seymour Duncan modified with humbucking pickups to give to him, Beck gave the famously contoured '54 Esquire to the budding pickup designer as a gift, and it has remained in Duncan's possession ever since. ✪

While Yardbirds bandmates were seen with new Vox designs in this 1965 TV appearance, Beck was filmed with his 1954 Esquire. He had already swapped the white pickguard for a blackguard. *Michael Ochs Archives/Getty Images*

Petra Niemeier/K & K/Redferns/Getty Images

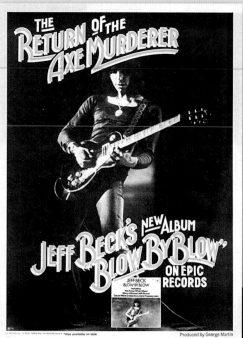

AS A YOUNG YARDBIRD, Jeff Beck began his career on Fender Telecasters and Esquires—and has come full semicircle to a Strat in his later solo work—but many fans will forever associate him with the thick, creamy Les Paul tone that formed the meat of much of his earlier playing in between. Beck bought his first Les Paul, a 1958 model with a deep sunburst finish, in 1966 at Selmer's in London, the same music shop where Keith Richards acquired his '59 Les Paul a few years before. In addition to using it prominently with the Yardbirds before departing that outfit, Beck played the guitar on much of the Jeff Beck Group's 1968 debut *Truth*, featuring it on songs like "Happenings Ten Years Time Ago," "Beck's Bolero," and "Over, Under, Sideways, Down."

Beck and the unusual '54 Les Paul he stumbled upon at Strings and Things one day in the early 1970s. *Robert Knight Archive/Redferns/Getty Images*

Through Beck's ownership of the guitar, its looks gradually evolved to fit the fads of the day: it lost its pickup covers to reveal two double-cream PAFs (a modification thought to induce improved high-end response), then was stripped of its characteristic sunburst top finish (a bid to enhance the wood's resonance). Sometime later, this first Beck Les Paul was damaged during a US tour, and it was replaced by another '58 Les Paul with a dramatically figured flame-maple top, which stood in for the damaged original until the Jeff Beck Group's demise in 1969.

For all these original late-'50s 'bursts, though, the guitarist is probably most often associated with modified '54 Les Paul that might have appeared a down-and-out working dog to some players of the day, but which spoke to the artist deeply. While recording in Memphis, Tennessee, in the early '70s, Beck paid a visit to the popular Strings and Things guitar store to check out the stock. He was captivated by a 1954 Les Paul that a customer had dropped in for some very specific modifications. One request was that its original goldtop be refinished to a deep chocolate brown, a color that turned out to exhibit some oxblood tints in certain light. Other modifications included the installation of full-size humbucking pickups in place of the P-90s, altering the full and rounded early-'50s neck shape to a slightly thinner profile, and changing the original tuners for modern replacements. Legend has it that the customer didn't like the results . . . but Jeff Beck did. He bought the adulterated Les Paul, played it extensively on tour and in the studio, and even gave it pride of place on the cover of his milestone 1975 album *Blow by Blow*.

While much of Beck's playing in the 1970s exhibits the incendiary tone that was common to Les Paul–dom that decade, much of it is also snappy, round, and lithe, and more akin to the semi-clean blues-rock tones prominent in the previous decade. Ultimately, all three of these Les Pauls have contributed to the work of an artist whom many fans still regard as one of the most skilled guitarists in the broad genre of rock-fusion. In 2009, the Gibson Custom Shop released its own tribute to the modified '54 goldtop as the Jeff Beck Oxblood Les Paul. ★

Beck's modified '54 goldtop, with chocolate-brown "oxblood" finish. *Backbeat UK/Outline Press*

Michael Ochs Archives/Getty Images

COUNTLESS GREAT RIFFS have fired up electrified music over the years, but if we were to choose just one to play to a landing party of benign, guitar-loving aliens in an effort to define the sound of rock 'n' roll, it would have to be the driving double stops that rev up the intro to Chuck Berry's "Johnny B. Goode." Hell, though . . . I guess you'd go on ahead and play them the entire song, then you'd play "Roll Over Beethoven," "Rock and Roll Music," and "Reelin' and Rockin'," explaining how this great originator morphed twelve-bar blues progressions into something the kids could groove to. Finally you'd throw in "Maybellene" to give a nod to country music's influence on Berry, and when they asked what was making that unearthly sound, you'd say, "Well, *that* is a Gibson ES-350T."

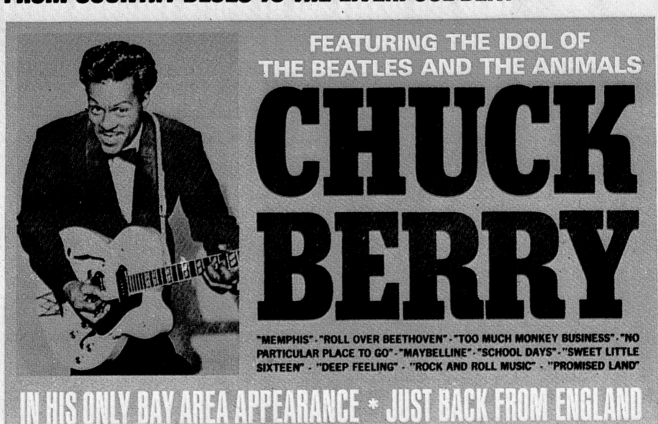

BLUES FESTIVAL '65
FROM COUNTRY BLUES TO THE LIVERPOOL BEAT

FEATURING THE IDOL OF
THE BEATLES AND THE ANIMALS

CHUCK BERRY

"MEMPHIS" · "ROLL OVER BEETHOVEN" · "TOO MUCH MONKEY BUSINESS" · "NO PARTICULAR PLACE TO GO" · "MAYBELLINE" · "SCHOOL DAYS" · "SWEET LITTLE SIXTEEN" · "DEEP FEELING" · "ROCK AND ROLL MUSIC" · "PROMISED LAND"

IN HIS ONLY BAY AREA APPEARANCE · JUST BACK FROM ENGLAND

A 1965 poster used an early promotional image of Berry. By the time of these gigs, Berry had switched to Gibson's semi-hollow double cutaways, usually the ES-355. *GAB Archive/Redferns/Getty Images*

Facing page: Berry gives one of his ES-350Ts the A-OK backstage at the Star Club, Hamburg, Germany. *K & K Ulf Kruger OHG/Redferns/Getty Images*

Berry has long had a reputation for being a hardnosed entrepreneur, and who can blame a musician who came up in an era when too many promoters and label execs would fleece an artist for all they were worth, given half a chance? This down-to-business ethos extended to his guitars, and Berry has gone from one to the other with little sentimentality. As he told Tom Wheeler in *Guitar Player* magazine (1988), when one wore out, he would "Get a new one! Uh, deductible, you know—tools!" From the early '60s Berry took up with Gibson's newer double-cutaway semi-hollow models, usually the up-market ES-355, but the instruments that powered those great mid- and late-'50s sides were Gibson ES-350Ts, first the early models with P-90 pickups, then the versions loaded with PAF humbuckers that arrived in mid-1957.

Introduced in 1955 alongside the Byrdland and the ES-225T, the ES-350T was the mid-range model in this trio of Gibson's first thinline hollow-body electrics, a style introduced to make the full-depth archtop electric a little less cumbersome for players who still wanted the look and amplified tone of that breed. Still deeper than the thinline semi-hollows that would follow, the ES-350T's reduced air space did help quell feedback to some extent and sharpened the sound through an amp (something the guitar's laminated maple top also aided). The decreased body depth also came with a shorter, 23.5-inch scale length and slimmer neck dimensions, features that might be considered unsuitable to a lanky, long-fingered guitarist, but which apparently didn't slow Berry down any.

Whether loaded with P-90s or humbuckers (both Gibson units had similar output levels in the mid- to late '50s), these ES-350Ts could induce some sting and grind in most combo amps of the day, and the guitar tone in the fills and solos of early tunes such as "Thirty Days," "Maybellene," and "Oh Baby Doll" certainly exhibit some bite. Add together the tone, the rhythmic momentum, the licks, and the street-poet lyrics, and rock 'n' roll couldn't have asked for a more expressive founding father. ♠

Eric Clapton and Keith Richards with their ES-350Ts at Berry's Los Angeles home during the filming of the 1987 documentary *Hail! Hail! Rock 'n' Roll. Terry O'Neill/Getty Images*

Jimmy Page plays an ES-350T said to have once belonged to Chuck Berry. The occasion is Led Zeppelin's rehearsal for their appearance at the Ahmet Ertegun tribute concert at London's O2 Arena, December 9, 2007. *Ross Halfin/Getty Images*

Berry poses with an ES-350T equipped with the PAF humbuckers that replaced the model's single-coils in 1957. *Michael Ochs Archives/Getty Images*

Blackmore with Deep Purple, circa 1973. *Ian Dickson/Redferns/Getty Images*

Rainbow

"Long Live Rock'n'Roll"

RAINBOW

STRAIGHT BETWEEN THE EYES

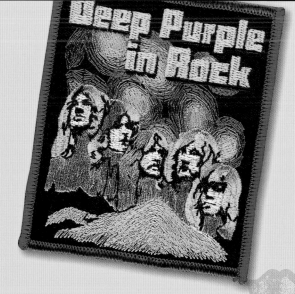

OFTEN TOUTED BY DEVOTEES of the form as the original god of the über-metal solo, Ritchie Blackmore kept the Fender Stratocaster in the fold when most stadium rockers where turning to the fatter tones of Gibson Les Pauls, SGs, and Flying Vs to pound their Marshall stacks into submission. First with Deep Purple in the early '70s, and then with Rainbow after 1975, Blackmore established himself as the dark master of the Stratocaster while also firming the foundations of a lead-heavy, medieval-influenced vein of hard rock and metal that has perpetuated to this day.

Like so many topflight artists, Blackmore modified his instruments considerably. He favored large-headstock, post-CBS Strats, mainly the early-'70s models with the "bullet" truss-rod adjustment points behind the nut, and is most noted for giving these a scalloped fingerboard. Created by filing away the wood between frets to create a concave fingerboard surface, the scalloped neck is said to aid speed and finger vibrato. Blackmore preferred a graduated scallop, which was fairly shallow up to the seventh fret and somewhat deeper thereafter. He also disconnected the middle pickup, which he never used; glued the necks in place, rather than relying on his Fenders' bolt-on attachments; and modified the vibrato tailpieces to achieve some up-bend in addition to the standard down-bend by removing some of the wood in front of the trem's inertia block in the back of the body. After they became available, Blackmore also added Seymour Duncan Quarter Pound Strat-style replacement pickups to the bridge and neck positions of his guitars, and these are retained in Fender's artist model, the Ritchie Blackmore Stratocaster. During Rainbow's heyday, Blackmore also took to smashing plenty of Strats, usually

as the grand finale to an explosive set, which would often culminate in a dummy amp stack bursting into flames after being assaulted with the unfortunate instrument. Rather than destroying one of his painstakingly modified guitars though, he would usually inflict such punishment on a Strat copy that would be pieced back together for further abuse night after night.

Translating Blackmore's six-string hellfire and fury to a 20,000-strong arena crowd obviously required some gargantuan amplification, and all needs were ably met with a pair of 200-watt Marshall Major heads, each of which ran through two 4×12-inch speaker cabs. To induce these extremely robust tube amps into early distortion, and to warm up the tone of the otherwise bright Strats, Blackmore played through an Awai reel-to-reel tape recorder, which he set to "pause" and used purely as a preamp.

In his more recent adventures with the Baroque-influenced outfit Blackmore's Night, Blackmore plays a range of acoustic instruments, although for his electric excursions he has lately taken to endorsing a model by German-made

Fin Costello/Redferns/Getty Images

RITCHIE BLACKMORE   31

Bloomfield and his whiteguard Telecaster perform with the Paul Butterfield Blues Band, New York City, circa 1966. *Don Paulsen/ Michael Ochs Archives/Getty Images*

BLUES MASTER Michael Bloomfield is perhaps most associated with "fatter" sounding Gibson Les Pauls, but his first ascent to worldwide fame was made with a Fender Telecaster in hand—and one formative such moment is firmly etched in the annals of rock history (and folk music infamy). When Bob Dylan boldly "went electric" before a raging crowd of folk purists at the Newport Folk Festival in 1965, a Telecaster was his weapon of choice. And right behind him, wailing on a matching whiteguard Tele, was his lead guitarist, Michael Bloomfield.

Born in Chicago, Illinois, in 1943, Michael Bloomfield was first drawn to the guitar at the age of thirteen by the sounds of seminal rock 'n' rollers such as Elvis Presley, and his guitarist Scotty Moore in particular. Soon, however, he was tapping into Chicago's huge, booming blues scene, and virtually ignoring his formal education in the process. Then again, what better education could there be for a burgeoning blues guitarist than hanging out in the many clubs on Chicago's South Side, digging the playing of legends such as Otis Spann, Howling Wolf, Muddy Waters, and several others? While still only in his mid-teens, Bloomfield himself became a fixture of sorts on the scene, a stand-out as one of few white youths in the crowd at the predominantly black establishments—and even harder to miss once he started hopping up on stage, guitar in hand, and asking to sit in with the greats (often digging in without awaiting the "yes" or "no" reply).

While still in his late teens, Bloomfield became widely accepted in Chicago, and soon beyond, as a musician in his own right. He performed and recorded with formative, if lesser-known, blues originators such as Big Joe Williams, Sleepy John Estes, and Little Brother Montgomery, and drew the attention of legendary blues producer John Hammond, who signed him to a contract with CBS in 1964. With his initial CBS recordings languishing unreleased, however, Bloomfield joined the Paul Butterfield Blues Band, providing an able foil for the singer and guitarist's own talents.

Although a Fender Duo-Sonic first accompanied Bloomfield into his professional career, in late 1964 or early '65 he acquired an "L" serial number whiteguard Telecaster with rosewood fingerboard, which would be his main squeeze until Les Paul fever won him over in 1966 in the form of a 1956 Les Paul goldtop, for which he swapped the Tele, and which he in turn swapped for a sunburst Les Paul Standard with humbuckers about a year later. In that brief span of time, though, the young blueser made some major noises with that Tele. Between fiery exchanges with Butterfield in the Blues Band—including the 1965 release *The Paul Butterfield Blues Band* and the more experimental, psychedelic-leaning *East-West*—Bloomfield and Tele trucked east for much of the summer of 1965. In June, he put the Tele to work recording the first batch of New York sessions that would become Bob Dylan's *Highway 61 Revisited*, then, after joining Dylan in Newport, Rhode Island, to be booed off stage by the sandals-and-beards crowd on July 25, returned to NYC for another week of sessions to complete the famous album. And all the while, as legend had it, Bloomfield dragged the Telecaster from gig to gig without a proper case to put it in, the journey taking its toll in the wear and tear soon evident on the guitar.

Even after revising his sound with the Les Paul in the late '60s, Bloomfield remained fond of the Telecaster, and occasionally dragged one back on stage. Existing photos of the band Mike Bloomfield and Friends performing live in 1973 show him wielding another old whiteguard example with rosewood fingerboard, first unmolested, then later in the year, updated with a crude psychedelic paint job. In the late '70s, he also occasionally played a later Tele with maple fingerboard, his legendary Les Paul having been surrendered in Vancouver, Canada, in compensation for an abandoned performance date in late 1974 or early '75. Michael Bloomfield was found dead in his car, having suffered an apparent drug overdose, on February 15, 1981. ♠

"A Long Time Comin'"

AFTER FAILING TO SET THE MUSIC WORLD alight upon its release in 1958—and suffering a premature deletion from the Gibson catalog in 1960 as a result—the sunburst Les Paul Standard's glories spread like a contagion in the mid-'60s, when its tonal splendor first became widely appreciated. Eric Clapton's use of a late-'50s 'burst on the Blues Breakers' so-called "Beano" album (a.k.a. *John Mayall Blues Breakers with Eric Clapton*) spread the bug like an uncovered sneeze in a crowded kindergarten classroom. The epidemic swept most virulently

An intent Michael Bloomfield picks his 1959 Gibson Les Paul. *Michael Ochs Archives/Getty Images*

through British blues-rockers, but notably caught up with plenty of American players too. Billy F Gibbons, for one, declared that he lusted after a Les Paul (and a few years later obtained an extremely fine one) after seeing Clapton play with the Blues Breakers, but ground zero for most US-based sufferers has to be Michael Bloomfield, who followed Clapton's lead into humbucker-fueled tone after wielding a slew of other guitars.

An avid blues fan from an early age, Bloomfield soaked up the work of countless blues originators in his hometown of Chicago and eventually made his own mark with the Butterfield Blues Band, the Electric Flag, Bob Dylan (most notably at the infamous electrified 1965 Newport Folk Festival set and on *Highway 61 Revisited*), and the *Super Sessions* album with Al Kooper and Stephen Stills (probably the most successful recording of Bloomfield's career). Having transitioned through a Fender Duo-Sonic, a Telecaster, and a 1956 Les Paul goldtop

with P-90 pickups, Bloomfield finally acquired his legendary sunburst 1959 Les Paul Standard with PAF humbuckers in the spring of 1967 in a deal made with acclaimed guitar technician Dan Erlewine, then an aspiring musician himself. Ironically, as David Dann writes at mikebloomfieldamericanmusic. com, Erlewine had acquired his '59 Les Paul partly in admiration of Bloomfield's tone on the goldtop, and bringing that guitar into the offer apparently sweetened the pot just enough to close the deal. Bloomfield gave Erlewine the goldtop plus $100 cash and got the 1959 Les Paul in return.

Bloomfield, who passed away in 1981, lost his 'burst in 1974 or 1975, when, as his brother Allen recalls at mikebloomfield.com, a venue owner in Vancouver retained it as compensation for an abandoned performance date. The iconic instrument is now believed to be in the possession of an anonymous US collector. Although outwardly "just" an excellent example of a '59 Les Paul 'burst with a striking flamed top, Bloomfield's former guitar is also distinguished by the Grover tuners that Erlewine installed shortly before swapping it, the lack of a tip on its pickup-selector switch, and a mismatched mix of top hat and speed knobs on its volume and tone controls (Bloomfield supposedly added these to better distinguish the controls without having to look down at them, but they were possibly just the best replacements he could find for missing knobs), and an inch-long crack near the treble-side post of the stop-bar tailpiece. ★

MOSRITE VENTURES MODELS

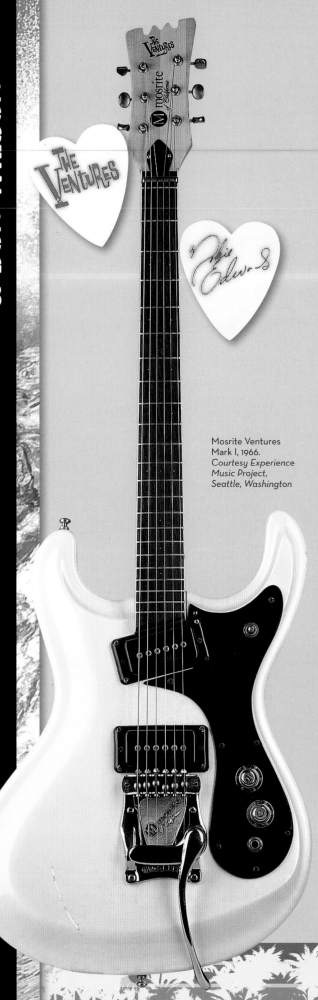

Mosrite Ventures Mark I, 1966. *Courtesy Experience Music Project, Seattle, Washington*

WHAT'S COOLER THAN being the world's biggest-selling guitar instrumental act? Being the world's biggest-selling guitar instrumental act with one of the world's coolest surf guitars named after you, of course. Formed in Seattle in 1958 by fellow masonry workers Bob Bogle and Don Wilson, the Ventures made a splash quickly and have sold more than 110 million albums to date, and the group logged a whopping thirty-seven albums on the Billboard charts. As big a hit as 1960's "Walk Don't Run" was for the band though, the Ventures didn't really hit their stride until bassist Nokie Edwards moved over to guitar in 1962, with Bogle taking up the bass. From this point until Edwards's temporary departure in 1968, the Ventures were on a roll, and things just got that much cooler when they strapped on those matching Mosrites.

Prior to picking up Mosrites, the Ventures played mainly Fender guitars, primarily Jazzmasters and Stratocasters. Shortly after his move to guitar, as Rich Landers wrote in *Modern Guitar Magazine* in 2005, Edwards borrowed an early Joe Maphis model from Mosrite founder Semie Moseley to test out in the studio, and he was hooked. Before the end of 1962, Edwards, Bogle, and Wilson began using prototypes of the Ventures model Mosrite guitars and basses, and the line was officially released in 1963. The original run of the signature model was actually short-lived and is believed to number only around two hundred guitars. Even within that modest production run, the guitar's specs and construction evolved. Nevertheless, the band's name and popularity helped put Mosrite on the map, and no doubt sent plenty of fans in search of the brand, even if it wasn't the Ventures model.

The original Ventures model was essentially an updated Joe Maphis model with the band's name positioned across the top of the headstock where the Mosrite logo would normally be. It had a set neck and the "reverse-bodied" asymmetrical lines of an upside-down Stratocaster (which, rumor has it, was what Moseley patterned it after), but with contoured body edges reminiscent of Rickenbacker's "German carve" and celluloid binding on both the body and neck. Mosrite manufactured most of its hardware and components in-house, and on early guitars Moseley's quirky but ingenious devices often have a rough-hewn look to them. The single-spring vibrato tailpiece suggests a slightly melted Bigsby; the roller-saddle bridge features six individual saddles that stand proudly above the bridge like miniature observatories; and lifting one of Moseley's bright but meaty-sounding P-90-like single-coil pickups from the guitar reveals a slathering of adhesive holding the bobbin together from underneath.

In 1964 Mosrite made several changes to ease production, and the Ventures model took on a bolt-on neck and a pickguard-mounted output jack in place of the side-mounted jack and lost its decorative body binding. Big in Japan? If you're the Ventures— or a Ventures model Mosrite—you'd better believe it. ★

From left: Don Wilson, Nokie Edwards, drummer Mel Taylor, and Bob Bogle. These post-1963 Mosrites have pickguard-mounted jacks and have lost their predecessors' decorative binding. *Michael Ochs Archives/Getty Images*

MID-1960s GIBSON FIREBIRD

Wearing his trademark grin, Clarence "Gatemouth" Brown picks his decorated Gibson Firebird. *Andrew Lepley/Redferns/Getty Images.*

THE TERM "MELTING POT" is perhaps over-used in describing America's cultural mélange, but it totally suits the musical cauldron in which Clarence "Gatemouth" Brown brewed up a style that was at once his own and an amalgam of almost all American music, including blues, country, bluegrass, jazz, and western swing. In many ways, it makes sense that this artist who defied categorization took up an instrument that relatively few guitarists accepted—at first blush at least—upon its initial release. The "reverse-bodied" Gibson Firebirds introduced in 1963 were just too far out for many players, and so evolved into "non-reverse" models in 1965, which themselves only held out until the end of the decade. The non-reverse Firebirds incorporated glued-in rather than through-body necks, and the lower models in the range (the I and III) carried P-90 pickups. The more deluxe Firebird V—Brown's choice—and VII retained the mini-humbucking pickups that had first appeared on the reverse 'Birds in 1963.

These bright, cutting mini-humbuckers proved the perfect pickup to translate Gatemouth Brown's chops into the unusual music that he became known for, and they served to further increase the quirk factor behind the playing of this utterly unique artist. Brown was also an accomplished fiddle player, and the dexterity honed on that instrument is evident in his guitar technique (as well as, perhaps, his penchant for using a capo high up the neck and playing in the upper register). Brown's playing style was unusual from the perspective of both his right and left hands. He picked the strings bare-fingered, mostly with the tip of a flitting index finger and his thumb braced on (and occasionally plucking) the low E string. To negotiate lower runs he often positioned the thumb and forefinger of his left hand *behind* the capo—something you don't often see—and used the remaining three

fingers of that hand to fret the strings as if the capo weren't even there.

Brown's Firebird was as unmistakable as his playing. Early on he stripped its finish to a mahogany brown, added a customized tooled-leather pickguard, and eventually replaced the Maestro Vibrola with an aftermarket tailpiece with fine tuners.

Like far too many great blues artists, Brown was rarely fully appreciated in his time, although his work with the Clarence "Gatemouth" Brown Big Band in the later years of his career brought him renewed recognition. For a quick hit of Brown's technique, dig up one of the several instances of video footage showing Gatemouth performing "Pressure Cooker" live. For fuller emersion, check out the late-'90s albums *Gate Swings* or *American Music, Texas Style*, recorded when Brown was already in his seventies.

Tragically, Brown's life and guitar both met sad ends. Brown was diagnosed with lung cancer in 2004, and after losing his home and presumably all his instruments in Slidell, Louisiana, to Hurricane Katrina, he grew ill and died on September 10, 2005. It's some small consolation that so many new fans were introduced to his music, and that unparalleled playing on a Firebird V, before his passing. ✪

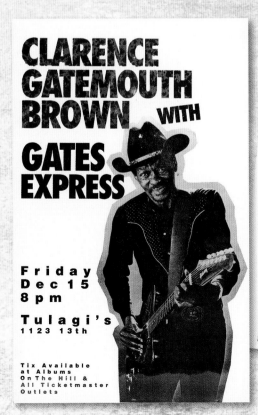

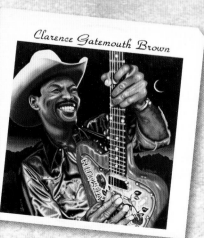

Clarence Gatemouth Brown

CLARENCE "GATEMOUTH" BROWN   39

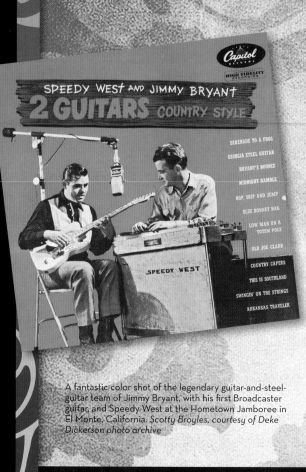

A fantastic color shot of the legendary guitar-and-steel-guitar team of Jimmy Bryant, with his first Broadcaster guitar, and Speedy West at the Hometown Jamboree in El Monte, California. *Scotty Broyles, courtesy of Deke Dickerson photo archive*

THANKS TO HIS Johnny-on-the-spot associations with Leo Fender and the preproduction development of the Broadcaster, Jimmy Bryant will forever be thought of as "Mister Telecaster." Even if he weren't hanging out in So-Cal to take up a prototype Fender solid body and display its capabilities for the masses, this fleet-fingered country, jazz, and Western-Swing soloist would deserve some attention for the sheer gymnastics of his playing.

Bryant was born in 1925 to a hardscrabble farming family in Moultrie, Georgia, and despite the encroaching Great Depression, managed to receive comprehensive musical education, and a deep appreciation of the art, from his musician father, Ivy. He played the guitar early on, and was a skilled fiddler even as a young child, playing on street corners at the tender age of five to supplement the family income, and performing at two World's Fairs with his father. Soon hailed as a fiddle prodigy in rural Georgia, Bryant's career on the violin was cut short when he was drafted into the army at the age of eighteen, and shipped out to the European front soon after. Head injuries suffered from a grenade blast

in Germany landed Bryant in the hospital, and he picked up the guitar during his long recuperation. Following his discharge, Bryant packed up his larger git-fiddle and headed west to Los Angeles, to get in on the burgeoning Western Swing scene.

Bryant's impressive guitar skills—blending country swing with a little be-bop influence and a clear love of Django Reinhardt–style hot jazz—helped him make a name on the circuit rather quickly, and he landed a string of prominent gigs even before taking up the Telecaster in 1950, so he was already something of a phenomenon when Leo Fender tracked him down to test out one of his early prototypes. Bryant was a member of Roy Rogers's band the Sons of the Pioneers, and was hired on for the band for Cliffie Stone's *Hometown Jamboree*, broadcast live on radio and then local television. While playing on the session and movie scene around L.A., Bryant would also make his most famous musical association, teaming up with steel-guitar whiz Speedy West to back a string of country artists, and eventually to be signed to Capitol Records as artists in their own right. Together, they cut more than fifty "sides" between 1951 and '56, including the showpieces "Stratosphere Boogie," "Speedin' West," "Bryant's Bounce," and "Frettin' Fingers," the latter a logic-defying blend of country tones and Eastern modality that displays Bryant's artistry at its peak.

Throughout the early '50s Bryant played, and promoted, the Broadcaster, then Telecaster, sporting a standard blackguard example early on, but replacing this with a custom-engraved white pickguard before that color became standard for the model. Bryant was purportedly a rather surly character, and difficult to work with. In his book *Fender: The Inside Story*, Forrest White, Fender's production manager through the mid- to late '50s and eventual vice president, tells of one awkward encounter with the guitar star. "I had been in charge of the operation for about three months and Jimmy brought his Telecaster in for some service work and new strings. He drove his Cadillac in through the side gate, rather than the front where it was plainly marked for visitors. He walked into the final assembly building with a can of beer and was walking by the assembly benches drinking his beer and shooting the breeze with anyone who would listen . . . . Jimmy was extremely obnoxious in those days. I found out later that he didn't have very many friends because of his attitude during that period of time. He looked at me and said, 'I don't need your help, I'm here to see Leo.'"

This attitude, it would seem, would lose Bryant his Capitol Records contract in 1956, and trigger his early departure from other prominent steady gigs. In the 1960s Bryant moved over to record production more than performing, and even moved from Fender to be an endorser for Vox guitars for a time in the late '60s. As an odd perk of this relationship, Bryant became owner of the Voxmobile built in 1968 by California's "King of the Kustomizers," George Barris, which he rode in parades to promote the hip British-gone-Californian brand. Bryant relocated to Nashville in the mid-'70s and reunited with former musical collaborator Speedy West in 1975. Rereleased as the CD *For the Last Time*, these tracks would be just that: Bryant, a lifelong smoker, would learn in 1978 that he had lung cancer, and would die in 1980. ♣

Custom Shop Jimmy Bryant Tribute Telecaster in white blonde. *Fender Musical Instruments Corporation*

SEVERAL OF THE GREAT pre-CBS Fender Telecasters have been owned and played by artists much better known than Roy Buchanan, but the 1953 Telecaster that he called "Nancy" is widely considered one of the most iconic vintage Teles in existence. Many factors contribute to Nancy's status, not least of which was Buchanan's raw skill as a Telemeister: Any early '50s Tele that is played so well, by a true apostle of the instrument, is going to be worthy of some serious adulation. Another factor is Nancy's condition; where the Telecasters and Esquires of Keith Richards, Danny Gatton, Andy Summers, Bruce Springsteen, and others were hacked, chopped, and modified over the years to suit their owners' requirements, Nancy, though heavily gigged, remained largely original, barring some necessary routine maintenance and one bungled modification.

Buchanan got his start in the early days of rock 'n' roll, recording and touring with Dale Hawkins from 1958 before jumping ship to tour with Dale's cousin Ronnie Hawkins's group alongside a young Robbie Robertson. Dissatisfied with life on the road, however, Buchanan eventually settled in the greater Washington, D.C., area, where he built a reputation as one of the hottest players on the scene and eventually gained some fame as "the world's foremost Tele master" (though no more mainstream success) after the broadcast of a 1971 PBS documentary entitled *The Best Unknown Guitarist in the World.* Somewhat parallel to Danny Gatton a decade later, Buchanan, with Nancy by his side, came to be known as a guitarist without parallel in any genre, his haunting pinched harmonics, faux-steel bends, and lightning-swift single-note runs unequalled by any other player in the jazz, blues, or country worlds. Also like Gatton, he failed to gain the recognition that players and fans in the know were convinced he deserved, or the adequate financial compensation that might have come with it.

Buchanan had long suffered from alcohol abuse, but was said to have been on the road to recovery at the time of the release of his twelfth album,

Hot Wires, in 1987. In August 1988, however, he was arrested in Fairfax County, Virginia, and found dead in his jail cell a few hours later, apparently having hanged himself with his own shirt. The official verdict of suicide has often been contested by those close to Buchanan.

Aside from its heavily worn finish and beautifully played-in neck, Nancy remains in much the same condition in which it left the Fender factory in Fullerton, California, in 1953. In addition to natural distress of the sort that would make the Fender Custom Shop's relicking team drool with envy, Nancy displays Buchanan's name crudely etched into its back at the bass-side upper bout, and

three characteristic friction marks behind the bridge where screwdrivers of old were used to adjust the brass saddles. In addition, Nancy appears to have had jumbo frets installed at some point and carries a hole that was drilled right through the headstock, piercing the *n* of the Fender logo, purportedly a botched effort by Buchanan to install a B-bender of his own devising (though he would often tease interviewers with the tale that he had "drilled that hole so he could hang Nancy up on a nail in the wall"). Nancy has recently been displayed at the Fullerton Museum Center in Fullerton, California. ✪

Roy Buchanan makes music on his beloved 1953 Fender Telecaster "Nancy" at the Newport Jazz Festival in 1973. *David Redfern/Redferns/Getty Images*

ARMADILLO WORLD HEADQUARTERS
PRESENTS
ROY BUCHANAN
The Bugs Henderson Group
AUSTIN, TEXAS
FRIDAY
9:00 P.M.
SEPT 1 1978
SEC   ROW   SEAT
01468
GEN. ADM.
SEPT. 1, 1978
ADMIT ONE ON ABOVE DATE ONLY
$6.00
ADVANCE
NO REFUND PRICE NO EXCHANGE
SEC   ROW   SEAT
01468
GEN. ADM.
ROY BUCHANAN
$7.00   DOOR
SEPT. 1, 1978
01468

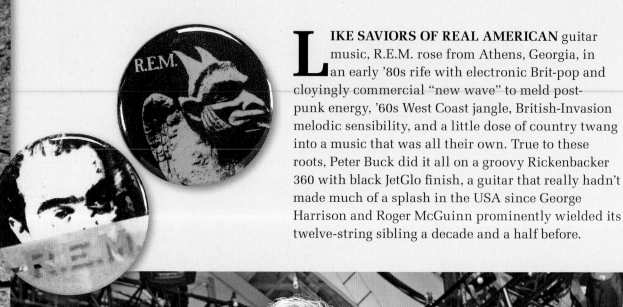

LIKE SAVIORS OF REAL AMERICAN guitar
music, R.E.M. rose from Athens, Georgia, in
an early '80s rife with electronic Brit-pop and
cloyingly commercial "new wave" to meld post-
punk energy, '60s West Coast jangle, British-Invasion
melodic sensibility, and a little dose of country twang
into a music that was all their own. True to these
roots, Peter Buck did it all on a groovy Rickenbacker
360 with black JetGlo finish, a guitar that really hadn't
made much of a splash in the USA since George
Harrison and Roger McGuinn prominently wielded its
twelve-string sibling a decade and a half before.

Peter Buck performs with R.E.M. at the Hollywood Bowl, Los Angeles, May
29, 2008. The "mudflap girl" is visible on the lower bout. © Kevin Estrada

As much as it echoed the look of the Rick 360 that helped give birth to jangle in the '60s, the '70s Rickenbacker that Buck used throughout R.E.M.'s debut album, *Murmur,* and beyond was a slightly different beast, thanks largely to its pickups. The 360 model of the '60s carried the "toaster-top" pickups beloved by fans of vintage Ricks. These are often mistaken for mini-humbuckers thanks to their dual-slotted covers, but are actually bright, crisp, single-coil pickups with alnico magnets. The Rickenbacker Hi-Gain pickups (a.k.a. "button tops") that replaced them in 1969 were more powerful ceramic-magnet single-coils that changed the core sound of the guitars somewhat. Hotter pickups or not, they still helped early-'80s indie players like Buck and, across the pond, Johnny Marr of the Smiths, to crank out the jangle. In addition, Buck's '70s-era 360 is known to have a slightly thicker neck than the narrow appendage that the '60s examples are known for. Otherwise, the 360 of the '70s was similar to the guitar of the previous decade, with a semi-hollow maple body and the five-knob control section and Rick-O-Sound stereo output that continues to confound players to this day.

As legend has it, Buck bought his black 360 in 1980 for $175 after breaking the neck of a Telecaster against the ceiling of an Athens club during an early R.E.M. performance. The Rick, which was stolen off a stage in Helsinki in 2008 but later returned anonymously, is notable for its reflective nude "mudflap girl" sticker in the upper corner of its lower bout and a small sticker of an alien playing a flute visible through its f-hole.

Buck has also played a MapleGlo (natural) 360, along with several backup Ricks, a couple of twelve-string models, and several other makes, including Fender Telecasters and Gibson Les Pauls. He is best known for playing through Vox AC30 amplifiers, although, according to producer Mitch Easter writing into rickresource.com, Buck recorded the majority of *Murmur* with an Ampeg Gemini II (although a small solid-state Kasino was employed for "Pilgrimage") and also frequently used Fender Twin Reverbs in earlier live performances. Add it all up, along with Buck's simple yet driving technique and a penchant for open-chord arpeggios, and you've got the sound that launched a thousand Ricks—and helped save American indie music in the process. ★

1954–1955 FENDER ESQUIRE

The Rock 'N Roll Trio at New York City's Pythian Temple during the band's May 7, 1956, recording session for Coral Records. Even in this photo, the bandmates seem to have a hard time keeping still.

AS A FOUNDING MEMBER of the Rock 'N Roll Trio, Paul Burlison was at the epicenter of the rock 'n' roll boom of the mid-'50s, and secured his place in history as a godfather of rockabilly, but the guitarist never achieved the wider fame that such eminence might be expected to bring. Even so, he was one of the first true rock 'n' rollers to ply his trade on a Telecaster (or originally, in his case, an Esquire), and left an indelible mark on popular music.

Burlison was born in Brownsville, Tennessee, in 1929, but his musical conscience was really formed by Memphis, the city to which his family moved in 1937. Burlison enlisted in the navy in 1946 at the age of seventeen, where he earned an all-navy runner-up boxing title as a welterweight a year later, and upon his return to Memphis following an honorable discharge in 1949 was introduced to brothers Dorsey and Johnny Burnette through the local Golden Gloves boxing association. In addition to boxing (older and younger brothers Dorsey and Johnny were Golden Gloves welterweight and lightweight champions, respectively), the Burnettes shared Burlison's interest in music, and, in particular, the blend of country and Beale Street blues that was then bubbling up around Memphis. While learning a trade as an electrician—the Burnettes themselves first worked as deck hands on Mississippi River barges, although Dorsey also later trained as an electrician—Burlison pursued his interest in the guitar, which he had learned as a teenager before joining the navy. In 1952, the three formed The Rhythm Rangers, and Burlison also played with other groups around town, backing Howlin' Wolf briefly, and even working as a studio guitarist at Sun Records before Elvis Presley joined the label.

In 1956, the Burnette brothers and Burlison decided to leave their wives and young children behind and hit the road for New York City, ostensibly to find union work for Paul and Dorsey, the electricians of the group, but their guitars came with them. An audition for the *Ted Mack Original Amateur Hour* show on ABC-TV affiliate WHBQ in New York—where they were briefly billed as the Rock 'N Roll Boys of Memphis—landed three successive wins when the trio's performance of "Tutti Frutti" consistently slammed the applause meter into the red. Band leader Henry Jerome signed them to a management contract, and after several record labels came courting, the group signed to Coral, and was renamed the Rock 'N Roll Trio (often billed as "Johnny Burnette and . . ." for the singer and rhythm guitarist).

Although he briefly played a 1953 Gibson Les Paul prior to the big move east to NYC, Burlison's main instrument throughout his time with the Rock 'N Roll Trio was a whiteguard Fender Esquire, most likely made in late 1954 or early '55. In a 1978 interview with *Guitar Player* magazine's Jas Obrecht, Burlison said, "I never did like [the Les Paul] because I got bad feedback . . . so as soon as that Fender came out, I traded it for a Fender." Early studio sessions in the spring of 1956 at the Pythian Temple in New York resulted in the singles "Midnight Train," "Tear It Up," "Oh Baby Babe," and "You're Undecided," and although none topped the charts, they achieved reasonable commercial success, and the Rock 'N Roll Trio set out on a whirlwind tour of stage, television, and radio appearances. Much of the playing on later sessions, however—which produced, among others, one of the Trio's biggest hits in their rendition of the blues song "Train Kept A-Rollin'"—is often credited to Nashville session guitarist Grady Martin. Indeed, many such studio sessions back in the day required the backing musicians behind the singer to step aside and let professional players record their parts,

and the complex chord work and fleet, confident solos do sound like more what we know Martin to have been capable of than what we hear elsewhere from Burlison. Nevertheless, Burlison's style on the Esquire, defined by boogie lines behind the rhythm guitar, and driving single-note and double-stop solos, are clear precursors of the style that would soon after be known as archetypal rockabilly, and certainly seminal rock 'n' roll by any standards.

After tiring of the road late in 1957, Burlison headed back home to Memphis, and aside from a brief jaunt to California to join the Burnette Brothers (as Johnny and Dorsey were now calling themselves), that was essentially the end of the Rock 'N Roll Trio. "I enjoyed it, but the main thing was I missed my family," Burlison told Obrecht in 1978. "I was married and I had children. I missed my wife more than anything else. As far as the playin' and everything, I'll tell you what I really wanted to do: I enjoyed the playin', but I enjoy playin' just sittin' around. I really do. And the fame—or whatever you want to call it—I don't really think it ever affected me at all. I was really wanting to make enough money out of the thing to come home and open up an electrical supply company. . . . That's really why I headed back to my hometown." And when he got there, that's exactly what he did. For some twenty years Burlison played music only "on the side," for the fun of it, and concentrated on his electrical business. In the 1980s he revived his career and performed and recorded with several other artists, although the deaths of Johnny Burnette in a boating accident in 1964 at the age of thirty, and of Dorsey Burnette of a massive coronary in 1979 at age forty-six meant the Rock 'N Roll Trio would never ride again. ★

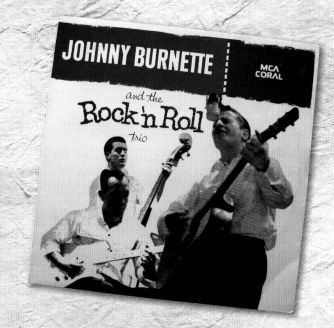

James Burton's country guitar licks were an essential part of Emmylou Harris's famed Hot Band in the late 1970s.

James Burton and his Paisley Red Telecaster back Emmylou Harris in The Netherlands, February 1976. *Gijsbert Hanekroot/Redferns/Getty Images*

FROM MAKING TV APPEARANCES on one of the nation's most popular shows while still in his teens, to being first-call sideman for massive stars from Elvis to Emmylou, James Burton was born to twang and was a Telecaster player right from the start. Born in 1939 in Dubberly, Louisiana, Burton expressed his musical drive early on. He took up the acoustic guitar while his age was still in the single digits, and first fell in love with a solidbody electric as a fourteen-year-old—at about the same time he turned professional—when he saw a new '53 Telecaster hanging on the wall of J&S Music in Shreveport, Louisiana.

Although he was younger than most significant players on the scene at the musical crossroads of the mid-1950s, Burton soon found himself right at the front edge of the rock 'n' roll boom. Shortly after turning pro, Burton was asked to join the house band for the *Louisiana Hayride*, broadcast from KWKH in Shreveport, Louisiana, on which he backed several renowned stars and began to make a name for himself as a reliable sideman. In 1955 he joined Dale Hawkins's band, and started

Burton and his Telecaster back Ricky Nelson in this classic Fender advertisement.

A young Burton added his defining Louisiana swamp riff to Dale Hawkins's rockabilly classic "Susie Q."

developing his rock 'n' roll chops more fully. Playing his own distinctive style using both a flatpick and a fingerpick on his middle finger, with light-gauge banjo strings on his Tele's D through high E for easy bending, the youngster was soon displaying one of the more distinctive sounds of the period. Together Hawkins and Burton cut the hit song "Susie-Q" at the KWKH studio in 1957, featuring an archetypal rock 'n' roll lick penned by Burton himself. Shortly after, Burton left Hawkins's band to form rockabilly wailer Bob Luman's backing band the Shadows, who scored minor hits with "My Gal Is Red Hot" and "A Red Cadillac and a Black Moustache" before heading west to appear in the largely forgotten 1957 Roger Corman film *Carnival Rock* (in which the eighteen-year-old Burton can frequently be seen squeezing out pyrotechnical riffs on a custom-colored Telecaster with a blackguard sporting "James" in white script). The film itself has largely disappeared in annals of B-movie mediocrity, but Burton's Hollywood debut brought him to the attention of Ricky Nelson and, soon, a much more long-lasting dose of national fame.

In joining Ricky Nelson's band—first as rhythm guitarist to Joe Maphis's lead, then as lead guitarist himself—James Burton found himself periodically in front of the camera on one of America's most popular TV shows of the 1950s and early '60s, *Ozzie and Harriet*, as well as performing on numerous hit recordings, and he even lived with the eponymous

Nelsons (a real family) for two years before finding his own digs in Tinseltown. Burton stayed with Ricky Nelson until 1967, but continued to play with Luman's band, as well as making more and more studio appearances as a first-call L.A. studio player. In 1968, Elvis Presley tapped Burton for his famous *Comeback Special*; he joined The King again for his Las Vegas shows of the following year. Burton remained Elvis's guitarist until Presley's death in 1977, although he found time between tours and recordings to make country-rock history first with Gram Parsons, then as a member of Emmylou Harris's original Hot Band (in which he frequently sported a Paisley Red Telecaster from the late '60s). A lifetime Telecaster player, Burton is an uncontested entry into the annals of the original solidbody, and even boasts a decorative signature model from the contemporary Fender company. ★

Burton Signature Telecaster in Red Flame.
Fender Musical Instruments Corporation

The Carter Family, circa 1937. From left: Maybelle and her L-5, A. P. Carter, and Sara Carter. *Frank Driggs Collection/ Getty Images*

THE MAJORITY OF GUITARS that have become legendary have achieved that status at the hands of renowned soloists: rock gods, blues wailers, country pickers, or jazz virtuosi who have dazzled us with their speed-of-light chops and otherworldly sonics. But one humble, late-'20s archtop acoustic has arguably seen more American musical history in the making than any other single guitar the world over and was itself responsible for a large slab of that history in the hands of "Mother" Maybelle Carter.

Country music originators the Carter Family—Maybelle, her brother-in-law A. P., and his wife Sara—made their first recordings in 1927 (the now-famous "Bristol Sessions," recorded in Bristol, Tennessee), and one year later their singer and guitarist Maybelle Carter used a little of the cash they earned from the records to trade in her Gibson L-1 flat-top for a brand-new L-5 archtop acoustic guitar. Carter's L-5 would be used throughout the Carter Family's recorded catalog of more than three hundred songs and her tenure as "Mother" Carter with her daughters Anita, Helen, and June. It also would help lay the foundations of country, bluegrass, and American folk music, earning Carter the title of "Queen Mother of Country Music" in the process. But in 1928 she was just a girl of nineteen with a new guitar—and, boy, could she play it.

Six years young at the time, Gibson's L-5 debuted in 1922 as part of designer Lloyd Loar's Master Series of instruments. The model represented some of the most significant advancements ever brought to the archtop acoustic guitar, and although it didn't retain quite the seminal status that its sibling the F-5 mandolin enjoys to this day, it did lay the groundwork for the great Gibson archtops of the '30s, which were leaders in their field. Carter's 1928 L-5, made just four years after Loar left Gibson, was a fairly austere instrument by the standards of later archtops, with simple dot inlays on the fingerboard, unbound f-holes, and a basic three-ply binding around its carved solid spruce top, but it did sport a very resonant, lively construction, and innovations such as an adjustable bridge and an adjustable truss

rod (both firsts for the archtop guitar when Gibson brought them to the L-5 shortly after its release).

Although today we think of archtops like the L-5 as "jazz boxes," in the early to mid-'20s the guitar was still a minority player in the jazz world, and fighting for a foothold in popular music in general. Arched top aside, Maybelle Carter established a playing style that echoes forth on countless flat-top dreadnoughts even today. Her technique, dubbed the "Carter scratch," was a form of fingerstyle that involved thumbing the bass note while her fingers picked a sort of hybrid lead and rhythm on the higher strings. Although it sounds rather simple on first listen, Carter's playing packs a lot of melodic nuance and a driving rhythmic momentum, and it is a clear precursor to many other great country playing styles to come, from Merle Travis's "Travis picking" to Chet Atkins's own fingerstyle. Listen to any of the Carter Family's legendary songs—"May the Circle Be Unbroken," "Wildwood Flower," and "Bury Me under the Weeping Willow Tree" among them—and you hear how confidently Carter's playing propels both the melody and the rhythmic motion of the song. ✦

Close-up images of Maybelle Carter's left-hand technique were taken for *Life* magazine in 1941. Carter is often credited with introducing the guitar as a lead instrument in country music.
Eric Schaal/Time Life Pictures/Getty Images

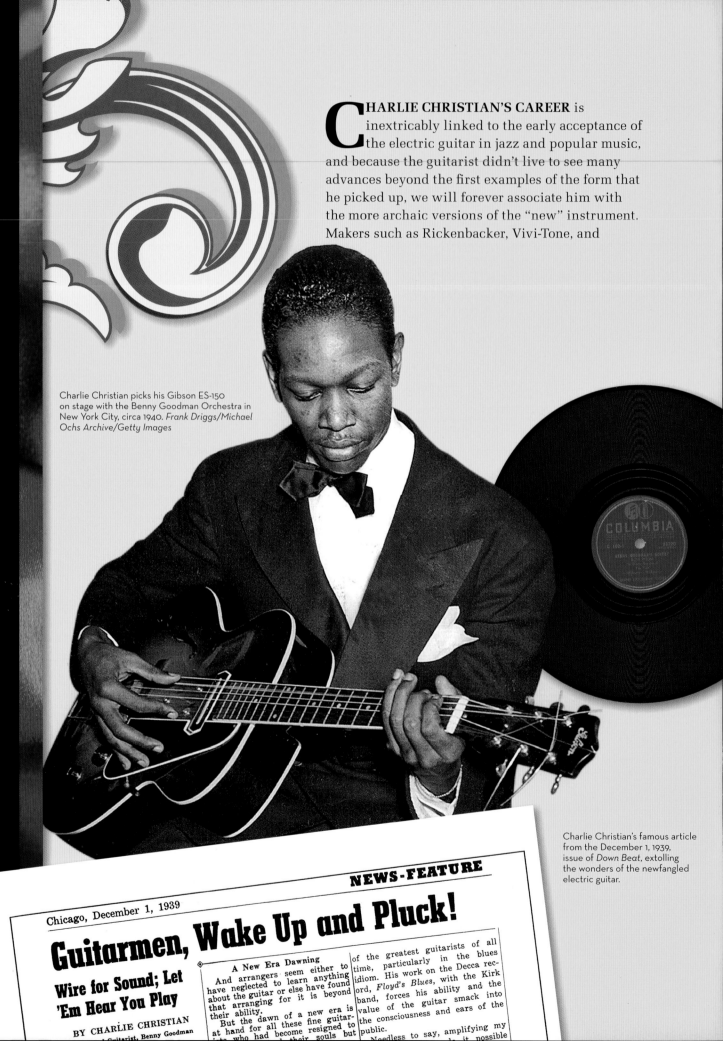

CHARLIE CHRISTIAN'S CAREER is inextricably linked to the early acceptance of the electric guitar in jazz and popular music, and because the guitarist didn't live to see many advances beyond the first examples of the form that he picked up, we will forever associate him with the more archaic versions of the "new" instrument. Makers such as Rickenbacker, Vivi-Tone, and

Charlie Christian picks his Gibson ES-150 on stage with the Benny Goodman Orchestra in New York City, circa 1940. *Frank Driggs/Michael Ochs Archive/Getty Images*

Charlie Christian's famous article from the December 1, 1939, issue of *Down Beat*, extolling the wonders of the newfangled electric guitar.

NEWS-FEATURE

Chicago, December 1, 1939

Guitarmen, Wake Up and Pluck!

Wire for Sound; Let 'Em Hear You Play

BY CHARLIE CHRISTIAN
Guitarist, Benny Goodman

A New Era Dawning

And arrangers seem either to have neglected to learn anything about the guitar or else have found that arranging for it is beyond their ability.

But the dawn of a new era is at hand for all these fine guitar-ists who had become resigned to their souls but

of the greatest guitarists of all time, particularly in the blues idiom. His work on the Decca rec-ord, *Floyd's Blues*, with the Kirk band, forces his ability and the value of the guitar smack into the consciousness and ears of the public.

Needless to say, amplifying my

Stromberg-Voisinet had experimented with electric guitars a few years before and released short runs of "semi-production" models, but the notion didn't catch hold until Gibson released its ES-150 in 1936, a guitar that has the distinction of being the first widely produced electric guitar from a major manufacturer.

As if waiting there at the end of the assembly line to receive the handoff and run with it, Eddie Durham took to the model immediately and is credited with recording the first electric guitar solos. But once Durham hipped fellow jazzman Charlie Christian to Gibson's new electric, the ES-150 really flew, and today Christian remains far and away the best remembered early electric jazz player. The ES-150 and accompanying EH-150 amplifier paved the way for the guitarist as a soloist in a full-band context, and for the first time Christian could be *heard* pulling off the fleet, fluid, single-note breaks that were previously the sole territory of horn players. Check out any of Christian's notable early works, such as "Air Mail Special" or "Solo Flight," and you hear classic swing solo work and also trace a direct line forward to the playing of rockabilly and early rock 'n' roll guitarists some fifteen years later.

The ES-150 itself was a far more basic model than traditional big Gibson archtops, such as the Super 400 and the L-5 (to which many players were attaching add-on pickups anyway). It still had the carved solid spruce top, but only a flat maple back and no decorative trim to speak of other than its single-ply binding and simple dot position markers. What it *did* have though was that honking single-blade pickup, and that made all the difference. Designed by Gibson's Walter Fuller and known forever after as the "Charlie Christian pickup," this unit is different from anything widely made today (though reproductions of the design are available). It comprised two large bar magnets suspended under the top of the guitar with three adjustment bolts, and a coil wound with relatively few turns of a much thicker gauge of wire than is used in contemporary pickups. The result was a fat, rich tone that plenty of players still seek.

After playing his ES-150 for three years, Christian moved up to the fancier ES-250 upon its introduction in 1939, and played this model—with a carved arched maple back and upgraded cosmetic appointments—until he succumbed to tuberculosis in 1942 at the age of twenty-five. ◆

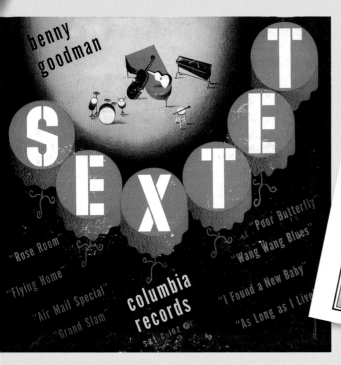

LONDON

BLUES BREAKERS JOHN MAYALL WITH ERIC CLAPTON

THROUGHOUT HIS CAREER, Eric Clapton has been an arbiter of tone, and while he has moved through several different makes and models of guitar over the past forty-five years, he has been extremely devoted to each at certain periods and has inspired major guitar lust in the hearts of many at every stop along the road. Clapton was already recognized as a leading blues-rocker while wielding a red Telecaster and a double-cutaway Gretsch 6120 with the Yardbirds in the mid-1960s, but he first established a must-have sound in the hearts and minds of other tonehounds when he took up a late-'50s sunburst Gibson Les Paul to record *John Mayall Blues Breakers with Eric Clapton*, otherwise known as the "Beano" album, in 1966. Clapton's exemplary Les Paul, believed to be a late-'59 or '60 model because of his descriptions of its thin neck profile, served as the midwife that took blues into blues rock when the star rammed it through a cranked Marshall 1962 combo (forever after known as a "Bluesbreaker") and warned the recording engineer that he intended to play loud. The result was one of the first widely chased guitar tones in the history of rock, and from thence forward, the previously underappreciated Les Paul Standard was a very well-appreciated guitar indeed. Clapton himself, however, was forced to evolve somewhat, due to the theft of said Les Paul in the summer of 1966 while he was rehearsing for Cream's first shows. ✦

Facing page: Clapton lost his "Beano" Les Paul during a short tour of Greece in the summer of 1966, as he relates in his autobiography. Returning to England, he borrowed a number of other Les Paul Standards, but none lived up to the "Beano" guitar. On July 31, 1966, he played one of the trial Les Pauls (with a Bigsby vibrato tailpiece) at the Windsor Festival, which was Cream's first live appearance. *David Redfern/Redferns/Getty Images*

BLUES BREAKERS JOHN MAYALL ERIC CLAPTON

In John Mayall and Eric Clapton we have the two most dedicated blues musicians in this country. Together with John McVie and Hughie Flint, they make up John Mayall and the Bluesbreakers. To hear them play can be a thrilling experience. Playing the blues is such a complex business, involving so many personal and external conditions, that it is never certain how well you are going to play until the first number of the evening is over. Watching the Bluesbreakers perform, you are immediately aware of their intense search for new ways in which to interpret their material. In fact, it is surprising to learn how little of their music is arranged and how much is improvised. It is because of this phenomenal ability to improvise that John Mayall and the Bluesbreakers are the premier blues group in England. On this record we have captured some of their best performances on numbers which they feature regularly in their club appearances.

The person responsible for much of the improvisation is Eric Clapton. Two years ago I stuck my neck out to say that Eric would become one of the top blues guitarists in the country. Now I know I was right – he *is* the best, damn it. A lot of people wondered why Eric left the Yardbirds just as they were hitting big. But Eric had an inevitable course to follow, and at the time it led him to the Bluesbreakers, as no doubt it will lead him elsewhere in the future. Since joining the group, his technique has improved beyond recognition, and on his best nights Eric can make time stand still. Some idea of this can be gained by listening to his solo on "Have You Heard". But even without stopping the clock his playing can be both breathtakingly beautiful and savage, as on "All Your Love", "Double Crossin' Time" and his two instrumental features, "Hideaway" and "Steppin' Out". As if this wasn't enough, this record marks the first occasion on which the Clapton voice has been aired on disc. For his debut, Eric chose the Robert Johnson number, "Ramblin' On My Mind", which has a very sympathetic piano backing from John.

Because a lot of the spotlight is thrown on Eric, we tend to overlook the fact that John himself is a most capable musician. Besides doing all of the singing (well almost), his piano, organ and harmonica playing provide much of the driving force of the group. His flair for composition, with some unusual chord progressions, is also shown to good advantage on "Little Girl" and "Key to Love". The two harmonica features on this record, "Another Man" and "Parchman Farm", usually develop into tours-de-force in a club performance, but here John remains short, sharp, but very much to the point.

It is a measure of this group's capabilities that they can inject new life into such cobwebbed numbers as "What'd I Say", and make them sound even more vital than the original. And perhaps this is why John Mayall and the Bluesbreakers are such an exciting group to watch and hear, and why they are the only group in Britain today whose music closely parallels that being produced by the blues bands of Chicago.

NEIL SLAVEN

SIDE ONE
1. ALL YOUR LOVE (3:33)
   (Rush/Dixon)
2. HIDEAWAY (3:15)
   (King/Thompson)
3. LITTLE GIRL (2:35)
   (Mayall)
4. ANOTHER MAN (1:45)
   (arr. Mayall)
5. DOUBLE CROSSING TIME (3:02)
   (Mayall/Clapton)
6. WHAT'D I SAY (4:25)
   (Charles)

SIDE TWO
1. KEY TO LOVE (2:06)
   (Mayall)
2. PARCHMAN FARM (2:20)
   (Allison)
3. HAVE YOU HEARD (5:55)
   (Mayall)
4. RAMBLIN' ON MY MIND (3:07)
   (Johnson)
5. STEPPIN' OUT (2:30)
   (L.C. Frazier)
6. IT AIN'T RIGHT (2:40)
   (Jacobs)

JOHN MAYALL, vcl/piano/organ/harmonica.
ERIC CLAPTON, vcl/guitar.
JOHN McVIE, bass-guitar.
HUGHIE FLINT, drums.
on Tracks 1, 3, 5, 6, 12.

Augmented by: JOHN ALMOND, baritone sax on Track 5

ALAN SKIDMORE, tenor sax; JOHN ALMOND, baritone sax;
DENNIS HEALEY, trumpet
on Tracks 7, 9, 11.

Layout: JOHN MAYALL.
Produced by MIKE VERNON.
Engineer: GUS DUDGEON.

LONDON RECORDS, INC.
539 West 25th Street
New York, N.Y. 10001

AFTER THE BLUES BREAKERS, Clapton gigged and recorded with a few borrowed Les Pauls, but, unable to find one that he liked as much as his lost "Beano" guitar, eventually settled in with a Gibson SG and an ES-335 for the majority of his work with Cream. The SG, a 1964 or '65 model, became famous for the paint job given to it by the Dutch artists collective known as The Fool, a name also given to the guitar itself. When Clapton owned the guitar, the remains of the framework of its original Maestro "lyre" vibrato tailpiece could still be seen. Todd Rundgren acquired the SG in 1974, and its bridge, tailpiece, and paint job were updated sometime after. It is currently on loan to the Hard Rock Café in San Francisco. ✦

Eric Clapton's 1964–1965
Gibson SG, "The Fool."
*Courtesy Nigel Osborne/
Jawbone Press*

"THE FOOL"

Cream performs on TV in November 1967. From left: bassist Jack Bruce, drummer Ginger Baker, and Clapton playing "The Fool."
Jan Persson/Redferns/Getty Images

DESPITE THE SG'S MEMORABLE **APPEARANCE,** the cherry-red ES-335 that Clapton used toward the end of the Cream era and early on with Bonnie & Delaney is arguably more memorable in a tonal sense, at least in the ears of many fans. This 1964 ES-335 with small-block fingerboard inlays is perhaps best known for its appearance at Cream's farewell concert at London's Royal Albert Hall in November 1968, but it was also used throughout Cream's US tour of 1968 and on several studio recordings, notably the monstrous "Badge" from *Goodbye.* Purchased new by Clapton during his tenure with the Yardbirds (though it was more often seen in the hands of bandmate Chris Dreja at the time), the red ES-335 has had the longest tenure of any of the artist's guitars to date and was only surrendered in the 2004 Crossroads guitar auction, where it sold for $847,500. ★

Eric Clapton's 1964 Gibson ES-335, which he played with Cream and Blind Faith. *Collection Guitar Center/Photo Robert Knight Archive/Redferns/Getty Images*

Eric Clapton plays his
1964 Gibson ES-335 with
Blind Faith in August
1969. *Richard Upper/
Redferns/Getty Images*

DEREK IS ERIC LONDON JUNE '70

ec.

461 TOUR 1974

THERE'S ONE IN EVERY CROWD 75

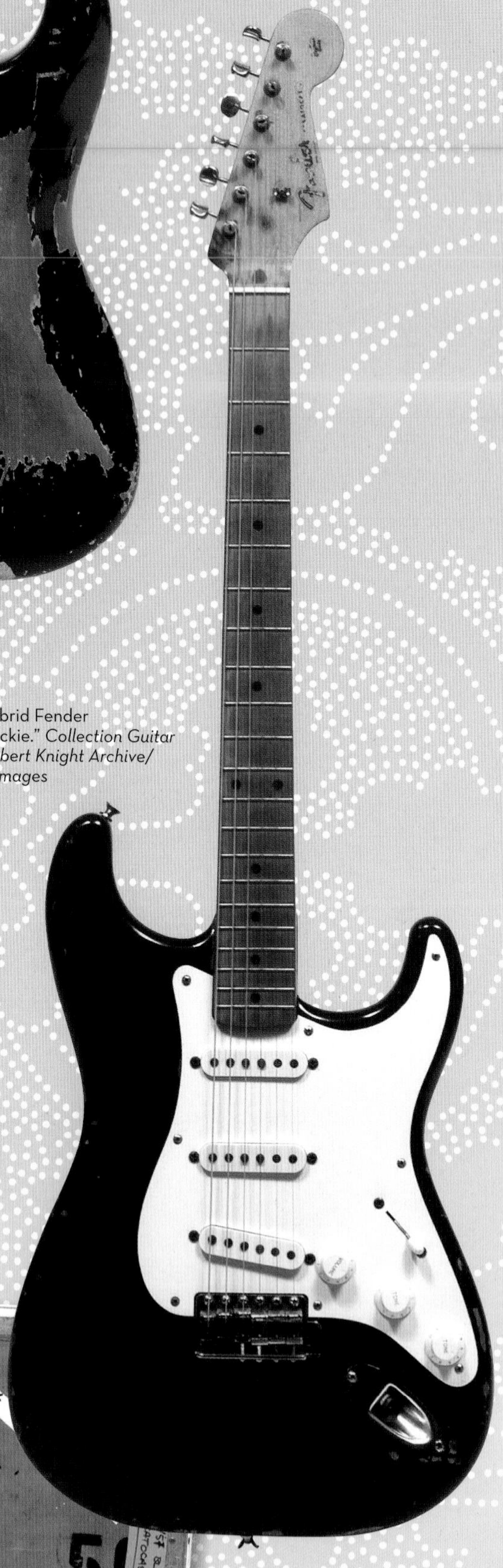

Eric Clapton's hybrid Fender Stratocaster "Blackie." Collection Guitar Center/Photo Robert Knight Archive/ Redferns/Getty Images

Fender STRATOCAS
WITH SYNCHR
Contour Body

FRAGILE ELECTRONICS

THE DUCK BROS.
LONDON 01 486 8056

"BLACKIE"

THE END OF THE '60s signaled Clapton's movement, by and large, from Gibson to Fender, and in 1970 he acquired the instrument that would become one of the most famous electric guitars of all time. His Stratocaster "Blackie" was pieced together after Clapton purchased six late-'50s Strats at a guitar store in Nashville and combined the best elements from his favorite three of the bunch (the other three were given to Pete Townshend, George Harrison, and Steve Winwood). Being a parts guitar, Blackie is unique, blending elements from these three '56 and '57 Strats, the modifications and repairs required to keep it serviceable over the years, and plenty of wear, sweat, and mojo from Clapton's own hands.

Clapton bends strings on "Blackie" during a 1978 concert.
Richard E. Aaron/Redferns/Getty Images

In heavy use from its first live appearance at the Rainbow Concert of 1973 until its semi-retirement after 1985, Blackie was the star of the same auction that saw the sale of the '64 ES-335 in 2004, and it fetched the highest price paid for a guitar at auction to date, going to Guitar Center for $959,500. ♦

LOS ANGELES NATIVE NELS CLINE forged a career as a hotly tipped avant-noise rocker and free-jazz experimentalist before gaining wider recognition in recent years as a member of the latest configuration of the Chicago-based band Wilco, which he joined in 2004. Though he has been tabbed as everything from "New Guitar God" (*Rolling Stone*, 2007) to "one of the best guitarists in any genre" (*New York Times*, 2009), Cline confesses

Battle-scarred though it may be, Cline's '59 remains his number-one guitar among a host of guitars he plays with Wilco. © *The Fretboard Journal*

Artist: John Lackey (www.homegrownpress.com)

Cline's '59 Jazzmaster bears the mark of its previous owner, bass legend Mike Watt. © *The Fretboard Journal*

Cline with Wilco in Cincinnati, Ohio, June 12, 2009. © *Richie Wireman*

that he was largely afloat in unfamiliar waters, gear-wise, throughout his earlier days as a player, and he remained somewhat oblivious to the tools of the trade through semi-success with his rock band Bloc in the late '80s and early '90s, the Nels Cline Trio after that, and even up to the time of his mid-'90s collaborations with some of his own early heroes, Mike Watt of the Minutemen and fIREHOSE and Thurston Moore of Sonic Youth. Then, in 1995, during the course of these projects, Cline picked up Watt's old, semi-beat 1959 Jazzmaster. "The whole time I was growing up, Fender Jaguars and Jazzmasters were considered joke guitars, not serious guitars," Cline told Bill Milkowski in *JazzTimes* in 2001. "They were generally twangy sounding and associated with surf music. But to me, just the whole shape of it, the neck, everything about it felt perfect."

While the Jazzmaster, introduced in 1958, was indeed embraced by many surf bands of the late '50s and early '60s, it was originally designed—appropriately enough for Cline's frequent endeavors—as Fender's bid to enter the jazz market. In fact, very little about the Jazzmaster addresses the needs of traditional electric jazz players, other than perhaps the rosewood fingerboard and the slightly warmer tone produced by the wide coils of the Jazzmaster single-coil pickups. Although it has been used by a few prominent jazz players over the years, the guitar has been less of a fixture in the genre than even Fender's countrified Telecaster, for example. Indeed, the Jazzmaster does prove too bright and twangy for most die-hard jazz player's needs, but therein lies its strength for many other players—the Jazzmaster has a lot of the characteristic Fender bite and definition that helps an instrument cut through a noisy alt-rock mix, and it has become a favored weapon of more than a few indie and experimental players over the years. The fact that it never appealed much to rock and blues artists helped keep the prices of vintage Jazzmasters at reasonable levels and therefore within reach of said notoriously shabby-heeled indie players. With its fluid vibrato unit and versatile switching, it's also a great guitar on which an aspiring avant-garde noisemaker might ply his trade.

Cline's pre-CBS Jazzmaster sports a much-abused purple-black finish (Cline says it's like eggplant) and replacement tuners and switches, and it carries several gouges in the headstock from where he fell on it at a Geraldine Fibbers show in the late '90s. However, it remains his number-one guitar, although he plays a wide range of others in the course of his duties with Wilco. Hear it on many of the standout tracks from critically acclaimed Wilco releases *Sky Blue Sky* (2007) and *Wilco (the Album)* (2009), or in much of Cline's more experimental work with The Nels Cline Singers. ✪

KURT COBAIN

1969 COMPETITION SERIES
FENDER MUSTANG

Kurt Cobain clowning with a tapestry on the set of the
"Smells Like Teen Spirit" video, August 1991. © *Kevin Estrada*

FLASHBACK TO SEPTEMBER 1991: Loud guitar music was, in the view of many rock fans, in dire straits. In the UK, shoe-gazing indie bands were afraid to be heard producing anything remotely resembling a guitar solo, while in the US plenty of commercial rock bands were more than happy to solo all night, so long as it didn't take the bounce out of their perms. Enter Nirvana's second album, *Nevermind*. Virtually overnight the kids were ready to rock again. The "grunge" phenomenon not only brought big, crunchy guitars back onto the radio and into the charts, it did so by appealing to a vast swath of music fans—punks, metalheads, alt-rockers, and classic rockers alike—thereby ushering in a new golden age of guitar rock. One of the really fun things for guitar nuts was that Nirvana main man Kurt Cobain produced much of this sonic mayhem on an underappreciated student model guitar from the late '60s: a Fender Mustang.

Cobain played, or more appropriately *went through*, a great many guitars in his all too short career, but the humble Mustang was one of his favorites, and one particular Mustang was especially close to his heart: a left-handed 1969 Competition Series Mustang in Lake Placid Blue, with a distinctive racing stripe and matching headstock. This Mustang was in Cobain's hands for much of the *Nevermind* recording sessions and was also seen on stage for several performances, as well as appearing, perhaps most famously, in the "Smells Like Teen Spirit" video.

Designed as a student model for younger players and built with a downsized body, a slim neck, and a shorter, 24-inch scale length, the

Mustang might have seemed an unlikely source of Nirvana's ferocious sonic assault, but it suited the guitarist's tastes and temperament to a T. A rather slight figure himself, Cobain clearly found the Mustang's body and neck dimensions comfortable, and attitude-wise, well, he wasn't the type to latch on to top-of-the-line models or current trends in gear. Making a big noise on a little guitar with low-output, single-coil pickups was just the thing for this self-proclaimed anti-guitar hero. Similarly, he performed and recorded with just about any amp that happened to be available and made them all sound like custom-made grunge machines in the process. Fittingly, though tragically, Cobain smashed the blue Mustang onstage during the infamous October 1991 concert at Tree's in Dallas, Texas, damaging part of the body and the neck joint, but apparently had it repaired and kept it, still cherishing the guitar and leaving it in storage for future tours and recording sessions. The Mustang was paid homage, in Cobain's own off-kilter way, in the creation Fender's Kurt Cobain Jagstang model, a design which the artist initiated, allegedly by cutting photos of a Mustang and a Jaguar in half, taping them together, and presenting them to Fender. Either way, the Mustang and the man made a big noise in their time and burned out too soon. ✪

Eddie Cochran rocks his Gretsch Model 6120 during a concert in Chadron, Nebraska, on October 3, 1959.

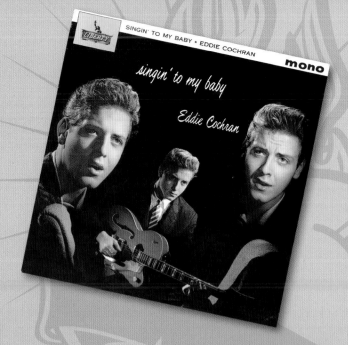

A SEMINAL ROCK 'N' ROLLER, Eddie Cochran has also been a major influence on countless rockabilly purists. As such, there's really no other guitar he could have played but a Gretsch 6120 Chet Atkins Hollow Body—*the* guitar to be seen with in the mid-1950s.

Born in Albert Lea, Minnesota (although he often referred to himself as hailing from Oklahoma, his parents' home state), Cochran followed an early interest in country music and segued into rock 'n' roll after his family moved to Bell Gardens, California. After playing a Gibson archtop electric with dual P-90s for a time, Cochran acquired his Gretsch 6120 in 1956, and like a talisman that foretold fame and fortune, he kept it with him throughout his brief but luminous career and even had it by his side at the time of his death in a car crash in England in April 1960.

As much as Cochran clearly cherished the 6120, he had obviously developed a taste for the P-90 pickups in his previous guitar too, and almost immediately upon acquiring the 6120 he replaced the neck pickup with one of the Gibson-made single-coils, as can be seen later that year in his performance of "Twenty Flight Rock" in the 1956 movie *The Girl Can't Help It*, a major debut achieved while the would-be star was still in his late teens. The pickup swap is slightly ironic, given that Gibson had recently sought more clarity and definition from that pickup position, developing the Alnico V pickup, made with alnico bar magnets somewhat in the image of the DeArmond Model 200. Otherwise, Cochran's 6120 remained stock, with the fixed-arm Bigsby vibrato, block position markers, and steer's-head headstock inlay that denoted a late-'55 or early-'56 model.

While plenty of rockers—then and now—showed little regard for their instruments, Cochran clearly cherished his Gretsch. A British newspaper account of one stop on his final English tour told of how a fan came across Cochran shielding the Gretsch with his own body backstage during a fight that had erupted in the theater, and the guitar even survived the crash that took Cochran's life, as if his love of the instrument carried it through the ordeal (Gene Vincent, on tour with Cochran in England, also survived the crash). It can be seen in action in film footage of the late '50s, notably Cochran's rousing performances of "C'mon Everybody" and "Summertime Blues" on TV's *Hadley's Town Hall Party*, and a visit to the Rock and Roll Hall of Fame in Cleveland, Ohio, will afford a look at this iconic 6120.

Program for a 1957 package tour including Eddie Cochran, Chuck Berry, Fats Domino, Buddy Holly, and more.

APPROPRIATELY KNOWN AS THE "ICEMAN" for his blistering treble-heavy tone, bluesman Albert Collins also wore the honorary a.k.a. "Master of the Telecaster," a tribute to his association with the debutante Fender solidbody that he made very much his own. Born in Leona, Texas, in 1932, Collins was actually led to the Telecaster by his love for the playing of fellow Texan Clarence "Gatemouth" Brown, an early Telecaster proponent who would be better known in later years for his use of a Gibson Firebird. In emulation of Brown—with whom Collins had performed on stage at the age of fifteen, during both players' pre-Tele years—Collins capoed his own Telecaster high up the neck, and developed a boppy, horn-lick-inspired blues style that was one of the most distinctive in the genre.

At the age of seventeen, Collins formed his own band, The Rhythm Rockers, which made a name for itself in Houston's Third Ward before he jumped ship to record and tour with a string of other artists, including Big Mama Thornton and Little Richard (where he filled Jimi Hendrix's rather large shoes). In the late 1950s Collins had the first glimmer of solo success in the form of a single called "The Freeze." The Iceman theme gained momentum with a million-selling single, "Frosty," in 1962, followed by his first major solo album, *Truckin' with Albert Collins*, released on Blue Thumb Records in 1965.

In the early '50s, unable to afford the object of his desires, Collins had put a Fender Telecaster neck on the body of a lesser make of electric guitar. He bought his first proper Fender Telecaster in the late '50s, but was ultimately best known for his use of a 1966 Telecaster Custom with a maple-capped neck and a Gibson humbucker added in the neck position, the guitar on which the Fender Custom Shop Albert Collins Signature Telecaster would be based. Even though the blues boom of the late '60s helped to give Collins more recognition, and a career boost of sorts, the fleeting nature of "success" on the blues scene of that time meant that he had to labor on the side as a house painter and construction worker to supplement his income right up to the late '70s. Appearances at the Newport Jazz Festival in 1969, the Filmore West in 1971, and the Montreaux Jazz Festival in 1975 further solidified his status, however, as did the Grammy Award–winning album *Showdown*, recorded at the

Collins's best-known guitar was a 1966 Telecaster Custom with a maple-capped neck and a Gibson humbucker in the neck position. This guitar is now part of the Steven Seagal collection. *Paul Natkin/Getty Images*

peak of his career in 1985, with Robert Cray and Johnny Copeland. By this time, Collins's formidable presence in the blues world was well established, as was his flamboyant persona as an artist. Always a dazzling live performer, Albert Collins was known for his interactive approach to the stage as much as for his frenetic, electrifying playing style and searing tone. Using an extra-long cable between his Telecaster and his amplifier up on stage (a blisteringly loud Fender Quad Reverb from around the mid-'70s onward), Collins would strut down into the audience while still playing, or even leave the stage at the end of the set while the band still played, without dropping a lick. Collins became ill while on tour in Switzerland in the summer of 1993, and was soon after diagnosed with lung cancer that had metastasized to his liver. He died the following November at the age of sixty-one. ✪

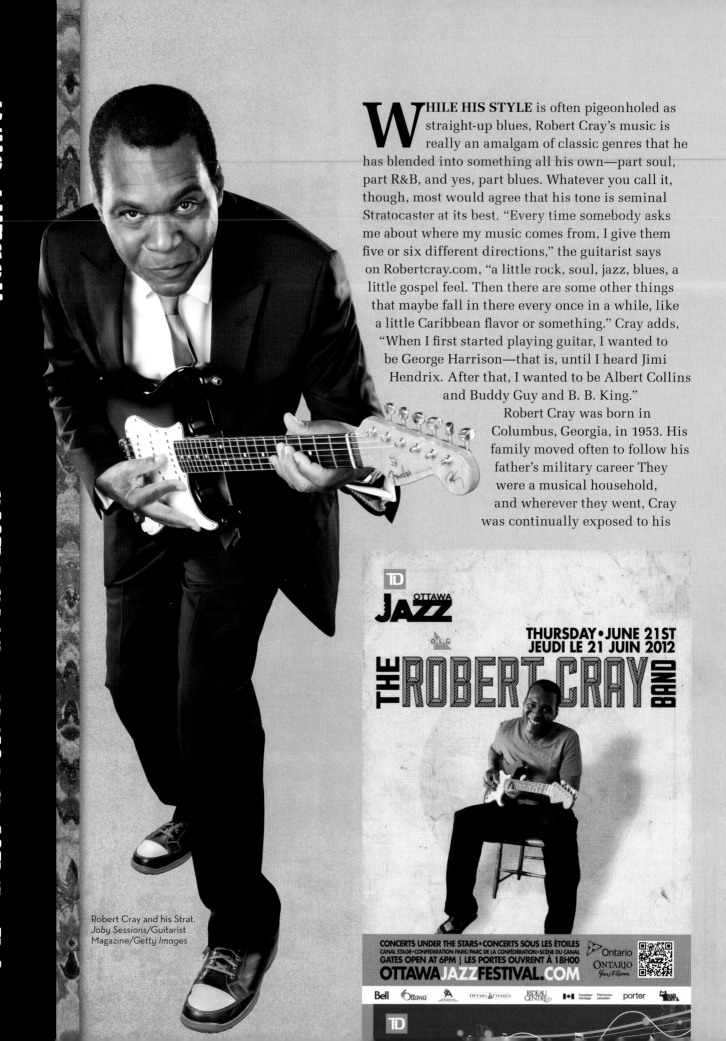

WHILE HIS STYLE is often pigeonholed as straight-up blues, Robert Cray's music is really an amalgam of classic genres that he has blended into something all his own—part soul, part R&B, and yes, part blues. Whatever you call it, though, most would agree that his tone is seminal Stratocaster at its best. "Every time somebody asks me about where my music comes from, I give them five or six different directions," the guitarist says on Robertcray.com, "a little rock, soul, jazz, blues, a little gospel feel. Then there are some other things that maybe fall in there every once in a while, like a little Caribbean flavor or something." Cray adds, "When I first started playing guitar, I wanted to be George Harrison—that is, until I heard Jimi Hendrix. After that, I wanted to be Albert Collins and Buddy Guy and B. B. King."

Robert Cray was born in Columbus, Georgia, in 1953. His family moved often to follow his father's military career They were a musical household, and wherever they went, Cray was continually exposed to his

Robert Cray and his Strat.
Joby Sessions/Guitarist Magazine/Getty Images

2004 Robert Cray Signature Violet Stratocaster. *Fender Musical Instruments Corporation*

parents' broad tastes, absorbing everything from pop to rock 'n' roll, to jazz to blues, to gospel and soul. Cray started playing the guitar in his early teens, joined his first band while still in junior high school in Newport News, Virginia, and moved to the Northwest at the age of twenty-one, where he soon formed the Robert Cray Band in Eugene, Oregon. Several years of paying dues all along the West Coast led to a deal with Mercury Records in 1982, but Cray's star truly ascended in 1986 with the release of his third album, *Strong Persuader*, which earned him a Grammy Award. Since then, Cray has gone on to earn another four Grammy Awards, fifteen nominations, and sold more than twelve million records.

From the start, Cray was drawn to the Stratocaster, and for many listeners, his playing has come to define the clean-yet-rich nature of the guitar's natural voice. His spare, tasteful playing style enables that guitar to be heard in a pure setting too—classy enough to make do with a few powerful, well-landed notes where less mature players might assault you with a blizzard of riffage, Robert Cray's playing is a virtual lesson in elegant restraint, yet manages to be utterly moving every time. His intimate technique is enhanced by his use of the bare flesh of his right-hand thumb rather than a pick and running it all through both a Matchless Clubman and a Fender Vibro-King set relatively clean, with just an edge of breakup when he picks hard. Rather than using the Strat's vibrato (he removes the bar from his own guitars or chooses hardtail variations), Cray induces an emotive shake in his tone, using a classic left-hand finger vibrato, although he is also fond of bringing in the Vibro-King's tremolo to assist in some classic retro tones. Fender released the Custom Shop Robert Cray Signature Stratocaster in 2003, a hardtail model with vintage-wind pickups and Cray's favorite Inca Silver finish, which is flanked by the more affordable standard-run Robert Cray Stratocaster. ★

Crayton's "The Telephone Is Ringing" on Vee-Jay featured one of the first—if not *the* first—recorded Strat. The tone is unmistakable.

2009 Custom Shop 1958 Candy Apple Red Stratocaster with gold-anodized pickguard, inspired by Pee Wee Crayton's guitar. *Fender Musical Instruments Corporation*

SWINGING BLUESMAN PEE WEE CRAYTON'S 1955 recording of "The Telephone Is Ringing" on Vee-Jay 214 just may be the premiere recording of a Stratocaster. Whether it was indeed the first or not—we may never know—the song showcased a tone like no other record before. Crayton played his big bends and bluesy pentatonic riffs, punctuated by shimmering ninth chords, with a unique, biting sound. The tone was unlike that of T-Bone Walker's archtop Gibson ES-5 with its woody, out-of-phase-pickup voice or Clarence "Gatemouth" Brown's snarling Fender Esquire. It was a sound all its own.

Connie Curtis Crayton was Texas born and influenced primarily by Texan guitar slingers, such as Walker and jazzman Charlie Christian. He began by emulating T-Bone, playing his jazz-inflected blues licks on a big archtop Gibson before he was given a Stratocaster and a tweed Twin amp by the factory, likely in 1954. No one seems to remember the circumstances behind the present—how, where, or when Leo Fender or anyone else from the factory met Crayton. In fact, as Leo was a staunch country music fan, his giving such an early and special Strat to a bluesman seems odd in retrospect. Nevertheless, Crayton's gift was one of the first Strats given to a musician by Fender, alongside the golden '54 given to Eldon Shamblin. And like Shamblin's guitar, Crayton's boasted a custom-color paint job and other special features.

Crayton's Strat was painted a bright red hue, a color some have suggested was a Studebaker car color. Bill Carson had a similarly colored red Strat, which he termed "Cimarron Red," perhaps inspired by the band Leon McAuliffe and His Cimarron Boys, as McAuliffe played a red Fender Stringmaster. The color was also close to what would years later appear in Fender color charts as Dakota Red.

Crayton's Strat featured a gold-anodized metal pickguard in place of the typical Bakelite plastic pickguard. The rest of its features toed the line with production Strats, including the chrome-plated hardware, rather than the special gold plating.

Crayton had moved from Texas to California during the Depression years of the 1930s, and that's where he started seriously playing guitar. He was often known as T-Bone Walker Jr., a name that was somewhat derisive, but also of prime promotional benefit. In later years, he and the real T-Bone shared the bills in hard-fought fret wars.

Crayton signed on with Modern Records in 1948, playing T-Bone-inspired jump blues. One of his earliest sides was the instrumental, "Blues after Hours," which hit No. 1 on the *Billboard* R&B chart. In the 1950s, he cut sides for other labels, including T-Bone's home, Imperial, as well as Jamie and Vee-Jay.

Crayton was often pictured with the special Strat in hand, Crayton himself usually wearing a lean, shiny sharkskin suit, the consummate bluesman. He cradled it on the cover of his early eponymous Crown LP in 1960 and still held the guitar on the 1971 Vanguard album, *Things I Used to Do*. During the years in between, Crayton's Strat had obviously been well used, the red paint chipped away, the neck and headstock smoke and time darkened. ✪

—*Michael Dregni*

Looking sharp in a sharkskin suit and toting his red Strat with gold-anodized pickguard, Pee Wee Crayton was ready to take on his archrival, T-Bone Walker, in a battle of the jump blues kings.

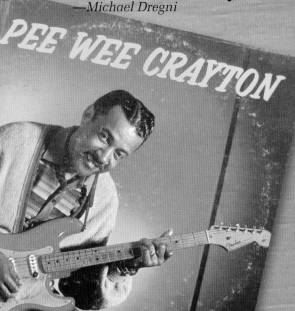

73

"HIP-HUG-HER"
IN PERSON
THE FABULOUS
BOOKER T
"KING OF THE HAMMOND ORGAN"
AND THE MG'S
★"BOOTLEG" ★"GREEN ONIONS"
"THE MG'S ARE" STAX RECORDING STAR
OTIS REDDING RECORDING BAND
LITTLE BAND & SHOW

STAX
S-127
Time: 2:45
Pub.-East BMI
STX-6295
GREEN ONIONS
(Jones, Cropper, Steinberg, Jackson)
BOOKER T. AND THE MG'S
DISTRIBUTED BY ATLANTIC RECORD SALES, 1841 BROADWAY NEW YORK, N.Y.

NO SHREDMEISTER, nor merchant of incendiary blues or rock riffs, Steve Cropper has nevertheless authored some of the most distinctive guitar parts, both solo and rhythm, in all of popular music. What Cropper might lack in flash he makes up for in an abundance of cool taste. Witness the sleek, spare licks on everything from Sam & Dave's "Soul Man" to Otis Redding's "(Sitting on the) Dock of the Bay" (which Cropper co-wrote) and "I've Been Loving You Too Long (To Stop Now)," to Booker T. and the M.G.s' instrumental classic "Green Onions," and you'll instantly hear what players in the know have been talking about since Cropper laid down these cool sounds in the early to mid-'60s. You don't have to play a flurry of notes to be a genius on the guitar—and when you want to keep it simple, there's arguably no better instrument than the Fender Telecaster.

On those early Stax recordings, including 1962's "Green Onions," Cropper is known to have played a 1956 Fender Esquire, the single-pickup version of the Telecaster. In 1963, however, he acquired the blonde Telecaster with rosewood fingerboard that would be played on the majority of the many hits to which he contributed and seen in most of his live performances for many years. Both were simple, solid, roadworthy workingman's guitars, and both would have sounded roughly similar, especially in Cropper's very able hands, which happened to be very busy too—in addition to recording and performing, Booker T. and the M.G.s, along with a rotating assembly of other musicians, served as the Stax Records house band in the label's Memphis studio and on tour throughout the 1960s.

In this role, Cropper and that blonde '63 Tele contributed their lithe, slightly countrified R&B licks to an unprecedented number of hits by other artists who, in addition to Sam & Dave and Otis Redding, included Carla and Rufus Thomas, Wilson Pickett, Johnnie Taylor, Eddie Floyd, Albert King, the Staple Singers, and several others. In the course of doing so, Cropper and his bandmates helped lay the foundations of soul music.

In addition to the Tele's twangy yet punchy single-coil pickups, Cropper's distinctive recorded tone had some help from an evolving array of classic amplifiers. In the early to mid-'60s he mostly used a small tweed Fender Harvard, later moving to a brownface 2×10-inch Super combo and a larger 4×10-inch Super Reverb combo after that. Whatever he played through, though—and whoever he played with—those tasteful licks were always pure Cropper. ♦

Cropper with the '63 Tele that helped contribute writhe licks to so many great Stax recordings. *Michael Ochs Archives/Getty Images*

ARGUMENTS ABOUT WHO originated surf guitar continue to rage, but for pure kinetic energy few would argue with crowning Dick Dale the "King of the Surf Guitar." Dale enjoyed a career resurgence after his signature tune, the eastern-inflected "Misirlou," was featured prominently in the 1994 film *Pulp Fiction*, but from late 1959 to early 1961 Dale (born Richard Monsour) and his Del-Tones packed the Rendezvous Ballroom in Balboa, California, and for a time after that, the Pasadena Civic Auditorium with upward of three thousand to four thousand young patrons nearly every weekend night of the year. To satisfy their lust for action, he generated furious levels of energy—and copious amounts of sheer volume—to translate surfing's extreme physical experience into a representative musical performance. Naturally, Dale's guitar choice was an important part of the process, but the need to satisfy such vast crowds

Dick Dale played music by surfers, for surfers. Armed with his trademark lefty Fender Stratocaster, also known as "The Beast," Dale and the Del-Tones rocked coastal ballrooms and school gymnasiums. The volume came courtesy of Leo Fender's hot-rodded Showman amp; "wave" sounds were thanks to the newfangled Fender reverb unit.

with the volume and power that the music demanded meant that he also became one of the first proponents of the entire rig, and arguably the first artist to front a truly arena-worthy backline.

Fender's Jazzmaster and Jaguar have come to be known as classic surf guitars, alongside the Mosrites that other artists (most notably the Ventures) also gravitated toward, but Dick Dale played a Stratocaster from the outset of his professional career and has stuck with it for fifty-plus years. Having started out as an aspiring country singer and guitarist, Dale was drawn to the Strat shortly before solidifying his stance as a surf guitarist. As a left-hander, he played the guitar strung "upside down," the way many lefties would approach the instrument upon flipping over a right-handed guitar. After initially being given a right-handed Stratocaster by Leo Fender in the late '50s and told to "beat it to death," as Dale recalls on his website, dickdale.com, he moved over to left-handed Strats (most notably a chartreuse metalflake example known as "The Beast"), but continued to string the guitar with the low E on the bottom.

Other than this quirk, Dale's use of a Strat for the bright, cutting tones of surf guitar really isn't all that unusual—the model is designed to excel in these tones just as much as the Jaguar and Jazzmaster. The bigger part of Dale's sonic revolution came in his amp of choice and his promotion of that super-wet, reverb-laden sound, although it was not always thus. In order to broadcast his big sound to the big crowds he was drawing, Dale used his budding relationship with Leo Fender to acquire a suitable amp. Fender had always turned directly to musicians for feedback about his developments, and Dale's pleas for more punching power made an impression. Accounts of how much input the guitarist himself had on the development of the Showman amp vary greatly (with Dale's own recollections often putting him right there at the drawing board, while those of other Fender employees occasionally minimize his role), but the powerful new Fender model, introduced in the new blonde Tolex covering in 1960, was undoubtedly designed specifically to belt the young surfing guitarist's music to the masses.

As wet as the surf sound eventually became, however, Dale's first hit single, "Let's Go Trippin'"; his entire first album, *Surfer's Choice*; and his

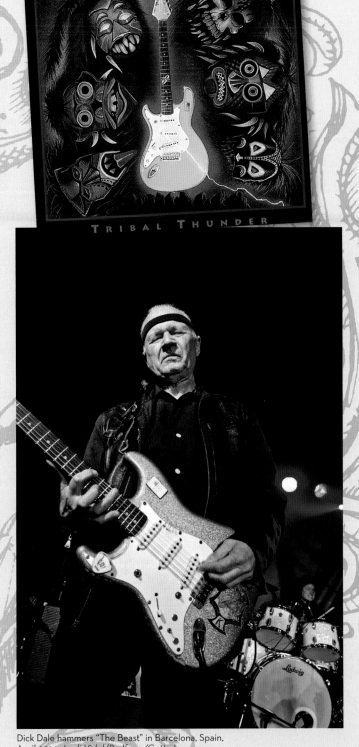

Dick Dale hammers "The Beast" in Barcelona, Spain, April 2014. *Jordi Vidal/Redferns/Getty Images*

legendary early Rendezvous Ballroom shows were all performed sans reverb. Once the Fender Reverb Unit hit the streets in early 1962 though, with prototypes road-tested by Dale, there was no turning back from the big splash. ✪

FROM HIS EARLIEST DAYS as the skinny, big-haired kid in thrash-metal sensation Pantera, Dimebag Darrell rocked Dean ML model guitars like they were made for him—and, one day, they would be. Dimebag (born Darrell Abbott, and initially nicknamed Diamond Darrell while in Pantera) received his first Dean as a much-anticipated gift from his father in the early '80s, just as Pantera was getting rolling in its hometown of Arlington, Texas. His most famous Dean, however, came hot on the heels of this gift, but would only secure a place in the Dimebag annals after a circuitous sidetrack and a striking new paint job.

Just days after receiving the gift guitar from his dad, and while still only in his mid-teens, Darrell entered and won a shredding contest in Dallas and took home, as grand prize, a maroon Dean ML. In need of a car more than a second guitar, Darrell sold the maroon Dean to Pantera's original lead singer, Terry Glaze, for enough cash to buy a used

Dimebag performs with Pantera, New York City, April 1992. *Ebet Roberts/Redferns/Getty Images* yellow Firebird; Glaze eventually sold the Dean on to friend and Pantera fan Buddy Blaze.

And, one might think, that was that. Darrell and Pantera transitioned from glam-metal to groove-driven thrash-metal, and Blaze went on to indulge his own love of metal guitars by refinishing and building his own (he would eventually move to New Jersey to custom-build instruments for Kramer). Several years passed and Darrell, who had remained friends with Blaze, found an occasion to borrow an electric-blue Dean ML with distinctive lightning-bolt graphics, a reshaped V-profile neck, and an added Floyd Rose vibrato that he had been coveting during recent visits to the guitar maker's shop. Speaking to Chris Kies in *Premier Guitar* magazine, Blaze recalled Darrell calling him over the ensuing weeks, begging to buy the guitar because he just couldn't part with it. As the reality set in that this guitar really was meant for hands other than his, Blaze finally told the up-and-coming metal star, "You got lucky this time because that lightning guitar is your red ML, your trophy guitar, so just keep it man. It was always yours and it's yours again."

Darrell used the modified Dean ML on 1988's *Power Metal* album and 1990s major-label breakthrough *Cowboys from Hell* (it famously

appeared on the cover of the latter). The guitar was also used as the basis for several Dimebag Darrell signature models that have since been issued by Dean, and it is best represented by the Dean from Hell CFH model, with lightning-bolt paint job and Darrell's preferred Bill Lawrence XL500 humbucker in the bridge position.

In December 2004, Darrell Abbott was shot and killed less than a minute into a performance by his new band, Damageplan, at the Alrosa Villa in Columbus, Ohio. His blue 1981 lightning-bolt Dean ML is on display at the Hard Rock Café in Dallas. ★

This performance photo provides a great view of the wear on the back of the '81 Dean ML's neck. *Marty Temme/ImageDirect/Getty Images*

Artist: Lee Bolton

LATE-1950s GIBSON FLYING V

Dave Davies performs with the Kinks, Tivoli Gardens, Copenhagen, Denmark, July 1, 1969. *Jan Persson/Redferns/Getty Images*

The Kinks perform on *Top of the Pops* in the late 1960s. From left: Ray Davies, Pete Quaife, Dave Davies with his Flying V, and Mick Avory. *David Redfern/Redferns/Getty Images*

AS LEAD GUITARIST WITH THE KINKS, Dave Davies was an early proponent of ear-catching guitar tones. He is widely credited as having recorded the first heavily distorted electric guitar sound to appear in the British pop charts, in the form of his chunky riffs on "You Really Got Me," released in August 1964. (For the record, and before the arguments begin, Dave Davies has flat-out denied on several occasions that Jimmy Page played the guitar on "You Really Got Me," as has been rumored and written in the past.) To achieve this nasty, ragged tone, Davies slit the cone of the speaker in a small Elpico practice amp, patched that through a Vox AC30, and laid down his historic power chords on a 1962 Harmony Meteor. In addition to these standout sonics, he and brother Ray Davies—the band's singer, rhythm guitarist, and main songwriter—like so many British bands of the day, were also big on standout styles. Rather than dedicated followers of fashion, however, the Davies brothers looked to be leaders, and Dave knew a radically stylish guitar when he saw one.

Davies used a handful of guitars in the early '60s, but his mainstay of the time, after the Harmony Meteor, was a black Guild archtop electric with two Guild humbucking pickups. The Kinks only traveled with one guitar at the time, and on a US tour in late 1964 or early 1965, an airline lost the Guild. Davies rushed to a Los Angeles guitar store, but didn't initially see anything he liked. "I saw this odd, dusty case under the counter, and said, 'What's in there?'" he told this writer in 1999. "The salesman said, 'Oh, that's some strange old guitar . . .'" The proprietor revealed the contents, Davies's eyes lit up, and $60 later he walked out the door with the most distinctive instrument in British rock music of the day. Later that year, when Davies appeared on the British TV show *Shindig* in 1965 and in other live and broadcast performances, his new acquisition, an original, late-'50s Gibson Flying V, made an enormous splash on the scene.

Used throughout the mid-'60s, Davies's Flying V was eventually retired from service, stored safely away from the rigors of touring, and he moved on to playing Les Pauls, Telecasters, Stratocasters, and a host of other guitars. Largely unappreciated before Davies picked one up, the radical Flying V certainly left its mark on the style and the music of the swinging '60s. ★

1958 RECTANGULAR GRETSCH

Gretsch, circa 1960,
formerly owned by
Bo Diddley. *Courtesy
Experience Music
Project, Seattle, WA*

Diddley with one of his pinstriped
and decaled rectangular
Gretsches, circa 1958. *Gilles
Petard/Redferns/Getty Images*

By this time of this 1963 show, Diddley had segued into other futuristic guitars, notably the Gretsch Jupiter Thunderbird. *GAB Archive/ Redferns/Getty Images*

AT THIS STAGE IN THE GAME there are plenty of guys with guitars named after them. Bo Diddley, on the other hand, has an entire *beat* named after him. *Bum-da-bum-da-bum, da-bum-bum.* That infectious jungle beat—with Diddley (born Elias McDaniel) gliding between low-position rhythm chords and higher slide stabs, Frank Kirkland pounding the drums, and Jerome Green emphasizing the syncopation on the maracas—not only launched the artist's first major hit, 1955's "Bo Diddley," but underpinned many of his equally addictive follow-ups and even helped give birth to rock 'n' roll itself. Paid tribute to by everyone from Buddy Holly to the Rolling Stones to U2, Diddley founded his own boastful, beat-heavy breed of music, and his nickname, "The Originator," couldn't have fit better if it were tailored on Savile Row. Diddley, who passed away in 2008, played a number of guitars during his run, but he launched his professional career on a Gretsch Duo Jet and a red Gretsch Jet Firebird. When fame earned him enough cash to commission something appropriately flashy, Diddley turned to Gretsch for his trademark rectangular guitar.

Diddley's first release, "Bo Diddley," May 1955. *Michael Ochs Archives/ Getty Images*

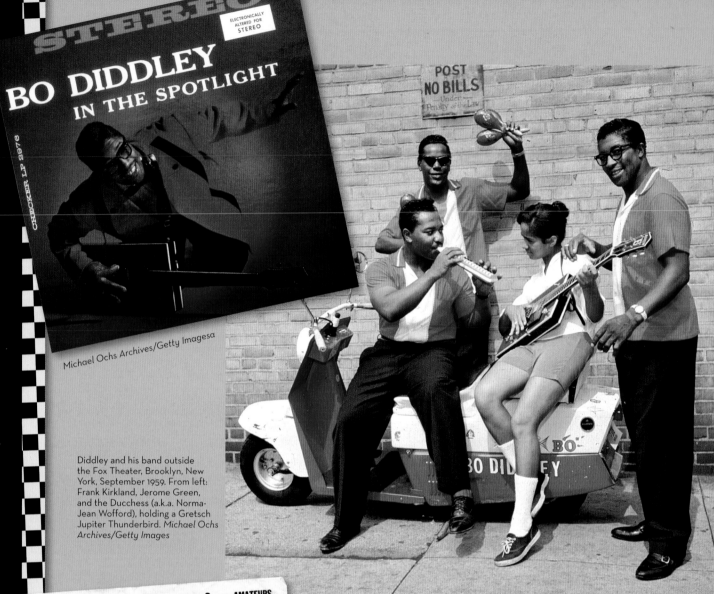

Michael Ochs Archives/Getty Imagesa

Diddley and his band outside the Fox Theater, Brooklyn, New York, September 1959. From left: Frank Kirkland, Jerome Green, and the Ducchess (a.k.a. Norma-Jean Wofford), holding a Gretsch Jupiter Thunderbird. *Michael Ochs Archives/Getty Images*

Gilles Petard/Redferns/Getty Images

Diddley owned several of the rectangular guitars, which were patterned after an instrument he had made for himself earlier (and much like others he would build in later years). The first was a red number made by Gretsch in 1958. It carried features from the models he had played earlier, including a pair of DeArmond-made Dynasonic single-coil pickups, an adjustable Melita bridge, and thumbnail position markers on its '57-spec neck. As he was prone to do, Diddley further adorned the guitar with stickers and pinstripes and modified its pickguard with an early example of a peace sign, a symbol that

Artist: Justin Hampton (www.justinhampton.com)

One of Diddley's late-career rectangular Gretsches. *Rick Gould*

had originated only a couple years before in 1956 as the emblem of the UK's Campaign for Nuclear Disarmament (not a surprising display of pacifism when you consider that, as the artist himself was fond of saying, "Bo Diddley is a lover").

Through the '60s and into the '70s and beyond, Diddley segued through other guitars, notably another modernistic Gretsch, the Jupiter Thunderbird, and other rectangular axes of his own devising, but he returned to the fold shortly before

his death to endorse the Gretsch G6138 Bo Diddley (which now carried Filter'Tron humbucking pickups). Diddley and Gretsch further ramped up the fun quotient, with Billy F Gibbons joining forces for good measure, with the G6199 "Billy-Bo," a reissue of the Space Age Jupiter Thunderbird. Throw either into open tuning, hit 'em with that "hambone" beat, and you just might feel the spirit of Mr. Bo Diddley himself moving through the room. ★

PRIOR TO DRAWING JEERS from swarms of (arguably small-minded) folk fans by going electric in 1965, Bob Dylan presented himself as the hard-traveling folk troubadour, an image he established while largely playing a vintage Gibson Nick Lucas model flat-top guitar.

The young Dylan had played Martin and other Gibson models in the late '50s and early '60s, but in those final years before taking up first a sunburst

Dylan performing on BBC with his Nick Lucas Special, 1965. *Val Wilmer/Redferns/Getty Images*

Fender Stratocaster, then a "blonde on blonde" whiteguard Telecaster and ushering in a new folk-rock sound, the Nick Lucas was his instrument of choice. He played this guitar in the studio and on tour from 1963 to 1966, and he used it for the legendary albums *Another Side of Bob Dylan* and *Bringing It All Back Home*. And, although it didn't appear on the covers of either of these releases, it is frequently seen in much of the live performance footage from the day, including broadcasts of the Newport Folk Festival in 1964 and 1965, Dylan's famous appearances on BBC TV in England in 1965, and in the documentary film *Don't Look Back*. While in hindsight the Gibson Nick Lucas seemed just right for the young Dylan, and has become an iconic folk guitar as a result, the model's origins suggest that it was perhaps an unlikely choice for the scruffy young folky.

By the mid-1920s Gibson was the top name in archtop guitars, and it had yet to offer a quality flat-top, but that market was showing signs of blooming. To help sell the format, Gibson turned to sideman and early jazz star Nick Lucas, whose 1929 recording of "Tiptoe through the Tulips" (a song that sounded considerably less camp in its day than it did when Tiny Tim re-recorded it in 1968) was featured in the Warner Bros. musical hit *Gold Diggers of Broadway* and had gained Lucas massive popular exposure. The Nick Lucas model (also referred to as the Gibson

Hutton Archive/Getty Images

Special, as were many signature guitars of the day) went into production in 1928. The instrument evolved during its lifetime, but consistent throughout was its notably deep body—a little over 4 inches at the deepest point—which made it an impressively loud, rich guitar for an acoustic whose dimensions were otherwise those of a small-bodied flat-top, such as the more cheaply made L-1, introduced two years before. Measuring 13.5 inches across the lower bout and with an original scale length of 24.25 inches, the Nick Lucas was born with twelve frets clear of the body but eventually gained a thirteen-, then fourteen-fret neck, all of which featured fretboards with distinctive and subtly elegant position marker inlays.

Dylan's own Nick Lucas, which he is said to have acquired in 1963 in a Greenwich Village, New York City, music shop after losing his Gibson J-50, has been variously reported as originating from 1929 and 1933. While its headstock logo—"The Gibson"—would seem to indicate a guitar from the earlier era, its thirteen-fret neck would push it into the '30s. Writing at dylanchords.info, Eyolf Østrem notes that reports made by those who have examined Dylan's Gibson in person reveal that the guitar's flat-top pin bridge is a Guild item that must have been added as a repair or modification. Also noteworthy is the fact that the guitar's original dark sunburst finish had given way to a stripped natural finish by the time it arrived in Dylan's hands, perhaps in conjunction with the bridge replacement.

The whereabouts of Dylan's Gibson Nick Lucas are currently unknown. ✦

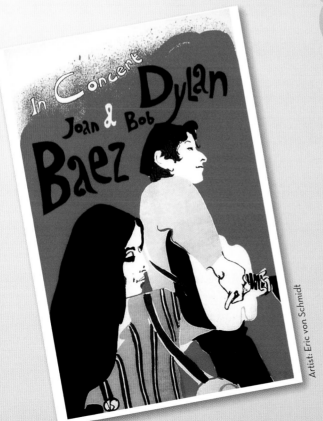

Artist: Eric von Schmidt

IN AN ERA WHEN "TWANG" almost universally means a country picker attacking a Fender Telecaster, it's worth revisiting the time when a teenage guitarist, his Bigsby-loaded Gretsch, and a 2,000-gallon water tank out in the Arizona desert helped establish twang as a formative rock 'n' roll style.

Perhaps ironically, a teenage Duane Eddy had set out very deliberately to be a country singer and guitar star in the mid-'50s. In 1957 he purchased a Gretsch 6120—paid for with a loan cosigned by his father—specifically because it was the model that Chet Atkins played and endorsed. Some career guidance and thoughtful record production from local

Duane Eddy's original Gretsch Chet Atkins Model 6120, which he used on most of his hit songs, starting in the 1950s. Courtesy Nigel Osborne/Jawbone Press

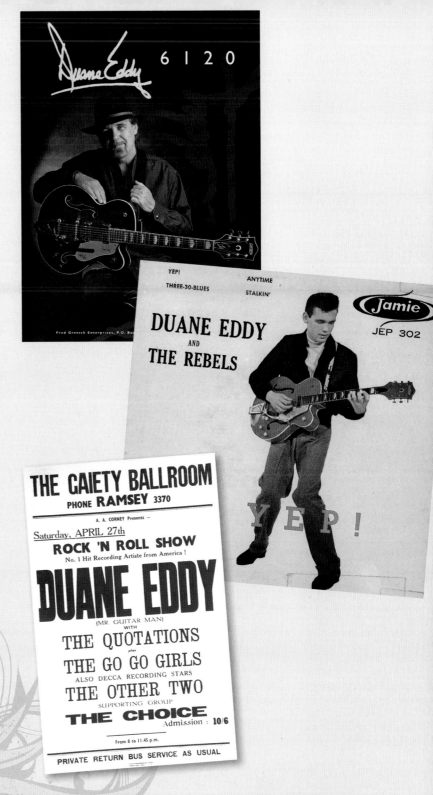

disc jockey Lee Hazlewood, however, put him on a new and rewarding path. Eddy's 1958 release "Rebel Rouser" set the standard for hard-edged, low-string, twangy rock 'n' roll instrumentals. Follow-ups such as "Peter Gunn" and "Cannonball" further affirmed this infectious new style, and an instrumental star was born. Eddy scored a whopping fifteen Top 40 singles in the first five years of his career, and he has gone on to sell more than 100 million records . . . and counting.

Eddy's breed of twang was not born out of mere treble bite, but it combined a number of elements that gave plenty of motion to his guitar tone. His '57 Gretsch 6120 was one of the last of the line to carry DeArmond Model 200 (a.k.a. Gretsch Dynasonic) single-coil pickups, which helped give it plenty of snap and definition, but Eddy's use of the Bigsby vibrato defined his sound as much as any electronic component. Rather than merely using the Bigsby to add a dip and a wobble to the tails of notes and phrases, as many artists had done before and still do today, Eddy dipped the bar to spring into notes, creating a lively, dynamic start to his riffs and adding plenty of shimmer and the occasional deep bend to keep things rolling mid-phrase. His propensity for low-string riffs also gave a rumbling menace to many tunes and increased the sense of size and muscle in his music. Pump it all through Hazlewood's clever early reverb system, which comprised a guitar amp at one end of a big, empty water tank and a microphone at the other, and Eddy's sound was larger than large for its day and plenty dynamic.

Like most guitar stars, Eddy was received with open arms by manufacturers eager to build him a signature model. In 1961 he signed with Guild, which released the Duane Eddy 500, complete with many of the 6120's appointments, including DeArmond pickups, master volume control, and a Bigsby tailpiece

(the model carried Guild humbuckers after 1964). Later, Eddy was wooed by Gibson, and the union gave birth to the Gibson Duane Eddy Signature Hollowbody with Seymour Duncan–designed single-coil pickups and, yes, a Bigsby vibrato. For fans of vintage rock 'n' roll instrumentals though, the "Titan of Twang" will always be posed with a '57 Gretsch 6120—even if that guitar carried another star's name. ★

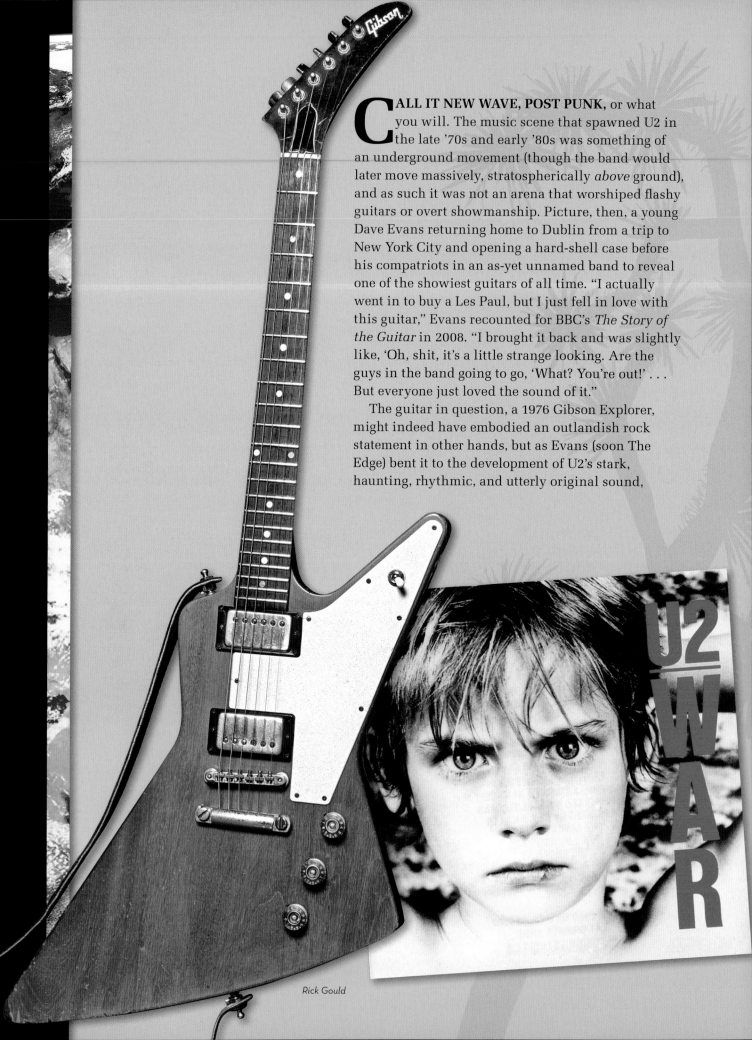

CALL IT NEW WAVE, POST PUNK, or what you will. The music scene that spawned U2 in the late '70s and early '80s was something of an underground movement (though the band would later move massively, stratospherically *above* ground), and as such it was not an arena that worshiped flashy guitars or overt showmanship. Picture, then, a young Dave Evans returning home to Dublin from a trip to New York City and opening a hard-shell case before his compatriots in an as-yet unnamed band to reveal one of the showiest guitars of all time. "I actually went in to buy a Les Paul, but I just fell in love with this guitar," Evans recounted for BBC's *The Story of the Guitar* in 2008. "I brought it back and was slightly like, 'Oh, shit, it's a little strange looking. Are the guys in the band going to go, 'What? You're out!' . . . But everyone just loved the sound of it."

The guitar in question, a 1976 Gibson Explorer, might indeed have embodied an outlandish rock statement in other hands, but as Evans (soon The Edge) bent it to the development of U2's stark, haunting, rhythmic, and utterly original sound,

Rick Gould

it took on the stance of the anti-guitar hero who wielded it and proved a cornerstone in the early career of one of the world's most popular and influential bands.

The Edge used this Explorer on the majority of U2's early recordings, often swapping it for a mid-'70s Fender Stratocaster and partnering the guitars with an Electro-Harmonix Memory Man echo unit and a Vox AC30 amplifier. Not simply either a lead or rhythm guitarist, The Edge's role in the band really incorporated elements of both, often simultaneously, as he set a driving momentum that incessantly propelled songs like "I Will Follow," "Gloria," "Sunday Bloody Sunday," and "New Year's Day" just as much as did Larry Mullen's drums.

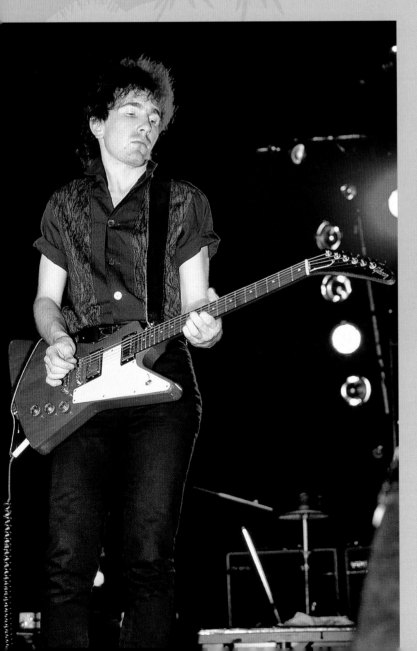

Royal Oak Theater, Royal Oak, Michigan, November 1981. *Robert Alford*

As U2 ascended dizzying heights of success, The Edge indulged in every rock star's prerogative to explore a wide number of makes and models of guitars. He has notably been seen cradling instruments such as a Gretsch White Falcon, 6120, and Country Gentleman; several Gibson Les Pauls; numerous Rickenbackers; and myriad Fenders (the total haul for 2009's 360 Tour numbered more than forty guitars). But the 1976 Explorer remains a standout in the minds of many fans and apparently remains dear to the artist as well. While recording 2000's *All That You Can't Leave Behind*, an album that signaled yet another evolution of the band's sound, The Edge found himself seeking just the right tone for a song that didn't quite want to gel. Out came the Explorer, the echo pedal, and the Vox AC30—and the layered, atmospheric guitar parts to "Beautiful Day" fell right into place. ★

IN THE ALTERNATIVE PUNK and new wave scenes of the late 1970s and early 1980s, the Stratocaster was often seen as a square traditionalist, the conventional weaponry of classic rockers and bluesers like Jimi Hendrix, Ritchie Blackmore, Yngwie Malmsteen, and Eric Clapton. As such, for a time there at least, it just wasn't much in favor with what you might call the "hip crowd"—players who were taking up the big names' alternatives like the Jazzmaster and Jaguar, the Les Paul Special and Junior, and other "second-tier" electrics. In using a 1970s Stratocaster to log many of

his most notable tones, however, U2's the Edge (a.k.a. Dave Evans) helped drag this seminal Fender toward indie's cutting edge, making it once again acceptable to a younger, up-and-coming generation of players.

While The Edge is reported to own more than two hundred guitars and commonly takes more than forty on tour at any time, Stratocasters take up a bigger chunk of his collection than any other model. As is the way with so many struggling musicians, though, the Strats that peppered the most notable early U2 recordings weren't the prized pre-CBS models. In the early days, he plied his trade on several workaday 1970s Stratocasters with large headstocks, three-bolt necks, and bullet-head truss rod adjustment nuts and forged an instantly recognizable signature sound in the process. Some of the earliest U2 photos from around 1977 and 1978 show the guitarist wielding a mid-'70s Stratocaster with sunburst finish, and a black '73 Strat was often his main squeeze through the 1980s, when the '76 Gibson Explorer was resting. And if an Electro-Harmonix Deluxe Memory Man delay pedal and Vox AC30 give a certain homogeneity to many of the early recordings, the Stratocaster's bright, glassy cutting power can certainly be heard amid the whirl of much of it.

Where the Stratocaster had previously been known primarily as a lead instrument, The Edge took its percussive rhythmic capabilities to new heights. Neither a "lead" nor a "rhythm" player, per se, he established a rhythmic momentum on the instrument that allowed U2's early songs, in particular, to display plenty of air and space, while retaining a compelling forward motion and simultaneously eliminating any real need for solos or chord parts in the traditional sense. Listen, for example, to his churning, bouncing performance on "Where the Streets Have No Name" from 1987's *The Joshua Tree*, and hear how well Leo's goal for a "bright, cutting" tone works in a context he could in no way have envisioned when designing the guitar in 1953 and 1954. In its own way, and for its time, it was as fitting a tribute to the traditional that the alternative could make. ★

The Edge and U2 perform at the US Festival in San Bernardino, California, May 1983. *Ebet Roberts/Redferns/Getty Images*

YOU'D BE HARD-PRESSED to cruise your AM or FM radio dial in America in 1976 or '77 without landing on one of the three mammoth hits from Peter Frampton's *Frampton Comes Alive!* album, which launched him into the pop-rock idol stratosphere. The singles "Do You Feel Like We Do," "Show Me the Way," and "Baby I Love Your Way" were everywhere, Frampton was selling out arenas across the country, and the artist's blond locks and jet-black Les Paul Custom gleamed out from the covers of the more than six million copies of the double album that were sold in its release year alone. But Frampton's chops had really solidified on one fateful night in California six years before, during the recording of a previous live album with a previous band—and while playing that same three-pickup Les Paul Custom for the very first time.

Frampton emerged as a young guitar star of '60s London in the wake of behemoth players such as Eric Clapton, Jeff Beck, and Jimmy Page. There, he caught the attention of singer and guitarist Steve Marriott of the Small Faces, who tapped the nineteen-year-old to form Humble Pie. Over the next couple of years, Humble Pie toured and recorded *hard*, and the creative juices were really flowing by late 1970 when Marriott, Frampton, and company found themselves opening for the Grateful Dead during a three-night stand at the Fillmore West in San Francisco, with a mobile recording unit pulled up outside.

On the first night, Frampton's Gibson ES-335 was plagued by feedback. After the Pie's set on the second night, a fan named Mark Mariana approached him and said he'd noticed that the guitarist was having some trouble. He offered to bring along a Les Paul the next day that Frampton could play for the third show, if he liked it. The following morning, Mariana met the guitarist in the hotel coffee shop and opened a new Gibson case to reveal a 1954 Les Paul Custom "Black Beauty," fresh from a factory refinish and its original single-coil pickups replaced with three PAF humbuckers. "As soon as he asked me if I wanted to try it, I said, 'Yeah, please!'" Frampton told

Steve Rosen for gibson.com in 2008. "And of course my feet didn't touch the ground the whole night. It was the most beautiful sound I'd ever heard."

Of course, Frampton couldn't imagine surrendering such an instrument, and he offered Mariana his ES-335 plus cash if he'd part with it. Mariana told the guitarist he wouldn't sell him the Les Paul—he would *give* it to him (unsurprisingly, the pair remain friends to this day). The live album gleaned from that first night that the Les Paul and Frampton joined forces, *Performance: Rockin' the Fillmore*, reached No. 21 on the Billboard album chart the following year, by which time Frampton had already departed Humble Pie for a solo career, throughout the zenith of which the modified '54 Les Paul Custom did him proud. The guitar was lost in 1980 when a cargo plane crashed in Venezuela, also claiming the lives of the pilot, co-pilot, and one passenger. ★

Facing page: Eastern Michigan University, Ypsilanti, Michigan, June 1975. *Robert Alford*

THE *NEW YORKER* once noted, "Bill Frisell
plays the guitar like Miles Davis played the
trumpet; in the hands of such radical thinkers,
their instruments simply become different animals."
It's hard to beat that for a definition of the otherwise
indefinable style of this elusive Tele-meister. Often
categorized as a jazzer, Frisell has offered stirring
support to rocking artists such as Elvis Costello,
David Sylvian, Ginger Baker, and Lucinda Williams.
Of course, he *has* also logged his time with jazz
greats, including his work with Jim Hall, Dave
Holland, Elvin Jones, and the occasional trio made up
of Ron Carter and Paul Motian. So ultimately we're
back where we started: you simply can't pin down

While the Telecaster may seem rather basic for a
versatile performer like Bill Frisell, the guitarist sites its
simplicity as its chief virtue. Here, he performs at the
Cheltenham Jazz Festival in Cheltenham, England, in
May 2008. *Steve Thorne/Redferns/Getty Images*

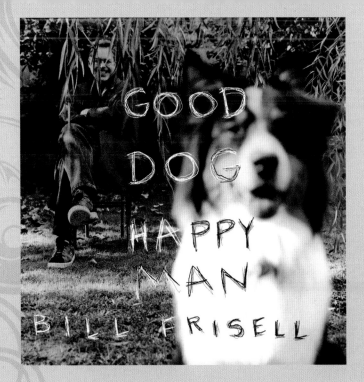

Bill Frisell. Except, that is, when you punch the category "Telecaster player." Frisell has played other guitars, but the Tele has returned time and again as his go-to instrument.

Frisell was born in 1951 in Baltimore, Maryland, and moved soon after with his family to Denver, Colorado. He first learned the clarinet, which he played in his elementary school band, but at the age of eleven he indulged in a longstanding desire to play the guitar. The first "real" guitar Frisell could call his own—after childhood experiments with box-bodied creations with rubber-band strings—was an archtop acoustic that he received as a Christmas present in 1962, and in 1965 he saved up his paper-route money to purchase his first electric, a newly released Fender Mustang. After attending the University of Northern Colorado, where he played clarinet, tenor saxophone, and guitar in the jazz and big bands, Frisell transferred to Berklee College of Music in Boston for a semester, then, deciding to concentrate on the guitar, traveled to New York City in 1972 to study with Jim Hall for eight weeks. For the rest of the '70s, Frisell lived a life familiar to many jazz artists who have struggled to scratch a living from their art: he bounced between further study in Boston, stints teaching and playing at home in Denver, and tours in Europe as a sideman. Then a move to New York in the early '80s, and a more concentrated effort at sinking his teeth into that scene, finally seemed to give the itinerant guitarist a more permanent home.

Frisell's first significant break in the NYC jazz scene came when young jazz-guitar star Pat Metheny recommended Bill to fill in for a session that he couldn't make. The gig resulted in Paul Motian's *Psalms* album for EMC Records, and landed Frisell a steady job as a house guitarist of sorts for the prominent jazz label, as well as sparking a longstanding association with Motian and other EMC artists. In 1982, Frisell recorded his first outing as a solo artist in his own right, again for EMC, and since that time—bouncing from collaborator, to sideman, to solo artist—he has never looked back.

He has owned and played several standout Telecasters throughout his career—including original examples from 1966 and 1974, as well as a Fender Custom Shop Relic Telecaster—but doesn't seem particular about vintage specs or high-end models. "Actually, my main Tele is a Mexican one," Frisell told *Fender News* in 2011. "It was like $500 and it's great! That's what I've been playing for the last few months. One time I tried to figure out how many Fender guitars I've had in my life, and it was kind of horrifying!" And if the Telecaster seems a rather basic instrument for such a versatile and eclectic player, Frisell's arguments for its merits put paid to such thinking pronto. "They're so simple and everything just works. . . . I can get from where it can almost sound like an acoustic guitar, or it can sound like a big, fat hollow-body guitar. Or it can have a 'stereotypical' Tele sound. People associate them with that 'twangy' thing, but they have this amazing clear low end. Just the range of what can happen with them is so extreme, without having eight-hundred pickups on it. . . . If something breaks on it, you can almost fix it with a pocket knife." ✪

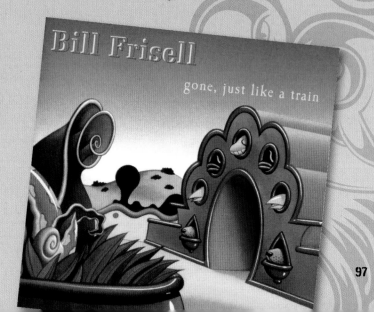

Rory Gallagher's well-used and much-loved 1961 Fender Stratocaster. *Geoff Dann/Redferns/Getty Images*

AMID ALL THE BATTERED STRATS that have made their marks in the annals of the electric guitar, Rory Gallagher's leaves a bolder impression than most. This road-worn 1961 Stratocaster epitomizes the instrument of the hard-traveling, hard-playing, hard-living blues-rocker and will eternally remain associated with the late Irish musician. Gallagher bought this guitar in 1963. It was not only the first Stratocaster he had ever seen, but it was believed to be the first Strat imported into Ireland. It was ordered for another local guitarist who thought he was buying a red Stratocaster (as recently popularized by Hank Marvin in England). When a sunburst instrument arrived, he played it for a time, then decided to pass it along to Gallagher and wait for a new red Strat. A fortuitous decision: Rory Gallagher and this passed-over Strat produced a mountain of fiery, emotive, heartfelt blues and helped to establish a Fender-based blues-rock tone that is idolized to this day.

A security guard holds Rory Gallagher's battered 1961 Fender Stratocaster while it is placed on display in Harrods department store's "Born to Rock" guitar exhibition in London in February 2007. Gallagher's Strat—along with 150 other star guitars, including those played by Jimi Hendrix, Brian Jones, Keith Richards, The Edge, Marc Bolan, Neil Young, and others—were kept under heavy, twenty-four-hour guard. *John D. McHugh/AFP/Getty Images*

In addition to its famous disappearing finish, Gallagher's Strat shows evidence of the wear and tear that will overcome any hard-gigged electric guitar. Its replaced tuners (mismatched, with five Sperzels and one Gotoh), single white-plastic fingerboard dot in place of one absent clay twelfth-fret marker, rewound pickups, and replaced potentiometers are all repairs of pure necessity, undertaken by an artist who made this his main instrument throughout his career (Gallagher owned but rarely played one other Strat, a 1957 sunburst with a maple neck, bought as a backup, as well as a Telecaster, a Gretsch Corvette, and a handful of other guitars). Mike Eldred, the head of Fender's Custom Shop, who examined the original item in the course of creating Fender's Rory Gallagher Tribute Stratocaster, relates that there were many further modifications under the hood too. "Inside it was pretty trashed. Replaced wood, bad wiring job, bits of rubber. It was a mess!" Eldred told Patrick Kennedy for *Strat Collector* in 2004.

The most notable aspect of Gallagher's '61 Strat's decay, however, was not the result of abuse (Gallagher doted on the instrument and cared for it lovingly), but of its owner's body chemistry. According to brother Donal, who now owns the guitar, Rory had a rare blood type that gave his sweat extremely acidic properties. Gallagher sweated *a lot* in the course of any performance, and his Strat's sunburst finish paid the price. (The artist himself spoke of having to remove the waterlogged neck to dry it out, sweat having penetrated the wood after wearing away the clear nitrocellulose lacquer from the maple.) The amount of bare wood on this legendary '61 Stratocaster has helped propagate the belief that guitars with thinner (or no) finishes resonate more freely and have a better tone than those with thick, non-breathable finishes. There might be something to this theory, but it's also a reasonable assumption that the magic that Rory Gallagher and his battered Strat made together had less to do with absent lacquer than it did with the artist's unchained heart, head, and hands. ⬟

Scheller present

SAARBRÜCKEN
OPEN AIR '79
18. Aug.
QUEEN.
RORY & HIS BAND
GALLAGHER
ALVIN LEE
TEN YEARS
LATER
MOLLY
HATCHET LAKE
VOYAGER RED BARON

präsentiert von
SR
EUROPAWELLE
SAAR

Samstag, 18. August '79 Start 13 Uhr
Einlaß/Doors open 10 Uhr   Ludwigsparkstadion

Facing page: Rory Gallagher on tour in the United States in 1970. *Richard Upper/Redferns/Getty Images*

POSSIBLY THE MOST HUMBLE GUITAR GOD ever to have planted a riff, "Galloping" Cliff Gallup had an enormous impact on rockabilly and rock 'n' roll of the '50s, '60s, and beyond. Even so, his time in the spotlight was relatively brief, and he ultimately rejected the music and lifestyle that he just couldn't jibe with. As a member of Gene Vincent's band, the Blue Caps, from 1956 to 1958, Gallup laid down some of the hottest guitar work that had yet been put to vinyl, using a black 1955 Gretsch Duo Jet. This semi-hollow guitar, ostensibly marketed by Gretsch as a solidbody, had a chambered mahogany back and laminated maple top, and carried two of Gretsch's bright yet meaty DeArmond single-coil pickups, along with a Bigsby vibrato that added further snap to the tone and plenty of rockabilly twang when in use. When Capitol Records signed Vincent (born Vincent Eugene Craddock), they were looking for a new young rock 'n' roll star to rival Elvis Presley over at RCA. As a bonus, they unwittingly landed a guitarist to rival Chet Atkins, Danny Cedrone, Jimmy Bryant, Carl Perkins, or any of the hottest pickers of the '50s.

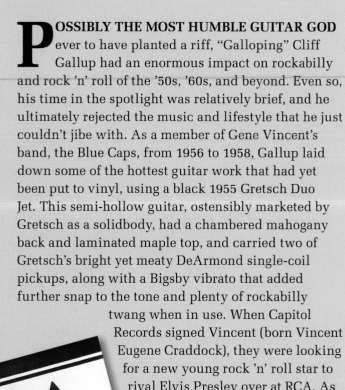

Facing page: "Galloping" Cliff Gallup—as he was listed on the Blue Caps' first LP—hits a rocking note on his Gretsch Duo Jet in this famous promotional shot from a Gene Vincent recording session.

STUDIO
A

Vincent and the Blue Caps' "Be-Bop-A-Lula" was a big hit in 1956, and one of the wildest, most raucous rock 'n' roll songs of its day, but Gallup struts his stuff more ferociously on songs like "Race with the Devil" and "Dance to the Bop," exhibiting lightning licks in the recording of the former song that have had rockabilly wannabes—and some major artists to boot—tying their fingers in knots for three generations. Eric Clapton, the three guitar-playing Beatles, and Jimmy Page all acknowledged Gallup as an influence, and his playing made such an impact on Jeff Beck that he recorded an album of Gallup-era Gene Vincent tunes in 1993, *Crazy Legs*, which was not a tribute album so much as an effort to precisely reproduce the guitarist's playing circa 1956. In the liner notes for that album, Beck wrote, "The guitar parts were all difficult to get right. Some of the harder

Jeff Beck paid tribute to Cliff Gallup in his 1993 album with the Big Town Playboys, *Crazy Legs*.

Jeff Beck's 1956 Gretsch Duo Jet, as used on *Crazy Legs*. *Courtesy Nigel Osborne/Jawbone Press*

sounding things like the triplet runs were not hard at all, but it's what you do after the runs that counts. I put myself in Cliff's shoes for a month and I've got to take my hat off to him—if he came out with those solos off the top of his head, then the guy was more of a monster than I ever believed."

Although he was only twenty-six years old when he recorded the first Blue Caps album in 1956, Gallup was nearly five years older than Vincent and the rest of the band, had a wife and child, and was reluctant to spend long stints on the road away from home. He eventually withdrew from the touring band in 1957, attended only a few recording dates after, and departed the Blue Caps altogether after 1958 and was replaced by Johnny Meeks. Gallup largely retired from music, although he continued to perform around Virginia in club bands over the years

(during which time he graduated to a later Gretsch Country Gentleman) while working as director of transportation and maintenance for the Chesapeake, Virginia, school district, before dying of a massive coronary in 1988 at the age of fifty-eight (Gene Vincent had died seventeen years before, in October 1971). At the time of his death, Gallup's wife asked that his time in the Blue Caps not be mentioned in his obituary in the local newspapers. ★

JUST AS THE GRATEFUL DEAD was no straightforward band, Jerry Garcia was never anything close to a straightforward guitarist. Certainly, his playing blended several relatively straightforward genres, incorporating rock, folk, country, blues, jazz, and bluegrass, but by the time the San Francisco native had processed it all through the melting pot of his creative consciousness, a music that was entirely *other* came out. Likewise, his gear choices were rarely anything you could label "standard." In the early days of the Dead, Garcia played a Guild Starfire, a Gibson SG and Les Paul, and a '57 Fender Stratocaster originally given to him by Graham Nash, but he was never quite satisfied with stock models. Rather than going the modding and hot-rodding route that so many players took in the early '70s, Garcia went whole hog, commissioning a series of custom-built guitars from luthier Doug Irwin. He played these guitars from 1972 until his death in 1995 (by which time they were supplemented by a similar guitar made by Steve Cripe).

This circa 1983 view of Tiger attests to its intricate woodwork and circuitry.
Larry Hulst/Getty Images

EURODEAD

Artist: Gary Kroman (www.garykroman.com)/
Courtesy Relix International, Inc.

The first of the four guitars Irwin made for Garcia was known as "Wolf," which he played extensively from 1972 until 1979, when the longest-reigning and best-known of Irwin's guitars hit the road with the Dead. Named "Tiger" after the tiger inlay on the preamp and battery cover mounted just behind the bridge, it was an extremely elaborate instrument in every regard. Like Wolf before it, Tiger was made from several exotic woods laminated together in a "hippie sandwich," a technique popularized by Alembic, where Irwin had worked briefly before going independent. The wood most visible in Tiger's top and back is cocobolo, while second most prominent is its figured maple core, visible at the sides of the body. Between this core and the front and back are fillets of maple and vermillion. Another oval of highly figured maple set into the back carries an elaborate floral inlay. Tiger's neck is made from maple with a center strip of padauk. Both its ebony fingerboard and the body are trimmed with brass binding, while the fingerboard carries elaborate pearl inlays. All this exotica made for a heavy guitar—Tiger weighed in at a whopping 13.5 pounds.

The guitar's electronics are as intricately wrought as its woodwork. Garcia favored high-output DiMarzio pickups—a single-coil SDS-1 in the neck position and a pair of Super II humbuckers in the bridge and middle positions (both wired for coil splitting)—all wired through a Strat-style five-way switch. But from here on out things got really interesting. From the selector switch the signal went straight into an onboard unity-gain buffer preamp, then out to Garcia's effects rig through the guitar's built-in effects loop. Post effects, the signal returned to Tiger and was routed through its volume control before finally leaving the guitar again on its way to the amp rig. This might seem like the long way around, but such routing allowed Garcia to maintain full signal strength through his effects setup so the tone of individual units wouldn't be altered by the setting of his guitar's volume control (which acted as a post-effects master volume), while the buffering preamp enabled the use of long cable runs without signal loss.

Hippie sandwich though it might have been, Tiger was no stoner's munchie-fest, but a well-thought-out performance tool that Garcia made brilliant use of for eleven straight years. After his death, Garcia's will dictated that Tiger be returned to luthier Doug Irwin. ☮

SURVEY AFICIONADOS' "titans of the Telecaster" lists, and more often than not Danny Gatton will be sitting right up there at No. 1. Previous to wedding the Tele, Gatton had unleashed his mighty chops on a modified Les Paul and a Gibson ES-295, but once the underappreciated picker took up with the humble Fender, the deal was sealed. It's sometimes surprising to find that a player of Gatton's magnitude was so devoted to a guitar as primitive as the Telecaster, the slab-bodied, bolt-neck design that really constituted the first commercially successful solid-body electric. But there's something magical about a good Telecaster that seems to draw in virtuoso pickers, and if you look past the plank styling, it's clear that the Tele has the chimey tone, ringing sustain, and solid, bend-friendly construction that appeals to players such as these.

The music that Gatton made on his 1953 Tele was nothing short of phenomenal, but that clearly had far more to do with the gargantuan talent of the artist himself than with the guitar on which he chose to ply his trade. Joe Barden, who worked as a self-appointed roadie while still in his teens and became Gatton's personal pickup maker toward the end of the guitarist's life, told this writer about the first time he experienced Gatton's stellar abilities: "It was one of the foremost moments in my life—I was completely transfixed. This was at a club called The Keg, in Georgetown, D.C., on a snowy Sunday night. I was one of two paying customers, and there was a drunk passed out, left over from the afternoon happy hour. I'm watching this short, stumpy little redneck, and he's covering everything . . . they were playing the most bizarre mix of shit, from straight-up 'Mystery Train' rockabilly to ancient chestnuts like 'Matilda' to slow blues. But none of this is 'normal' music at all. It's not rock and roll, it's not jazz. I thought I'd walked into a time warp or an alternative universe." Such was the power of Gatton's talent, which had reached far too few fans by the time he took his own life in 1995 at the age of forty-nine.

Danny Gatton's own favorite Danny Gatton Signature Telecaster was an unnumbered prototype. The Fender Custom Shop's ace luthier Mike Stevens personally built this guitar. It became Gatton's workhorse guitar, which he used to record *88 Elmira St*, *Cruisin' Deuces*, and portions of *Relentless*, and continued to play right up through his last tour. *Steve Gorospe*

Facing page, top: Playing alongside rockabilly singer Robert Gordon, Danny Gatton picks his 1953 Fender Telecaster onstage at the Ritz in June 1981. *Ebet Roberts/Redferns/Getty Images*

Facing page: Danny Gatton's original '53 Fender Telecaster, here fitted with the later Joe Barden neck pickup. Gatton played this Tele through most of the 1980s and 1990s; his Fender Signature model was then based on the guitar. *Steve Gorospe*

As much as Gatton loved his Telecaster, he was often chasing a fuller, fatter tone than the model was born with; he sought to attain it by modifying the instrument rather than by surrendering it entirely. For a time, he installed a large, cumbersome Gibson "Charlie Christian" pickup in the neck position of his Tele to bring that notoriously underpowered setting up to par. A more manageable solution eventually came in the form of the standard-sized, dual-blade pickups that Barden designed for him, which he took to using in both the bridge and neck positions from the early '80s onward. Gatton is believed to have sold his prized '53 Telecaster to a collector in 1990, after which he often played prototypes of Fender's Danny Gatton Signature Telecaster. ◆

Gatton's spruce-topped 1956 Gibson ES-350 was his first "real" guitar, given to him when he was twelve by his dad. Although he sold it in the 1960s to buy his first car—a 1958 Chevy Impala—he later reacquired it and played it the rest of his life. *Steve Gorospe*

Above: Gatton's favorite amp, a tweed 1956 Fender Twin. *Steve Gorospe*

Facing page: Danny Gatton's 1954 Gibson ES-295 with added Bigsby B6 tailpiece. He bought the ES-295 in Memphis in honor of Scotty Moore's playing behind Elvis Presley. *Thomas Gage/courtesy Arlen Roth and the Gatton Estate*

1959 GIBSON LES PAUL "PEARLY GATES"

FEW GUITARS IN ROCK ARE AS ICONIC as Billy F Gibbons's 1959 Les Paul Standard, named "Pearly Gates" by the Texas tonehound for its supposed divine connections. This guitar has been the subject of much adulation over the years, and no small portion of it gushes from the ZZ Top guitarist himself, who has conducted a forty-plus-year love affair with the guitar that he still refers to as "my beloved Miss Pearly Gates." As Gibbons told Alex Becker of gibson.com in 2009, Pearly Gates is not just *a* 1959 Les Paul Standard, "but *the* 1959 Les Paul Standard." Anyone who has seen or heard this incomparable electric guitar is likely to agree with him.

Gibbons formed ZZ Top in Houston, Texas, in 1969 with bassist Dusty Hill and drummer Frank Beard, but by this time he had already been on the prowl for a late-'50s Les Paul Standard after having seen Eric Clapton play one with John Mayall & the Blues Breakers some years earlier. As if a sign of this band's ascending fortunes, his opportunity came shortly after—and

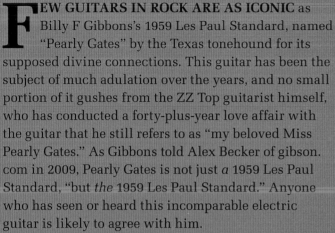

Facing page: BFG with Dusty Hill (left), Frank Beard (drums), and Miss Pearly, Chattanooga, Tennessee, October 1973. *Tom Hill/WireImage/Getty Images*

© David Perry
(www.davidperrystudios.com)

totally unexpectedly. Having traveled in an old 1930s Packard in their early days together, the band loaned the car to a member's girlfriend to make the trip out to Hollywood to audition for a role in the movies. The friend, Renee Thomas, arrived safely *and* got the part. Gibbons and company determined that the beat-up old car must have been a heavenly omen and named it "Pearly Gates." To pay back her friends, Renee sold the car to a collector and sent the proceeds to Gibbons. "The very day that the money arrived, a guy called me up wanting to sell an old guitar . . . a '59 sunburst Les Paul," Gibbons told Becker. The guitarist and a friend drove out to rural Texas, where the seller pulled a brown, form-fitting hard-shell case out from under the bed, where it had lain since the guitar's owner passed away several years before. The cash was exchanged, and the rest is history.

While all 1958–1960 Les Paul Standards are highly prized, slight irregularities of production, the variables in wood stocks and pickup windings, and other factors mean that some examples simply play and sound better than others. Pearly Gates is at the top of the heap, representing a fortuitous confluence of a gently figured maple top, a light and resonant mahogany body, a comfortably rounded neck profile, and two sweet, rich, vocal PAF humbucking pickups that stand as the epitome of the art form. "It was assembled on one of those fateful days when the glue was just right, the wood was just right, and the electronics were placed perfectly," Gibbons reflected in his 2005 autobiography, *Rock + Roll Gearhead*. "'Til this day, I have yet to find an instrument to equal its raw power." ♦

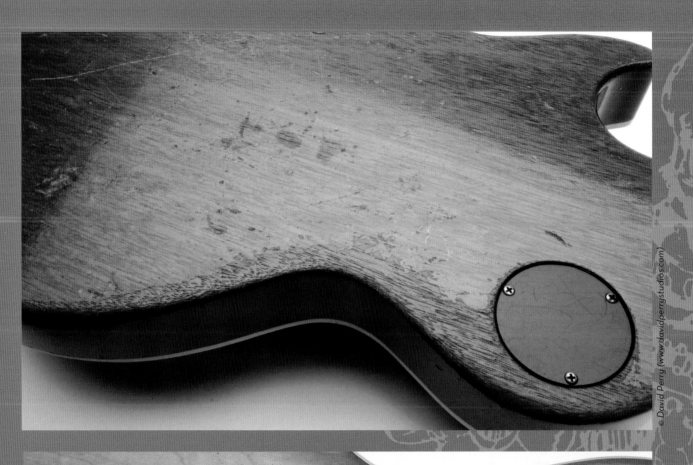

© David Perry (www.davidperrystudios.com)

© David Perry (www.davidperrystudios.com)

Gilmour rehearses at Black Island Studios in London for the September 23, 2004, Miller Strat Pack concert at Wembley Arena. *Jo Hale/Getty Images*

SOME ARE BORN WITH GREAT GUITARS, while others have great guitars thrust upon them. So it was, to some extent at least (and with Shakespeare's forgiveness), with David Gilmour, who made plenty of standout music with Pink Floyd on other instruments before acquiring a certain 1954 Strat toward the end of the '70s. Historic in its own right, now doubly iconic for its use on several classic Pink Floyd recordings, Gilmour's 1954 Stratocaster is a very early example of that model and carries the serial number 0001 on its neck plate, although these two facts don't have any real correlation.

This '54 Stratocaster, with a neck made in June of that year and a body dated in September, is certainly an early one (the Stratocaster was only released early in 1954 following several prototypes made in 1953), but it is not actually *the* first Strat made, as the

serial number implies. Gilmour's Stratocaster wears a nonstandard finish that is sometimes referred to as Desert Sand or faded Olympic White, but it is really not quite like either of those two later Fender custom colors. It also has a gold-plated vibrato unit and jack plate, and a gold-colored anodized aluminum pickguard like those that would later appear on the Musicmaster, Duo-Sonic, and Jazzmaster. The common wisdom in vintage-Fender camps is that the eye-catching serial number was used to denote a special-order model, indicating this perhaps was the first Stratocaster with gold-plated hardware, seen more often on the blonde "Mary Kaye" Stratocasters that became popular a couple of years later. In any case, Stratocasters made before Gilmour's have been seen wearing higher numbers, so the 0001 most likely wasn't intended to denote the guitar's chronology—at least not among all Strats.

Gilmour's 0001 Strat followed a rather circuitous route into his loving hands. Owned at one time by pickup maker Seymour Duncan, the Strat was purchased by Pink Floyd guitar tech Phil Taylor in the mid-'70s for a reported $900 (possibly from Pete

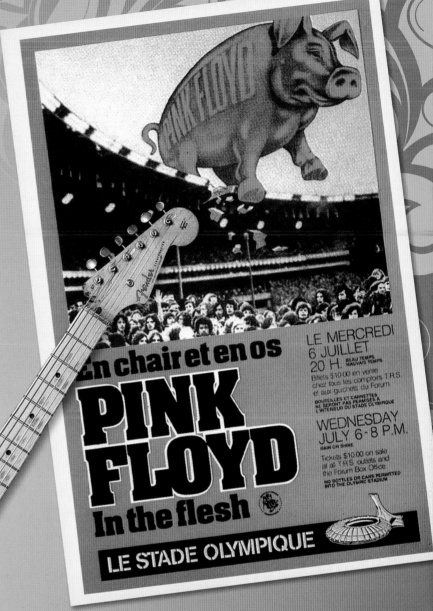

Townshend's guitar tech, Alan Rogan, who is credited in some versions of the history as having owned it between Duncan and Taylor). A couple of years later, Gilmour pried the instrument from Taylor by offering the tech the cash he was seeking toward the down payment on a house. The 1954 Strat was often used in the studio from around 1977 onward on several Pink Floyd recordings and on work Gilmour did for Paul McCartney and Brian Ferry. One of the easiest ways to see and hear it simultaneously, though, is to watch the video of the fiftieth anniversary concert for the Fender Stratocaster filmed at Wembley Arena, London, in 2004, when Gilmour picked up this legendary guitar for live renditions of "Coming Back to Life" and "Marooned." ★

Courtesy Nigel Osborne/ Jawbone Press

MOST INSTRUMENTS WORTHY of star guitar status are notable for the exemplary tones they put forth in the hands of the artists who made them famous. But in the minds of the fans who idolize them, some guitars have been elevated beyond mere celebrity guitar status. Peter Green's 1959 Les Paul Standard is one example that has been thus elevated, as has the tone he achieved with it in the early incarnation of Fleetwood Mac. In 1967, after leaving John Mayall & the Blues Breakers—that crucible of blues-rock guitar stardom—Green founded Fleetwood Mac alongside Mick Fleetwood, John McVie, and Jeremy Spencer (later replaced by

Green performs with Fleetwood Mac in a 1968 television appearance. Note the "backward" neck pickup.
Jan Persson/Redferns/Getty Images

Peter Green unceremoniously quit Fleetwood Mac in 1970 and faded into an obscurity that bottomed out with the former star being diagnosed with schizophrenia and eventually enduring several bouts of institutionalization. He famously sold his Les Paul to blues-rocker Gary Moore for around £110 (approximately $200), a paltry sum for a vintage Les Paul Standard even in the mid-'70s. Moore told *Guitarist* magazine in 1995 that Green himself insisted upon the figure because it was the price he had paid for the guitar in the first place. Moore used the Les Paul on several recordings with Thin Lizzy and later as a solo artist, but he eventually sold the guitar. Since the late '90s, Peter Green has reemerged as an artist, recording and performing with his own Peter Green Splinter Group and several collaborative projects. Of his legendary old partner, Green told Rick Batey of *The Guitar Magazine* in 1999, "I'm sick of Les Pauls. . . . You see them everywhere." ★

Danny Kirwan) in order to play "pure blues." In their company, Green recorded such classics of tone as "Need Your Love So Bad," "Black Magic Woman," "Albatross," "Oh Well," and several others. Amid a late-'60s scene in which other British blues artists were evolving toward high-gain blues-rock, Green's more purist stance, coupled with his more nuanced and organic tone, delicate touch, and plaintive melodic sense, helped him to stand out from the crowd.

His Les Paul was a standout instrument too, and it quickly drew the eye of many a guitar worshiper. While Green owned it, the guitar still maintained much of the richness of its sunburst finish, as would be expected in a guitar that was then only between eight and eleven years old, but this 1959 'burst is also famous for having faded later to a golden hue that beautifully showed off its gently tiger-striped maple top. Perhaps most notable from early on in Green's stewardship of the instrument, however, is the reversed neck pickup, which not only *appears* "backward"—with the adjustable pole pieces facing the bridge rather than the fingerboard—but also was rewound to reverse polarity by a misguided repairman. Possibly one of the more fortuitous mistakes in the annals of the electric guitar, the reversed neck pickup gave Green a distinctive out-of-phase tone when both pickups were used together, which helped to cement the mythos of this artist and has been copied by countless other players since.

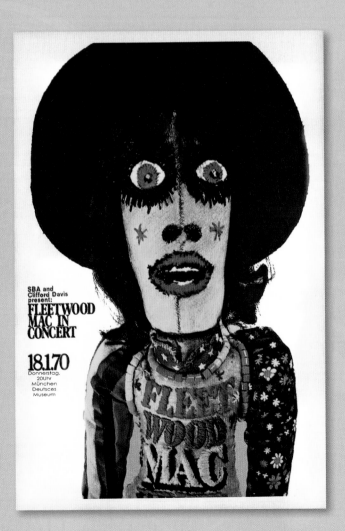

THIS MACHINE KILLS FASCISTS

TO SAY THAT WOODY GUTHRIE wasn't a materialistic guy might be the understatement of the millennium. Put simply, Guthrie was a people person, not a possessions person, and this attitude carried right through to his guitars. He cherished his instruments as music-making tools, but he didn't prize them as objects in and of themselves, and he is even known to have given away hundreds of guitars throughout his lifetime, mostly bestowing them on other musicians who were down on their luck.

Given this attitude, it might be surprising to learn that Guthrie usually played high-quality guitars, mainly a Gibson banner-headstock Southerner Jumbo and various Martins, although closer examination usually reveals that they were the more affordable examples of the Martin breed: smaller-bodied 0, 00, and 000 models with the simple woods and trim of the 18 series. Of course, there were far fewer options in serviceable acoustic guitars in the 1930s and '40s than there are today, and a hard-traveling, hard-playing soul like Woody Guthrie needed a guitar that could get the job done while surviving a pounding along the way. These better makes fit the bill. It would be hard to pin down one single guitar as *the* Woody Guthrie guitar, since he played—and was photographed

with—so darn many. Martin selected the 000-18 for its commemorative 000-18WG Woody Guthrie model, but we probably more often see photos of the artist cradling a slightly smaller 00-18. One thing is for certain though: whatever size and model Guthrie was playing, it had to be wearing his slogan "This Machine Kills Fascists," which he often painted right onto the top of the guitar.

In addition to giving voice to the lives of poor migrants and disenfranchised classes of the Great Depression and the early war years, the era in which some of its most powerful songs were penned, Guthrie's musical catalog represents a one-stop folk archive that not only chronicles the hard times but also celebrates the wonder and hope at the heart of the American spirit. Given this perspective, his road-worn Martin really does take on the mantel of a weapon of good in the hands of a vanquishing hero. Fellow hero of the twentieth-century working class, John Steinbeck, probably best described the spirit of Woody Guthrie in the foreword to *Hard Hitting Songs for Hard-Hit People*: "He sings the songs of a people and I suspect that he is, in a way, that people. Harsh voiced and nasal, his guitar hanging like a tire iron on a rusty rim, there is nothing sweet about Woody, and there is nothing sweet about the songs he sings. But there is something more important for those who still listen. There is the will of a people to endure and fight against oppression. I think we call this the American spirit." ◆

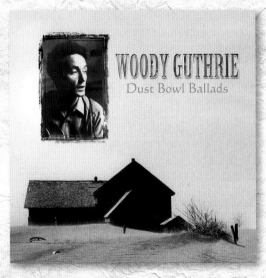

Left: Woody Guthrie performs in McSorley's Bar in New York City in 1942. *Eric Schaal/Time Life Pictures/Getty Images*

Facing page: Woody Guthrie with a fascist-killing Gibson in 1943. *Al Aumuller/World Telegram/Library of Congress*

THERE'S NO BETTER EXAMPLE of supercharged, hard-blowing, electric Chicago blues than Buddy Guy. His guitars of choice— and the amps he plays them through, for that matter—are staples of the bluesman's toolbox. As simple as these ingredients may be, they are capable of producing no end of firepower when used with attitude. Listen to any of Guy's early recordings for examples of his legendary stinging pick attack and extreme bends, then sample 2001's raw, stripped-down outing, *Sweet Tea*, for evidence that the artist retained that incendiary style five decades later. Although Guy has occasionally strutted his stuff with Guild Starfire semi-acoustics, he is far and away best known for his use of Fender Stratocasters, and he has played plenty of examples of this legendary model throughout his career. For many years Guy wielded vintage '50s Strats with maple fingerboards.

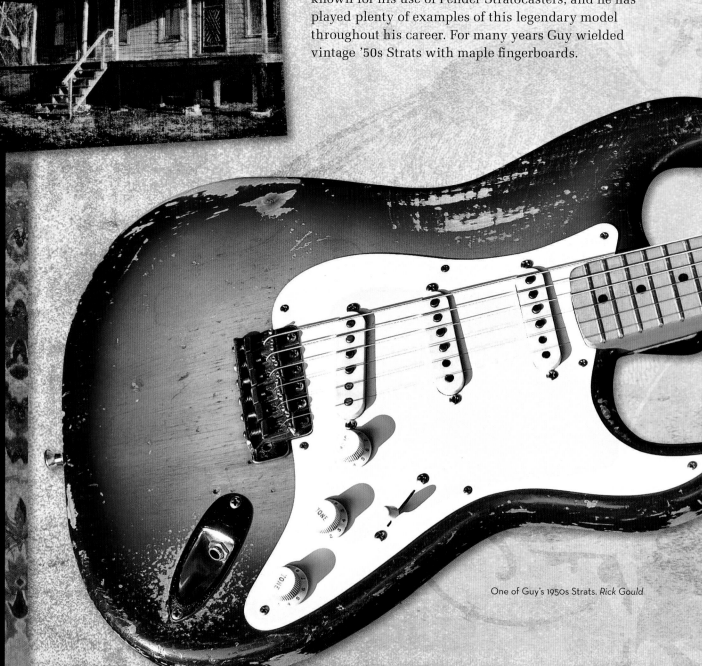

One of Guy's 1950s Strats. *Rick Gould*

122

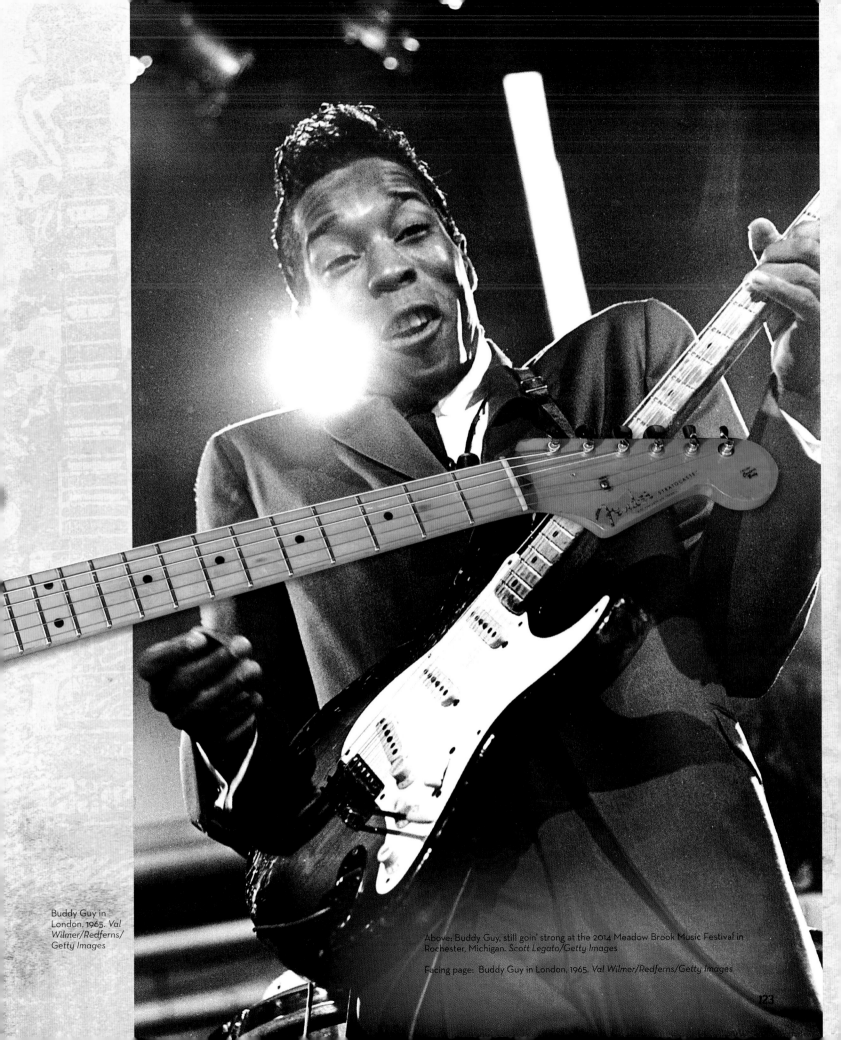

FENDER STRATOCASTERS

Buddy Guy, still goin' strong at the 2014 Meadow Brook Music Festival in Rochester, Michigan. *Scott Legato/Getty Images*

In recent years, Buddy Guy has been the subject of not one but two Fender signature models, and he has lately been most associated with the Buddy Guy Standard Polka Dot Stratocaster, which expresses his desires in a modified Strat, as well as his flair for fashion and performance.

The Polka Dot Stratocaster follows classic Strat lines, with an alder body and all-maple neck, vintage-style vibrato, five-way switch, and single volume and dual tone controls (for neck and middle pickup only), but its pickups gain a little extra poke courtesy of their ceramic magnets. The second of Guy's Fender signature models, the high-end Artist Series Buddy Guy Stratocaster, changes the alder body for ash, the ceramic-magnet pickups for three Lace Sensor Golds, and adds a mid-boost to the guitar's electrics. Both aim to offer classic Strat playability and versatility, but to hit the amp harder than many bluesmen might seek to do.

Guy's amps deserve some consideration in their own right, as does the way in which he uses them. Throughout his early career, Guy preferred a model that can lay claim to the tag "ultimate blues amp of all time": a late-'50s Fender Tweed 5F6-A Bassman. Purportedly, he played these 4×10-inch combos with all knobs wound up toward max save the bass tone control, which he kept down low. Like most artists with his sort of longevity in the business, Guy's arsenal has diversified over the years. In the late 1990s and early 2000s, Guy often played a Victoria 45410 (a hand-wired reproduction of a Bassman), and he has lately endorsed the Buddy Guy Signature Series Amp from Chicago Blues Box, which is modeled specifically on Guy's own favorite '59 Bassman. Between guitar and amp, Guy has often favored a Crybaby wah pedal, a duty now performed by the Jim Dunlop Crybaby Buddy Guy Signature Wah—in black with white polka dots, naturally.

As with most guitar stars, it's not so much the ingredients as the way the artist attacks them that accounts for the hot, stinging tone. And now into his seventies and counting, Buddy Guy is still hitting those strings hard. ✪

Guy, circa 2000. James Fraher/Michael Ochs Archives/Getty Images

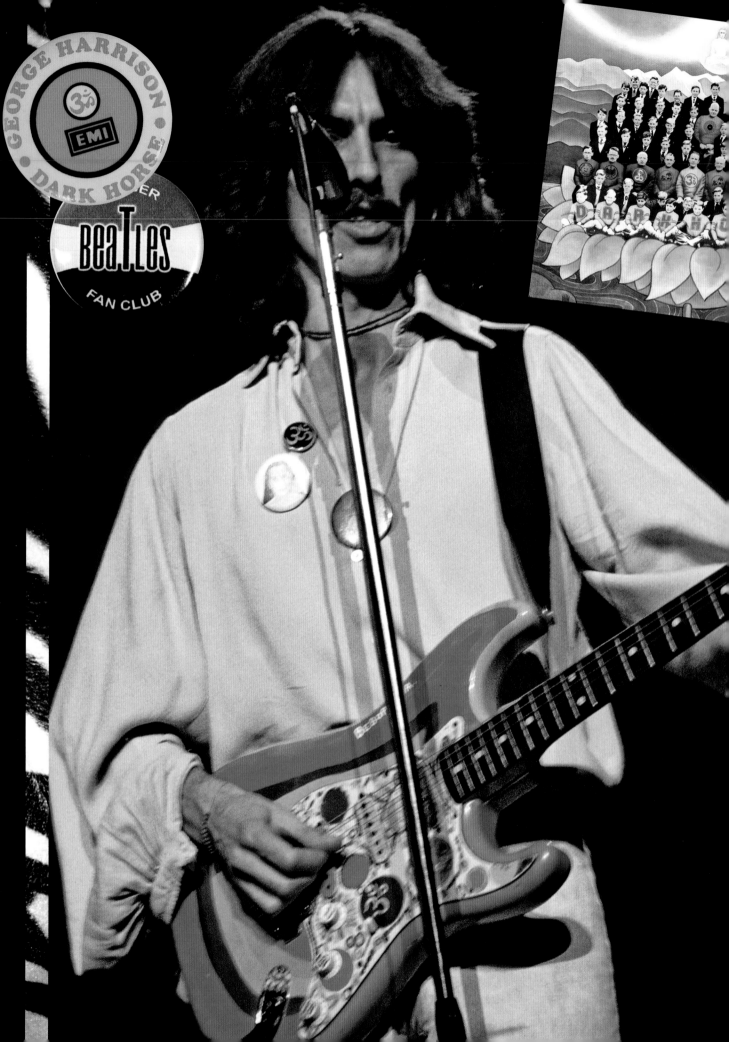

1961 FENDER STRATOCASTER GEORGE HARRISON

IT'S ALWAYS A LITTLE HEARTWARMING, somehow, to recall what gearheads the Beatles remained, even through careers graced with unfathomable levels of fame and recognition. They were, after all, musicians first and foremost, and the equipment used to make that music continued to be vitally important to them right up through the end of the band's run and beyond. When both George Harrison and John Lennon acquired Fender Stratocasters early in 1965, their childlike glee was virtually palpable. As revealed in Andy Babiuk's strenuously researched *Beatles Gear* (Backbeat Books, 2001), Harrison in particular had enjoyed trying a fellow musician's Stratocaster in Hamburg in 1960 and had been beaten out by a rival guitarist in an effort to purchase a used example in 1961. His subsequent use of Gretsch and Rickenbacker guitars through the early years of the band's success might have been a rebellion of sorts at his failure to acquire the original object of his desires: "I was so disappointed, it scarred me for life," the Beatle said in the TV documentary *The Story of the Fender Stratocaster*. When Don Randall sent a representative to New York to try to woo the Beatles to Fender mid-1964 during the band's US tour, the effort apparently never made it past an underling in the Fab Four camp. Yet around February 1965, both Lennon and Harrison decided to tap that jones for what was then arguably the world's most popular solidbody electric, and they sent Beatle roadie Mal Evans out to purchase a pair of Stratocasters.

The guitars were matching Sonic Blue examples with pre-CBS features, and Harrison's at least would prove to be a used 1961 model. Both got immediate use from the Beatle guitarists during the recording of 1965's *Rubber Soul* album—and can even be heard together in the unison solo on "Nowhere Man" (as, once again, noted in *Beatles Gear*)—but Harrison's Stratocaster would make a more famous reappearance two years later as a key visual amid the band's psychedelic phase.

As London's legendary swing took a decidedly hallucinogenic swoop in spring 1967, the Beatles decided to paint several of their guitars to match the overriding mood, many of which would appear in the *Magical Mystery Tour* TV special that aired in September of that year. Lennon blasted his Epiphone Casino with spray paint while his Sonic Blue Stratocaster was left untouched, but Harrison's formerly matching Strat underwent the most notable transformation of all. Harrison swathed the front of the Strat's body in several rainbow stripes of day-glow paint, adorned the pickguard with eastern imagery, rather touchingly evidenced his abiding love of seminal rock 'n' roll by gracing it with the slogans "Go Cat Go" and "Bebopalula," and rechristened the Strat "Rocky" on the headstock. In the hands of a nameless player this hippy sick-up paint job would today be seen only as spoiling an otherwise collectible pre-CBS Strat. On Harrison's guitar, it came to represent one of the most iconic images of the psychedelic era. Harrison set up the Stratocaster for slide from around 1970 on (following advice from Ry Cooder), and the guitar remains the property of the George Harrison estate. ★

Right: George Harrison's 1964 Stratocaster, Rocky. *Backbeat UK/Outline Press*

Facing page: Harrison plays his Strat, Rocky, on the *Dark Horse* tour, late 1974. *Steve Morley/ Redferns/Getty Images*

IMMENSE STARS THAT THEY BECAME, all three Beatles guitarists were enormous gearheads throughout their tenure with the band, and they seemingly maintained a sincere, almost childlike glee about the acquisition of any new guitar of worthy quality. As lead guitarist of the group, George Harrison was the Beatle most commonly assailed with offerings from guitar makers hoping to tap the invaluable free promotion that came from landing an instrument in the hands of a Beatle, and he frequently took them up on it, with apparent enthusiasm.

After struggling with a Hofner Club 40 and a Selmer Futurama, Harrison bought and paid for his first quality electric guitar, a 1957 Gretsch Duo Jet, which he tracked down in Liverpool in 1961. From that point onward, however, and certainly once Beatlemania bit, great guitars virtually fell into his lap. A Rickenbacker 360/12, Gretsch Country Gentleman, and Epiphone Casino famously all came his way. The last significant offering of his Beatle days, however, and the most unusual, was a Rosewood Telecaster, one of two prototypes of the instrument made in late 1968.

Legend has it that the George Harrison Rosewood Telecaster, constructed of the best body and best neck of the two prototypes, was flown to London in its own seat. According to the excellent book *Beatles Gear* by Andy Babiuk, it was delivered to The Beatles by company head Don Randall himself during a meeting at the Apple offices, at which time he also handed over a six-string bass, two Rhodes electric pianos, a Fender PA, and various amps in an effort to woo the Fab Four over to Fender. Harrison used the Rosewood Telecaster for the recording of *Let It Be* in January of 1969, as well as in the rooftop concert atop the Apple building in London on January 30, 1969, the Beatles' final live performance. In addition to Harrison's Rosewood Telecaster, photos from that performance show the band using Fender Twin Reverb amplifiers, two Rhodes pianos, and even the Fender PA head set off to the side of the stage, with the "hang tag" still

attached to the handle on top, so Randall's delivery clearly found its mark.

As a result of Harrison's prominent use of the instrument, Fender brought the Rosewood Telecaster into production from 1969 to '72. Early examples had a solid body made from two slabs of rosewood in a "sandwich" with a thin layer of maple in between—just like the prototype given to Harrison, which was made mostly by young Fender guitar builder Phillip Kubicki who later became a respected independent luthier in his own right—although the weight of that highly prized timber led to a use of chambered bodies later in the model's run. The guitars also had a solid rosewood neck, initially with a glued-on rosewood fingerboard, but later, with an integral rosewood fingerboard and a truss rod installed via a route in the back that was filled with a maple "skunk stripe." In addition to their exotic look, the density of the rosewood also gave these guitars a clear, crisp tone that is distinctive from that of ash or alder Telecasters.

George Harrison gave his Rosewood Telecaster to Delaney Bramlett of Bonnie & Delaney while performing with them later in 1969. The former Beatle died in 2001, and Bramlett sold the guitar at auction in 2003 for more than $470,000 (after a failed auction attempt in 1998). The guitar was bought on that occasion by actor Ed Begley Jr. on behalf of Harrison's widow, Olivia Harrison, and returned to the Harrison family estate. ✦

Delaney Bramlett, to whom Harrison gave the Rosewood Telecaster in 1969, sold the guitar at auction in 2003. It was bought by actor Ed Begley Jr. on behalf of the Harrison estate. *Courtesy Julien's Auctions (juliensauctions.com)*

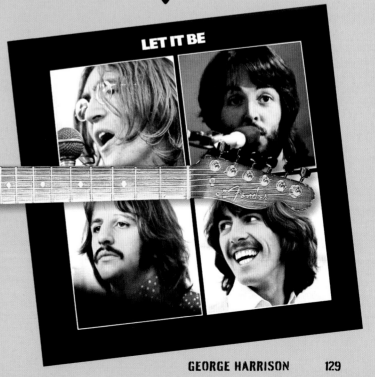

Facing page: The Dark Horse's Rosewood Telecaster was one of two prototypes produced by Fender in 1968. The guitar was most famously played in the Beatles' famous "rooftop" concert, their final live performance. Legend has it that a Rosewood Stratocaster was intended for Jimi Hendrix but never made it into his hands, and that its whereabouts are still unknown. *Daily Mail/Rex/Alamy*

GIVEN THE HOT PUNKABILLY and twisted honky-tonk licks the man has been laying down for twenty-some years, you'd think the Reverend Horton Heat and a Gretsch 6120 were a match made in heaven—or that other place, to get a little more *rock 'n' roll* about it. But it was not always thus. In the band's early days, the Rev (a.k.a. Jim Heath) toured with a Gibson ES-175D with Bigsby vibrato, a guitar that experienced heavy wear and tear from a months-long string of one-nighters out on the road. As Heath himself tells it, he was rolling through Illinois in 1989 or 1990, with paying gigs strung out ahead for several nights to come, when the faltering electronics in the ES-175D threatened to give up the ghost for good.

Facing page: The good Reverend, armed with his Gretsch 6120W sporting a Clay Smith Cams "Mr. Horsepower" sticker. *Atomic Music Group/courtesy Yep Roc Records*

REVEREND HORTON HEAT
WITH SPECIAL GUEST:
UNKNOWN HINSON
HOUSE OF BLUES - LAS VEGAS
3950 LAS VEGAS BLVD./MANDALAY BAY/(702) 632-7600

MONDAY DEC 30TH 2002

Johnny Ace Studios/www.acekustoms.com

Jim Heath's 1954 Gibson ES-175D fitted with a Bigsby B6 vibrato and strung with flat-wound strings. *Courtesy Jim Heath/Photo Michael Dregni*

"On a day off, I went into a Guitar Center in Chicago," Heath told this writer in 2009, "looked up on the wall, and saw a new Gretsch [6120W reissue: "W" for "Western maple stain," a.k.a. Gretsch Orange]. I was a little blown away by how it looked, and when they pulled it off the rack and let me try it, I was impressed, to say the least. It had the wide body and the Bigsby like I was used to, but it seemed to have a bit of a Telecaster spankiness to it. I thought to myself, 'This Tele-type thing is not real typical of old Gretsches, but I sure do like it!'" Gathering up his touring money and borrowing from the band fund, Heath was able to take away the new 6120, which he debuted at a gig in Champaign, Illinois, the very next night. "I plugged that baby in and hit a chord to get my sound," he relates, "and I'll never forget the look on Taz's [drummer Patrick Bentley] face. He looked up, very surprised, and just said 'Woo hoo!'" From that point on, Heath and a Gretsch 6120 went together like bourbon with a beer back.

To check out that big archtop-electric sound mixed with "a bit of a Telecaster spankyness," spin any of the Rev's standout tracks from the early '90s in particular, such as "The Devil's Chasing Me" from 1993's *The Full-Custom Sounds of . . .* or "Big Sky" from 1994's *Liquor in the Front*. Although this description of the 6120's tone might seem contradictory, Heath nails it on the head, and the guitar's thickness blended with plenty of cut, twang, and definition defines what has come to be known as "that great Grestch sound" over the course of five decades. His own 6120, made in Japan in the era when Fred Gretsch III had reacquired his family's company from Baldwin but not yet sold it to Fender, would have been made much in the image of the late-1950s original, although the Filter'Tron pickups of the late '80s and the '90s had ceramic magnets rather than alnico, and they were a little sharper and more aggressive-sounding. Other than adding some hot rod stickers—notably the Clay Smith Cams "Mr. Horsepower" decal—Heath kept the guitar stock. He still owns it, but he has been forced to retire it after several re-frets and now plays Gretsch's current G6120RHH (the Reverend Horton Heat Artist Signature model), which he cranks through the same 1978 Fender Super Reverb amp that he has used since he picked up his first Gretsch twenty years ago. ♠

Heath's current main touring guitars are his Signature Model Gretsch 6120RHH with TV Jones Filter'Tron pickups. "I run the 6120 through a 1978 Fender Super Reverb," Heath says. "That '78 Super has been the main amp on all of Reverend Horton Heat's recordings. In fact, that amp is really just as, or more, important to my sound than my guitar. I almost cannot live without that amp."
Courtesy Jim Heath/Photo Michael Dregni

THE GEAR OF ALL MAJOR GUITAR HEROES attracts some attention, but the equipment used by Jimi Hendrix, and his Fender Stratocasters in particular, has drawn more intense analysis than most. Hendrix played several Strats during his short time at the top, and he famously also used a Gibson Flying V and SG. His supposed preference for later-'60s CBS-spec Strats over early to mid-'60s Strats with pre-CBS (i.e., pre-1965) specs remains a hotly debated issue. Certainly the last Stratocasters the world saw him playing were CBS-era models with large headstocks, modern logos, and maple fingerboards. Among these, the white Strat played at Woodstock in 1969 and the black Strat played at the Isle of Wight in 1970 are the instruments he was most photographed with.

Above: Jimi Hendrix's 1965 Fender Stratocaster that he set alight onstage at London's Finsbury Park Astoria in 1967. *Peter Macdiarmid/Getty Images*

Left: Armed with one of his many Fender Stratocasters, Jimi Hendrix leads The Experience at the Civic Auditorium in Bakersfield, California, on October 26, 1968. Drummer Mitch Mitchell is at left. *Michael Ochs Archives/Getty Images*

Experience tour manager Gerry Stickells aids Jimi Hendrix in tuning up his Stratocaster onstage during a show at the Star Club in Hamburg, Germany, on March 16, 1967. *K & K Ulf Kruger OHG/Redferns/Getty Images*

A fragment of Jimi Hendrix's Fender Stratocaster that he smashed and then set aflame during "Wild Thing" at the 1967 Monterey Pop Festival. This Strat began as a Fiesta red example, but Hendrix painted it just before his performance. *Courtesy Experience Music Project, Seattle, Washington*

In the early days, however, around the time of *Are You Experienced* and his inflammatory performance at the Monterey Pop Festival in 1967, Hendrix was usually seen playing one of a handful of pre-CBS or transition-era Stratocasters with small headstocks and "spaghetti" or transition logos. Hendrix played two Strats at Monterey: a black mid-'60s model with characteristic rosewood fingerboard and small headstock and a guitar at the center of what is possibly the most legendary "Hendrix moment" of all—the Stratocaster that Hendrix doused in lighter fluid and lit on fire at the end of his performance of "Wild Thing," a transition-era '65 Strat, also with the early-style small headstock. This incalculably famous Hendrix Strat was photographed far less than his later instruments for the simple fact that

he wasn't yet as big a star at Monterey as he would be from that moment forward—and also because by the end of this climactic moment the guitar was charred and smashed to pieces. Seen little before the Monterey appearance, it had recently been customized by Hendrix, who painted approximately half of the Fiesta Red body white and adorned it with floral graphics. Otherwise, the standard late-'65 Stratocaster carried a short-lived combination of features, including a fatter, new-style gold logo with black outline on a small headstock and a rosewood fingerboard with pearloid inlays. Another '65 Stratocaster, a sunburst model, was also played, burned, and it was smashed by Hendrix at the London Astoria and later given to Frank Zappa, who left it to his son, Dweezil, upon his death.

While pre-CBS Stratocasters have attained far greater status as collector items, many Hendrix-philes believe Jimi preferred post-'65 guitars for tone-based reasons. One theory is that he found the extra wood in the larger post-CBS headstocks to increase sustain. Another holds that the slightly weaker single-coil pickups of the late-'60s Stratocasters added up to a bigger sound when injected through his 100-watt Marshall stacks (this might sound contrary to reason, but the theory itself is sound: weaker pickups prevent the signal from breaking up too early in the signal chain, so a little more fidelity is maintained through to the output stage of a large amp). Also frequently discussed is his preference for right-handed Strats played upside down, when left-handed Strats did exist. Among other observations, much is made of the fact that restringing the right-handed guitar with the low E back on top, and thus wound around the tuner post that was now furthest from the nut, created a change in the vibrational characteristics of that string.

Perhaps the best authority on these theories is the tech who worked with Hendrix live and in the studio and had hands-on experience with Jimi's guitars. British effects guru Roger Mayer not only built and modified many of the pedals that Hendrix used, but also worked as an all-round right-hand man and even helped select and set up many of the star's guitars. What does he have to say about the wide headstock/ greater sustain theory? "No, Jimi wouldn't have considered that," Mayer told this writer for *Guitar Rigs: Classic Guitar and Amp Combinations.* "All the guitars that we used were bought out of necessity; there weren't that many

Stratocasters around [in London] in those days, and they were very expensive. Also, in the 1960s nobody paid much attention to whether pre-CBS Fenders were any better than CBS Fenders. They were all about the same. I can't see a slightly bigger headstock making any difference anyway."

Of course, the final word in all of this is that the Strats Hendrix played are iconic simply because he played them—and whatever Strat Jimi wailed on, it was sure to make a heavenly sound. ♦

Right: Jimi Hendrix's 1968 Fender Stratocaster, serial number 240981, that he played at Woodstock in August 1968. *Courtesy Experience Music Project, Seattle, Washington*

Facing page: Jimi Hendrix with ubiquitous Stratocaster onstage at Fillmore East in 1968. *Elliot Landy/ Redferns/Getty Images*

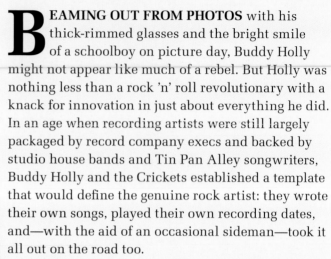

BEAMING OUT FROM PHOTOS with his thick-rimmed glasses and the bright smile of a schoolboy on picture day, Buddy Holly might not appear like much of a rebel. But Holly was nothing less than a rock 'n' roll revolutionary with a knack for innovation in just about everything he did. In an age when recording artists were still largely packaged by record company execs and backed by studio house bands and Tin Pan Alley songwriters, Buddy Holly and the Crickets established a template that would define the genuine rock artist: they wrote their own songs, played their own recording dates, and—with the aid of an occasional sideman—took it all out on the road too.

Holly's playing was likewise innovative, blending chunky rhythm and high-string lead work into a style that owed an equal tip of the hat to country, R&B,

Holly and his Crickets, Joe Mauldin (bass) and Jerry Allison (drums), appear on the BBC-TV program *Off the Record* in 1958. *John Rodgers/Redferns/Getty Images*

140

and rockabilly (and to his predecessor Bo Diddley, among others). Amid all this avant-garde behavior, his guitar choice was radical too: while other heroes on the burgeoning rock 'n' roll scene were playing Gretsches or big-bodied Gibson archtops, Holly—with a loan from his brother Larry—purchased a new Fender Stratocaster, a guitar that had been designed for country players and released onto the market just a year before. In doing so, Holly (born Charles Hardin Holley) also became the first household name in popular music to perform regularly on a Stratocaster.

Holly played his first Stratocaster, a late-1954 or early-1955 model, for about two years and used it to record his first hits, including "That'll Be the Day" and "Peggy Sue," before it was stolen from a tour bus in Michigan in the fall of 1957 during DJ Alan Freed's "Biggest Show of Stars" package tour. The 1957 Stratocaster that he acquired to replace it, however, purchased hurriedly in Detroit in time to make the show that evening, is possibly the most recognizable of all of the four or five Strats Holly owned. Another two-tone sunburst model with a maple fingerboard, it appears in several popular photos of Holly performing in 1957 and '58 and is notable for the wear that soon developed in the covers of the middle and neck pickups just below the high E string, which eventually revealed the black-fiber coil formers beneath.

This iconic 1957 Stratocaster accompanied Holly on many of his most prominent performances of the time and certainly helped to establish Fender's modernistic new model as a standard of solid-body design. It was played on TV appearances on *The Ed Sullivan Show* and *The Arthur Murray Dance Party* (with a tweed Fender Bassman amp visible in the background, finally earning a little spotlight time for the backline), and traveled to the UK with Holly for his historic British tour. In April 1958, Holly lost yet another Stratocaster when the 1957 instrument was stolen from the band's station wagon during a stop at a restaurant in St. Louis, Missouri. The star acquired at least two or three more Strats before his death in 1959. ✪

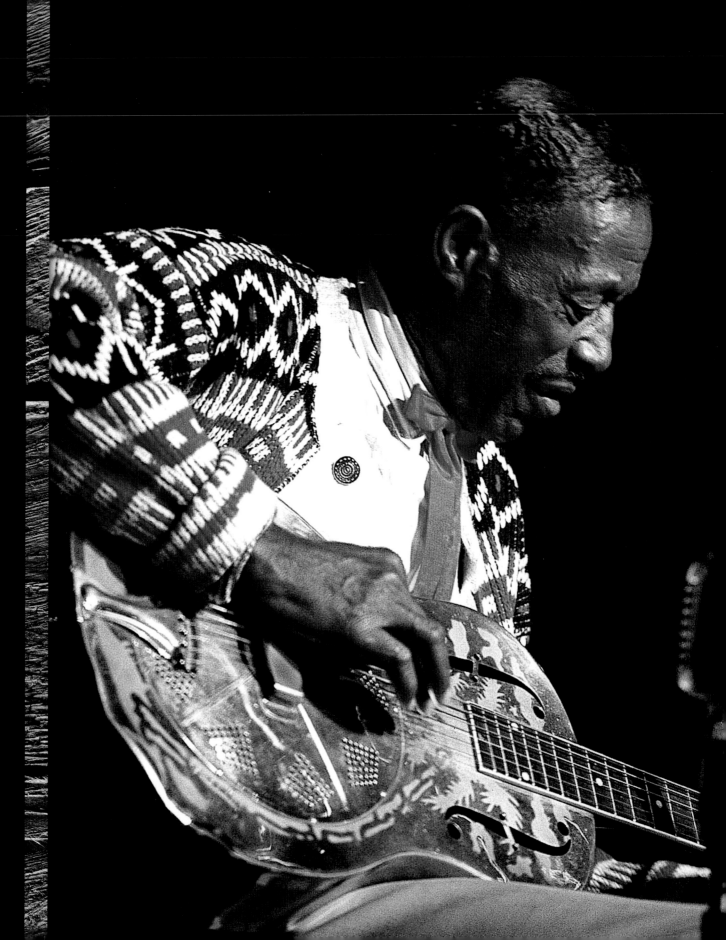

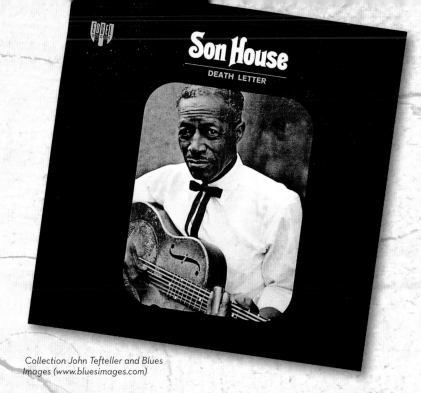

Collection John Tefteller and Blues Images (www.bluesimages.com)

AMONG DELTA BLUES SHOUTERS, Son House was the real deal. He epitomized the genre with his art, his life, and even his continual struggle with the music that he clearly loved, but also seemingly feared. Born in Mississippi in 1902, House vacillated between God's music in the church and "the Devil's music" in the taverns and roadhouses. He became a Baptist preacher in his teens but didn't learn to play the guitar until his early twenties, having avoided the instrument because of its secular associations. Eventually, though, he was hooked, and when he traveled to Grafton, Wisconsin, in 1930 to record his first sessions—resulting in three "sides" released by Paramount on 78 rpm and one unreleased tune—the guitar he took with him was a National Duolian.

National's Style O and Duolian models have become blues standard bearers, but House was one of the first Delta musicians to bend the loud, brash, yet extremely evocative instrument to the cause. His use of the single-resonator National exploited the guitar's strengths as one of the few six-string acoustics that could complement the volume levels that the man's voice could crank out. House tuned to open G (D-G-D-G-B-D) and played with a slide that was often cut from a length of copper pipe and worn on the ring finger of his left hand so he could fret notes both with his little finger in front of it and with his index and middle fingers behind it. His right hand set the pounding, driving, ever-shifting rhythm that he became known for, and he attacked the guitar with a lively, loose-limbed approach, using bare fingers—rather than the fingerpicks worn by many resonator players—to strum, slap, pluck, and snap the strings.

House's performances were packed with an unfettered intensity, and they have to be seen to be fully appreciated. As his latter-day manager, Dick Waterman, put it, "If blues were an ocean to be distilled to a lake, and a pond, and ultimately smaller and smaller until eventually it became a drop of water, then that is Son House."

Fortunately, after giving up music from the mid-'40s until the late '50s, House made something of a comeback amid the blues and folk boom of the '60s, and several live performances were recorded on film in the early and middle part of that decade. He was also recorded by Alan Lomax in 1941 and '42, and recorded several more songs for Columbia Records in 1965. For a dose of the good stuff, dig up "Death Letter Blues" or "Levee Camp Blues," both just as blue as the blues is ever likely to get. ★

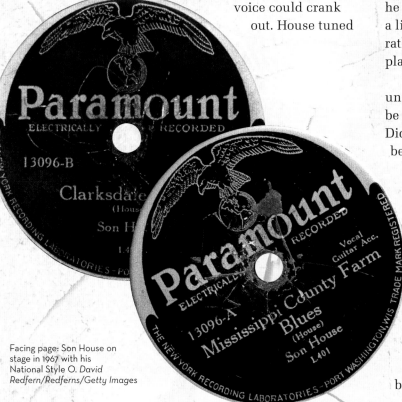

Facing page: Son House on stage in 1967 with his National Style O. *David Redfern/Redferns/Getty Images*

Chrissie Hynde has wielded numerous Telecasters,
but her blue model with a mirror pickguard has
long been a signature of the Pretenders. *Ebet
Roberts/Redferns/Getty Images*

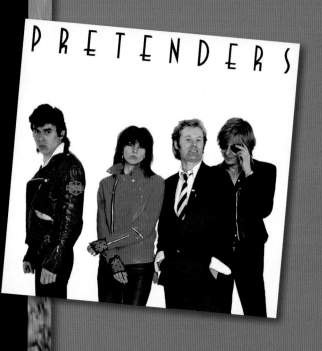

AFTER STRUGGLING through her efforts to
kick-start a career amidst London's punk
scene of the late '70s, Chrissie Hynde emerged
in the early '80s, Telecaster in hand, to offer some
of the most infectiously tuneful creations of the
early post-punk years. Born in Akron, Ohio, in 1951,
Hynde was the archetypal high-school outsider and
consummate music fan, irresistibly drawn to the
excitement she perceived in the rock music world
and, inevitably, her own part in the midst of it all.

While attending college at Kent State University
in Ohio, Hynde briefly formed a band with Mark
Mothersbaugh, later of Devo, then packed up and
headed east to London, where the real action seemed
to be in the early '70s. Even before forming the
Pretenders, Hynde was involved in musical projects—
often precursors to other punk and underground
bands that would later emerge—with Mick Jones
(The Clash), Nick Moss (Culture Club), Steve Strange,

members of The Damned, Tony James (Generation X), and future Sex Pistols manager Malcolm McLaren. Dave Hill, the owner of London indie label Real Records, took Hynde under his wing in 1978 and helped her form a band. Bassist Pete Farndon was first into the fray, followed by guitarist James Honeyman-Scott and drummer Martin Chambers—and the Pretenders were born.

Early in 1979, the band logged an early hit with a cover of the Kinks' "Stop Your Sobbing" (Hynde would be romantically involved with Kinks main man Ray Davies soon after, and had a daughter with him in 1983). The eponymous debut album released later that year received wide critical acclaim and reasonable commercial success, and issued hit singles in "Brass in Pocket" and "Kid," as well as containing several other stand-out tracks. In the early '80s *Pretenders II* was another strong showing, with solid singles in "Talk of the Town" and "Message of Love," but it failed to catch fire like the debut album had nearly two years before. Adding to the strains of "the difficult second album," interpersonal issues within the band, exacerbated by Farndon's drug abuse, were clearly taking their toll on the Pretenders. Farndon was fired on June 14, 1982—purportedly a crushing blow for the bassist who had been the first Pretender other than Hynde, and who had helped to shape the band—but more significantly, guitarist Honeyman-Scott was found dead of heart failure just two days later, following an apparent cocaine overdose. Less than a year later, drugs claimed Farndon's life, too, when he drowned in a bathtub after an apparent heroin overdose.

Although such twofold tragedy would be enough to put paid to most bands, the Pretenders got back to the grindstone pretty quickly. Hynde and Chambers were joined by Rockpile guitarist Billy Bremner and Big Country bassist Tony Butler to record the hit single "Back on the Chain Gang," released in November of 1982. A song that pairs an upbeat arrangement to the melancholy tale about getting back to work after the death of Honeyman-Scott, it would join the band's next album proper, 1984's *Learning to Crawl*, alongside another hit dedicated to the former Pretender guitarist, the haunting ballad "2000 Miles." Since then, the Pretenders have enjoyed relatively steady success, while Hynde has also turned her hand to several guest appearances and side projects.

From the start, Hynde's own guitar duties were primarily to cover the rhythm, while Honeyman-Scott laid down tasty hooks and solos that displayed surprising maturity and a keen melodic sense for his young years (he was just twenty-five at the time of his death in 1982). Even so, Hynde's blue Telecaster with a mirror pickguard has long been a signature of the band, both sonically and visually. Not that the instrument has been entirely sheltered from lead duties: Honeyman-Scott borrowed Hynde's Tele to record the catchy intro riff and solo to the song "Kid," and can be seen playing a whiteguard early '60s Telecaster with rosewood fingerboard (still with its original blonde finish and white pickguard) in photos shot in the studio from about that time—possibly Hynde's own Telecaster prior to modifications. Later, Hynde also took gold and silver sparkle Telecasters on the road, somewhat extending the theme, as well as a more originally equipped early '60s Tele. ◆

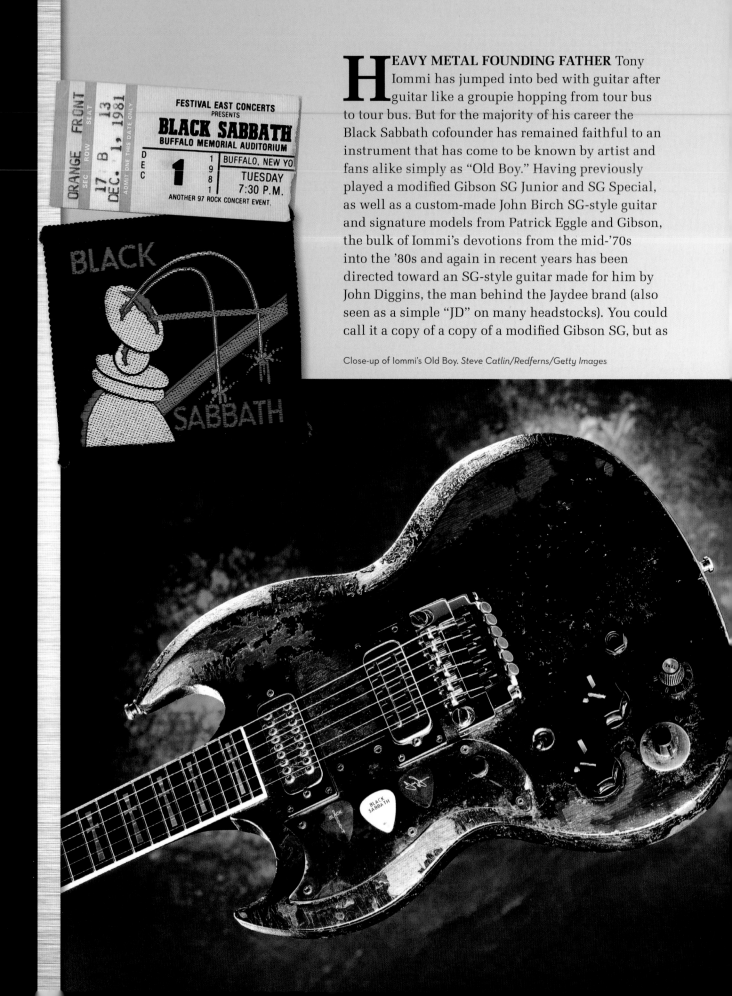

FESTIVAL EAST CONCERTS
PRESENTS

BLACK SABBATH
BUFFALO MEMORIAL AUDITORIUM

ORANGE FRONT
SEC 17 ROW B SEAT 13
DEC. 1, 1981

DEC **1** 1981 BUFFALO, NEW YO
TUESDAY
7:30 P.M.

ADMIT ONE THIS DATE ONLY

ANOTHER 97 ROCK CONCERT EVENT.

BLACK SABBATH

HEAVY METAL FOUNDING FATHER Tony Iommi has jumped into bed with guitar after guitar like a groupie hopping from tour bus to tour bus. But for the majority of his career the Black Sabbath cofounder has remained faithful to an instrument that has come to be known by artist and fans alike simply as "Old Boy." Having previously played a modified Gibson SG Junior and SG Special, as well as a custom-made John Birch SG-style guitar and signature models from Patrick Eggle and Gibson, the bulk of Iommi's devotions from the mid-'70s into the '80s and again in recent years has been directed toward an SG-style guitar made for him by John Diggins, the man behind the Jaydee brand (also seen as a simple "JD" on many headstocks). You could call it a copy of a copy of a modified Gibson SG, but as

Close-up of Iommi's Old Boy. *Steve Catlin/Redferns/Getty Images*

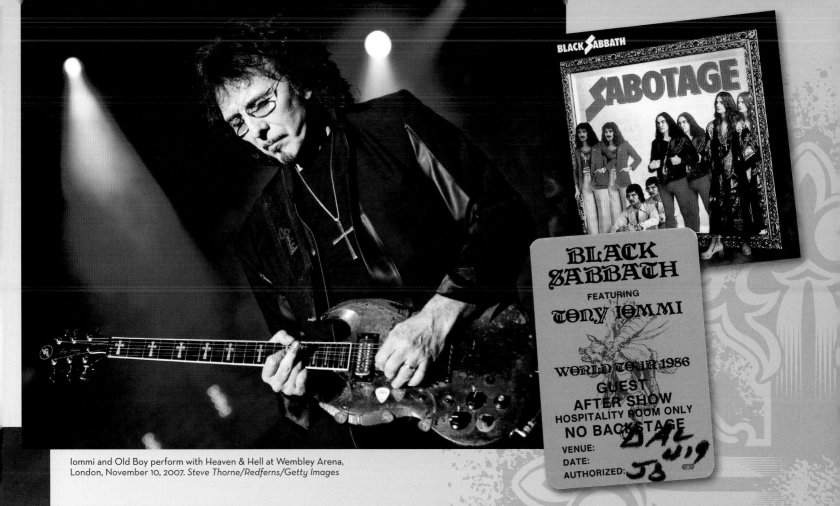

Iommi and Old Boy perform with Heaven & Hell at Wembley Arena, London, November 10, 2007. *Steve Thorne/Redferns/Getty Images*

any true Sabbath fan knows, Old Boy is so much more than that.

Iommi and Black Sabbath have always been known for making a sound that's monstrously huge but rather straightforward, and as such his demands from a guitar blend solidity, power, and simplicity. His battle-scarred Jaydee carries a pair of custom-made mini-humbucking-sized pickups: in the neck position, a Magnum X (a.k.a. Hyperflux) based on a John Birch design, and in the bridge, a custom-made John Diggins unit. Both high-output pickups have coils wound with extremely fine wire and often cobalt-steel magnets rather than the more traditional alnico or ceramic. The pickups are also designed to put less of a magnetic pull on the extremely light strings that Iommi uses, thus easing his playing with two prosthetic fingertips, a feature made all the more important by the extremely slack C-sharp tuning the Sabbath axeman often uses (at the age of eighteen, the left-handed guitarist lost the tips of the middle and ring fingers of his right hand in a machine-press accident). Today, Jaydee offers a signature Old Boy in both right- and left-handed models.

Old Boy also carries a Schaller combination bridge/tailpiece, with individually adjustable saddles and fine-tuners, and an odd-looking assortment of knobs that actually perform only straightforward volume and tone duties (the bridge pickup's tone control is disabled). Other than its distinctive crucifix fingerboard inlays though, Old Boy is probably best known for its worn, peeling finish. It would be easy to assume its paint has fallen prey to the rigors of touring with one of the world's fiercest metal bands, but the deteriorating finish was in fact the casualty of an early guitar that was rushed through production by Diggins to meet a Sabbath tour deadline. As Diggins recalls on jaydeeguitars.com, "The lacquer was still soft when it was taken to the US, and it was this factor combined with severe changes in temperature and humidity that caused the paint to crack and flake off, giving the 'Old Boy' the well-worn look that it has today."

Either way, the look suits a guitar that has peeled off some of the meanest riffs in the history of rock—with a little help from several mammoth Laney amp stacks and a left-handed metal maestro. ★

From a BACKWOODS HOOTENANY...
To the BIGTIME NASHVILLE SOUND!

...He drove his talent like a high-priced car on a reckless race to the top!

...They called him The

NASHVILLE REBEL

...and dared him to go all the way!

IN TECHNICOLOR® AND TECHNISCOPE®

AMERICAN INTERNATIONAL STARS

TEX RITTER · **SONNY JAMES** · **FARON YOUNG**
LORETTA LYNN · **PORTER WAGONER** · **THE WILBURN BROTHERS**
HENNY YOUNGMAN · and introducing **WAYLON JENNINGS** as Arlin Grove

FROM ORIGINAL STORY BY CLICK WESTON AND IRA KERNS AND JAY J. SHERIDAN · SCREENPLAY BY JAY J. SHERIDAN · DIRECTED BY JAY J. SHERIDAN · PRODUCED BY FRED A. NILES · AN AMERICAN INTERNATIONAL RELEASE

ONE OF THE ORIGINAL COUNTRY OUTLAWS, Waylon Jennings aligned himself throughout his long career with other anti-Nashville rebels such as Johnny Cash and Willie Nelson, and along the way he forged a breed of instantly recognizable spanky-twang guitar playing. Using a light touch that often incorporated bare thumb-and-finger playing for rhythm work and a pick for lead runs, Jennings combined driving low-string hammer-on and pull-off riffs with evocative upper-fret double stops, while making frequent use of the modulation effects of which he was fond (tremolo in

Jennings starred in the 1966 film *Nashville Rebel.* Interestingly, the film studio chose to depict his Tele's famous tooled-leather cover in red and white instead of its actual black and white.

An early image of Jennings in the recording studio. *Sony BMG Music Entertainment/Getty Images*

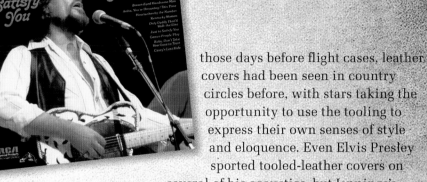

the early days, phaser pedals after these units reached the market), all of which gave his hallowed 1953 Telecaster, with its tooled black-and-white leather cover, a sound like no other guitar on the scene.

A native of Littlefield, Texas, Jennings played bass in Buddy Holly's band for what would be the star's final tour in late 1958 and early '59. When the band booked a small airplane to take them between shows mid-tour, Jennings famously gave his seat up to J. P. "The Big Bopper" Richardson, and in doing so he avoided the crash that took the lives of Holly, Richardson, and teen idol Ritchie Valens. Jennings laid low in the early '60s, moving to Phoenix, Arizona, working in radio, and putting Holly's death behind him. He slowly worked his way back into recording and live performance. By the mid-'60s he had developed his songwriting chops alongside inimitable singing and playing styles, catching the attention of the prevailing music scene. Jennings signed first to the newly formed A&M records, but his contract was bought out by RCA, and in 1965 he traveled to Nashville to begin a long and successful recording career (upon arriving in Music City, Jennings roomed with one Johnny Cash, and yes, wild times ensued).

Even before leaving Phoenix though, Jennings had partnered up with the guitar that would form a big part of his visual identity right up until his death in 2002. When he started to get serious about performing again, his bandmates decided he needed a good Telecaster and purchased a used 1953 Tele that they'd adorned with a custom-fitted, tooled-leather cover before presenting it to Jennings. Considered necessities by some, due to the hard knocks that guitars often received on the road in

those days before flight cases, leather covers had been seen in country circles before, with stars taking the opportunity to use the tooling to express their own senses of style and eloquence. Even Elvis Presley sported tooled-leather covers on several of his acoustics, but Jennings's eventual fame, and the unmistakable look of that black leather cover with white floral work, helped establish these erstwhile protective devices as badges of honor for country pickers everywhere.

Beneath the cover, Jennings's second-hand blackguard Tele remained largely unadulterated for years. In the early '80s he did eventually swap its original three-brass-saddles bridge for a '70s six-saddle Tele bridge, and EMG pickups finally replaced the thirty-plus-year-old Fender single-coils, but through it all, the guitar never lost that fluid, slappy, swirly twang that was so recognizable as "the Waylon sound." ★

Jennings, circa 1980, before he swapped the guitar's brass saddles for a six-saddle bridge. Stephanie Chernikowski/Getty Images

eric johnson
Live In Concert

with special guest

Saturday
April 19
Paramount Theatre
8 pm • $20.00

Budweiser

REGARDED IN GUITAR CIRCLES as a tone freak's tone freak, Eric Johnson is famous for such niggling tweaks as using a rubber band to hold the bottom plate on his Fuzz Face fuzz box because he doesn't like its sound with the standard screws and preferring the performance of his BK Butler Tube Driver when positioned on a wooden block that lifts it above the level of the rest of his effects pedals. Most players would be thrilled with *any* 1957 Strat, but with ears like these, and a discriminating sonic sensibility to go with them, you can be sure Johnson isn't likely to settle on just any 1957 Fender Stratocaster. It's well known that even valuable vintage guitars range from poor to mediocre to good to outstanding in the tone and playability stakes, and if Eric Johnson has chosen to ply his trade for years on one particular '57 Stratocaster, you can bet it's a breathtaking instrument. As such, this particular maple-neck sunburst Strat has become legendary among an elite crowd and is a fitting example of everything a great Strat should be.

As iconic a guitar as Johnson's Strat might be, it's no museum piece. Rather, it has been carefully modified to suit the needs of a hardworking and very discerning professional. Johnson has the guitar refretted with jumbo wire as often as necessary to keep it feeling meaty and playable. As Johnson explained to Dan Erlewine in *How to Make Your Electric Guitar Play Great!*, rather than having the fingerboard planed down to a flatter radius than the vintage 7.25-inch radius that Fender originally used, he has his frets milled down slightly lower toward the middle of the neck so they remain higher toward the edges, making it easier to grip the strings for extreme bends. Johnson famously leaves the cover off

Johnson at the Crossroad Music Festival in Dallas, Texas, June 5, 2004. Among the many modifications to his gear, Johnson leaves the cover off the tremolo spring cavity on the back of the guitar because he feels it hampers the tone. © David Atlas/Retna Ltd.

the tremolo spring cavity on the back of the guitar because he feels it hampers the tone, and he has had a nylon insert cut from an old Gibson bridge saddle installed in the high E string's steel saddle to soften its shrillness, a goal further pursued by rewiring the Strat's controls so the bridge pickup passes through a tone potentiometer rather than straight to the output, the way a '57 was wired at the factory.

Achieving Johnson's famous "thousand-pound violin" tone involves far more than just the guitar though, and several other elements of his rig deserve a portion of the credit. The essentials here are really rather simple, but they add up to a mammoth sonic assault. Johnson's guitar signal first runs through his choice of ingredients on a fairly basic but meticulously selected pedal board, including the aforementioned Fuzz Face and Tube Driver, a Crybaby wah-wah, a TC Electronic Stereo Chorus Flanger, and an Echoplex tape-delay unit. From there, Johnson selects between a pair of blackface 1966 Fender Twin Reverb amps with JBL D120F speakers or a 1968 Marshall 50-watt Tremolo head and 4×12 cab

and/or a 1969 Marshall 100-watt Super Lead and 4x12 cab. A mighty arsenal, yet for all this, we've perhaps got to credit the player's hands for just a *little* of the mighty tone this rig generates. ✪

Johnson's Strat alongside his SG. *Rick Gould*

EVERY BLUESMAN OF THE PAST seventy years who has gone "down to the crossroads" owes a direct debt to the legacy of Robert Johnson. But hell, every musician who has let slip a Delta moan or bent a blue note owes at least an indirect debt to this great originator. Johnson's influence on the blues is writ large, his short life is a thing of mythic proportions, and the scant firsthand history of the man and a musical catalog numbering just twenty-nine known recordings only serves to further inflate the legend. And if few veracious accounts were written, even fewer were committed to film. For many years only two verified photos of the blues legend were known to exist, although a third that possibly shows Johnson and fellow performer Johnny Shines surfaced in 2005. In the best-known of these images—a studio portrait taken in 1935

The Columbia LP collections that introduced much of the world to Robert Johnson's music.

by Hooks Brothers in Memphis, Tennessee, and best known for its appearance on the cover of *Robert Johnson: The Complete Recordings* in 1990—the unnaturally talented bluesman is playing a Gibson L-1 acoustic guitar.

As the inventor of the archtop guitar, the instrument it still held in highest esteem through at least the first third of the twentieth century, Gibson had little regard for the flat-top acoustic. Market forces, however, and no doubt the growing popularity of the instruments of rival C. F. Martin, pressured the company to release its own flat-top. Unveiled in 1926, the bare-bones L-1 (the model number was appropriated from Gibson's bottom-of-the-line archtop, which was discontinued in 1925) was just 13.5 inches wide and had either ladder or H-bracing (neither of which were as tone-enhancing as X-bracing or parallel bracing). The necks of early examples had no truss rod, even though Gibson had

invented the device four years before and was using it in most of its guitars by this time.

Nevertheless, the model apparently appealed to artists who wanted Gibson quality at an entry-level price. In addition to Johnson, Maybelle Carter of the Carter Family played an early L-1 before moving up to a sophisticated L-5 archtop. And if the actual tone of the instrument heard on Johnson's twenty-nine recorded songs and twelve alternate takes isn't exactly stellar, it certainly is at least evocative enough to express the artist's depth of feeling. The story of Robert Johnson's life and death is likely to remain wrapped in an enigma: there are at least three renditions of how he was killed, two gravesites in Mississippi that bear his name, and no birth certificate has ever been found to prove his supposed birth date of May 8, 1911. But at least the sound of that lonesome, emotive Gibson L-1 will forever help tether the ethereal legend to this earth. ★

Collection John Tefteller and Blues Images (www.bluesimages.com)

Johnson's famous "redguard" Tele takes a break. *Kevin Nixon/Guitarist Magazine/Getty Images*

WITH HIS SHAGGY BOWL HAIRCUT, black clothes, herky-jerky stage presence, and frenetic playing style, Wilko Johnson was considered by many to be the heart and soul of Dr. Feelgood, the band he cofounded in 1971. His black Telecaster with red pickguard was as much a part of his image as anything, and an even bigger force upon the music, given its punchy tone and the energy it injected into this seminal London pub-rock outfit.

The guitarist was born John Wilkinson in 1947 in Canvey Island, a 7-square-mile island just off the southern corner of Essex, England, that is known mainly for its large oil depot and flat, swampy land. Inverting his name to create his better-known stage moniker, Wilko Johnson launched his music career shortly after graduating from the University of Newcastle upon Tyne with an English degree. Settling back home in Essex, a county just east of London, he met up with two old acquaintances: singer Lee Collins (soon Lee Brilleaux) and bassist John Sparkes, whose group the Pigboy Charlie Band had just lost its guitarist. Johnson hopped aboard, and local working drummer John "The Big Figure" Martin was roped in to fill out the quartet, which opted to mark the personnel change with a name change. The new name—Dr. Feelgood—seems to have originated from a song by bluesman Piano Red, which was covered by English rock 'n' rollers Johnny Kid and The Pirates (themselves a significant influence on early Dr. Feelgood), although it is also the name given to any doctor on the rock scene who was willing to dole out "feel good" meds.

From the start, the members of Dr. Feelgood considered it an R&B band, but the tag might be misleading to R&B purists. Blending blues, rock 'n' roll, R&B and something distinctly *London* into their own original sound—buoyed by an electric stage presence in live shows—Dr. Feelgood became the central fixture of what would be known as the London pub-rock scene of the 1970s. Including bands like Ducks Deluxe, Brinsley Schwarz, Chill Willi and the Red Hot Peppers, and Nick Lowe, and later the likes of Ian Dury, Joe Strummer's 101ers, the Stranglers, and Elvis Costello, pub rock stood out as a back-to-basics reaction of sorts to the phoniness and glitz of the booming glam-rock scene, while earning its name from the venues that these smaller, more rebellious bands were forced to play, being largely

Johnson performs with Dr. Feelgood in Los Angeles, March 23, 1976. *Richard Creamer/ Michael Ochs Archives/ Getty Images*

shut out of the theater and arena concert circuit. Pub rock is also credited as the breeding ground for the riotous punk-rock scene that followed, and there was certainly some overlap between the genres in the mid-'70s, although punk purists largely rejected pub-rock as "dad's music," much as they rejected just about everything else.

Johnson bought his first Telecaster from a shop in Southend, Essex, in 1965 for £90 (then the equivalent of around $150), which he paid off in weekly installments by saving his school lunch money and, eventually, persuading his girlfriend—later to be his wife—to cash out her savings account. In 1974, after Dr. Feelgood signed its first record deal, he bought a second Telecaster. Originally a sunburst model from 1962 with rosewood fingerboard and white pickguard, the new guitar was painted black and a red pickguard was added once Dr. Feelgood got rolling so it would match his favorite black-and-red shirt. The choice of a Telecaster had been inspired by its use by guitarist Mick Green with Johnny Kidd and The Pirates, the band that had also, it seems, inspired Johnson's choice of band name. And, as Johnson told Richard Flynn of *Guitar & Bass* magazine in the United Kingdom in September of 2011, Green also had an enormous effect on Johnson's playing style. "I can remember discovering him and being intrigued by the way he played," said Johnson. "The thing that hit me was his style. It was so American. It was a rhythm and blues style, and

it didn't sound like what most people were doing over here. One of the many things that intrigued me was when I found out the Pirates didn't have a rhythm guitarist. It was all one guy, and I thought that was great and I started learning how to do it. . . . But I worked out a way of doing it, which of course was wrong—it's not the way he did it. So if you like, I've ended up with my own style." A big part of that "own style" also revolves around the fact that Johnson is a natural left-hander, but plays guitar right-handed, while also using his bare fingers and thumb rather than a pick.

Dr. Feelgood was on tour in the United States in 1976 when punk hit it big in the United Kingdom. Upon their return, they found a drastically altered scene, one in which they were a little less welcome than they had been in the years before. This, and increasing animosity between Johnson and signer Lee Brilleaux, led to Wilko's disenchantment with the band. In 1977, after several modest hit singles, three successful studio albums—*Down by the Jetty*, *Malpractice*, and *Sneakin' Suspicion*—and a 1976 live album, *Stupidity*, that reached No. 1 on the UK album chart, Wilko Johnson left Dr. Feelgood. Johnson continues to record and tour with his own band, figured largely in the award-winning pub-rock documentary *Oil City Confidential* (2009), and played the part of the mute executioner in the HBO TV series *Game of Thrones*. He still owns his original black Telecaster but has retired it from the road. ★

WHILE SEVERAL GUITAR HEROES HAVE LIVED into ripe old age, their gear preferences evolving with them, those who were taken from us too young are often cemented in the mind's eye with a single iconic guitar of choice. So it is with former Rolling Stones guitarist Brian Jones, who played several guitars in his short years but seems forever associated with that hip Vox Phantom, which, like his dapper outfits, became so

Jones and the Rolling Stones perform at the NME poll winners' party, Wembley Empire Pool, London, April 11, 1965. *David Redfern/Redferns/Getty Images*

THE ROLLING STONES

DECCA

23.634

(I Can't Get No) SATISFACTION

The under assistant west coast promotion

Photo Combs Press

MARK III PROTOTYPE

representative of swinging London in the decade that he failed to outlive.

The teardrop-shaped Vox Phantom Mark III that Jones played on and off for more than three years was actually a prototype of the model built for him by Vox designer Michael Bennett and presented to the star in late 1963. Vox capitalized on Jones's use of the guitar and used his photo in several advertisements throughout the mid-'60s, although close comparison of Jones's Mark III and the model that eventually hit the market, the Mark VI, show slight differences in the shape of the bodies (the actual production-model Mark III was more of a rounded pentagon too). Jones also played the production Mark VI and the twelve-string version, the Mark XII. Many existing photos show him live and in the studio with all of these Vox guitars.

Prior to the Phantom range, which were initially made in England, Vox and parent company JMI marketed several cheaper instruments made in Italy and went back to Italy later in the decade for guitar production. Jones is understood to have parted ways with his original prototype teardop-shaped Mark III well before his death in 1969, and many reports indicate that he traded it to a dealer in Glasgow for a Fender model in 1967. In 1984 the Hard Rock Café purchased a Vox Phantom Mark III that is believed to be Jones's original guitar; this instrument is now part of that restaurant chain's permanent collection.

Throughout the '60s Jones played a range of other interesting guitars, including a few Gibson Firebirds, a Les Paul, and an ES-330; a Rickenbacker 360/12 twelve-string electric; and a Gretsch Double Anniversary. A talented multi-instrumentalist, Jones also recorded notable parts for Stones tracks on harmonica, Mellotron, sitar, flute, and dulcimer, among other instruments. Amid all this, though, we still see him with that bright-white Vox Phantom. Together they make a guitar-and-star pairing that's about as iconic as they come. ◆

GAB Archive/Redferns/Getty Images

Rehearsal for ABC's *Thank Your Lucky Stars* TV program, 1964. *Terry O'Neill/Getty Image*

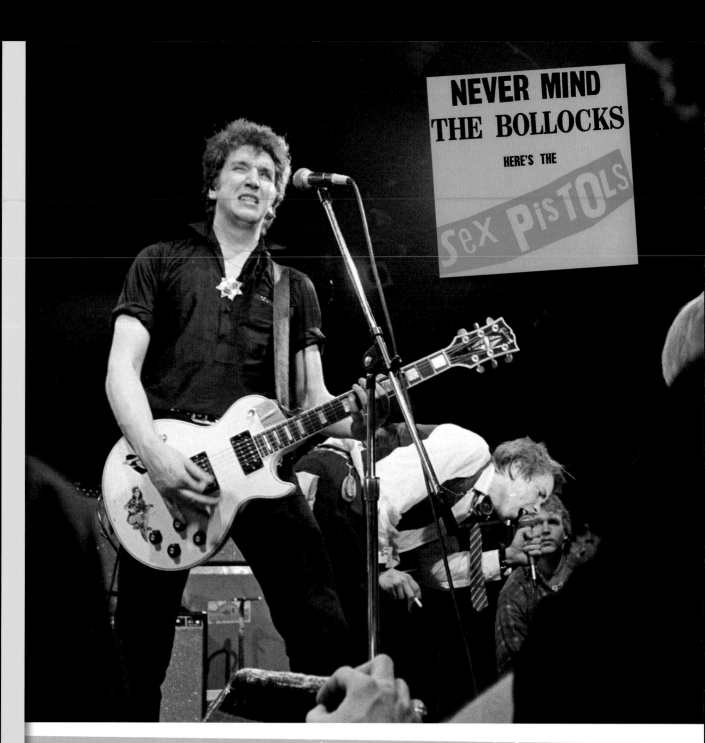

NEVER MIND
THE BOLLOCKS

HERE'S THE

Sex Pistols

Jones at the Sex Pistols' first US concert, Great
Southeast Music Hall, Atlanta, January 5, 1978.
Tom Hill/WireImage/Getty Images

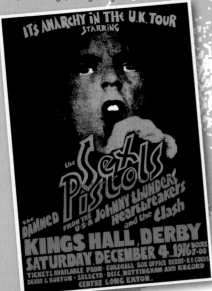

MORE THAN JUST A FOUNDING FATHER
of punk guitar, Steve Jones of the Sex Pistols
was arguably the ultimate anti-guitar
hero, a stance he was happy to ram home himself by
stenciling the ironic declaration "Guitar Hero" on
the grille cloth of his silverface Fender Twin Reverb
amp just months after he'd learned to play the guitar.
The instrument that he most famously injected into
this combo, though, was not the usual punk Mosrite,
Mustang, or Les Paul Junior, but a surprisingly exotic
offering: a Gibson Les Paul Custom. Of course, when
you're slinging such an up-market model, it's easier
to play down any accusations of being a well-heeled

muso or a punk in poseur's clothing if you bandy about an assortment of apocryphal tales of how you pilfered said guitar from a famous rock star, which is exactly how the Pistols played it.

Research Jones's gear and you'll encounter widely accepted stories of how he allegedly stole the Les Paul from Mick Ronson backstage at a David Bowie concert (or perhaps from Paul McCartney) and of how the Twin Reverb was likewise allegedly lifted from either (a) the back of Bob Marley's equipment truck or (b) backstage at a Bowie concert. (Bandmate Johnny "Rotten" Lydon was purported to have stolen PA equipment from Keith Richards's house.) Word is, though—and straight from the mouth of a sober, latter-day Jones himself—that the Les Paul Custom in question landed in his hands via a totally legitimate route. After declaring that, sure, he did swipe other guitars in his late teens, even before learning to play the instrument, Jones told Jerry McCully of gibson.com: "The one that I started playing was the one that Malcolm McLaren actually brought back from New York that he got off Sylvain Sylvain, which was the white Gibson Les Paul. A '74, I think it was, a white Custom." Sylvain, the New York Dolls' guitarist better known for playing Les Paul Juniors, purportedly added the two famous pinup stickers to the guitar and removed its pickguard and pickup covers before sending it across the Atlantic with McLaren, but Jones himself helped to expose it to the nicotine haze that would further yellow its original Arctic White finish.

Having originally been recruited by McLaren to sing lead vocals in the Sex Pistols, Jones moved to guitar when Rotten joined the band. The only problem was he couldn't really play the thing yet. Taking the '74 Les Paul Custom, Jones worked out the basics in only three months before the band started gigging, and he only had a year with it before carrying it into the studio to record the legendary *Never Mind the Bollocks, Here's the Sex Pistols* LP. Regardless of his apparent "beginner" status, Jones's tone throughout the Pistols' studio recordings is big, fat, gnarly, and downright infectious—and certainly sweeter and juicier than that of many punks of the day.

Sex Pistols' final show, Winterland Ballroom in San Francisco, on January 14, 1978. *Chris Walter/ WireImage/Getty Images*

A dapper Albert
King shows off
one of his Gibson
Flying V guitars.

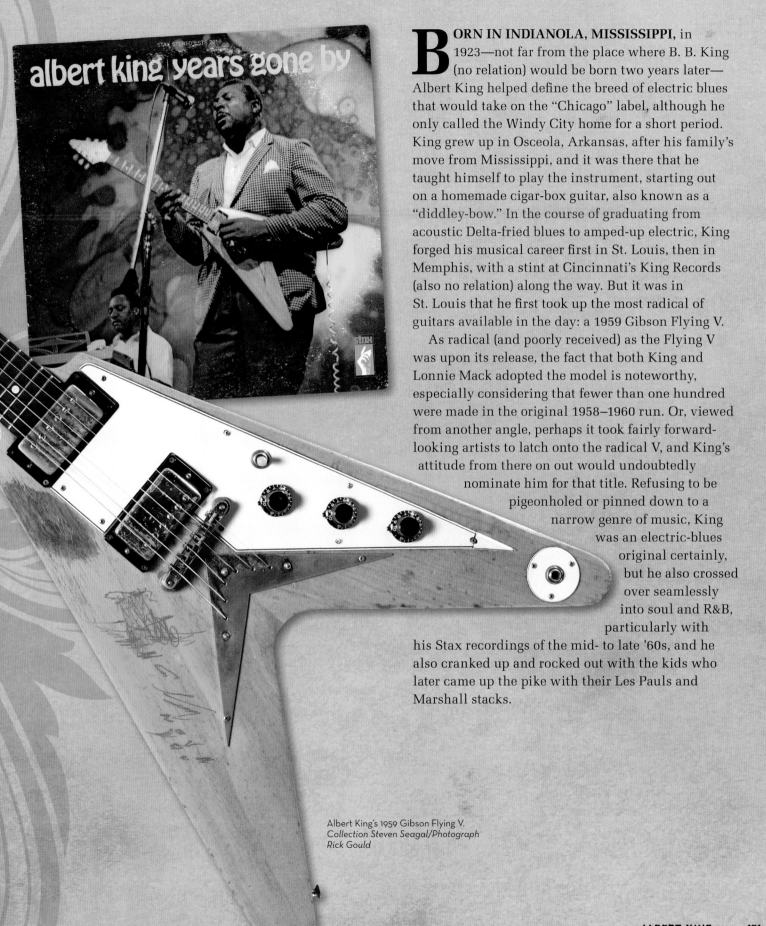

BORN IN INDIANOLA, MISSISSIPPI, in 1923—not far from the place where B. B. King (no relation) would be born two years later— Albert King helped define the breed of electric blues that would take on the "Chicago" label, although he only called the Windy City home for a short period. King grew up in Osceola, Arkansas, after his family's move from Mississippi, and it was there that he taught himself to play the instrument, starting out on a homemade cigar-box guitar, also known as a "diddley-bow." In the course of graduating from acoustic Delta-fried blues to amped-up electric, King forged his musical career first in St. Louis, then in Memphis, with a stint at Cincinnati's King Records (also no relation) along the way. But it was in St. Louis that he first took up the most radical of guitars available in the day: a 1959 Gibson Flying V.

As radical (and poorly received) as the Flying V was upon its release, the fact that both King and Lonnie Mack adopted the model is noteworthy, especially considering that fewer than one hundred were made in the original 1958–1960 run. Or, viewed from another angle, perhaps it took fairly forward-looking artists to latch onto the radical V, and King's attitude from there on out would undoubtedly nominate him for that title. Refusing to be pigeonholed or pinned down to a narrow genre of music, King was an electric-blues original certainly, but he also crossed over seamlessly into soul and R&B, particularly with his Stax recordings of the mid- to late '60s, and he also cranked up and rocked out with the kids who later came up the pike with their Les Pauls and Marshall stacks.

Albert King's 1959 Gibson Flying V.
Collection Steven Seagal/Photograph
Rick Gould

Lucy

Albert King

King of the Blues Guitar

ATLANTIC

CONTAINS BONUS TRACKS

ALBERT KING

A big man with a formidable
presence at six foot four
and 250 pounds, King put a lot
of muscle into his playing and
squeezed out a scorching tone
as a result. With the Flying V in
hand, and armed with his wide,
singing bends and deep yet
smooth vibrato, King went blow
for blow with blues-rockers
decade after decade, taking on
John Mayall and Jimi Hendrix
at the Fillmore in 1968, Stevie
Ray Vaughan on *In Session*
in 1983, and Gary Moore on
Moore's *Still Got the Blues*
in 1990. On the stylistic
flipside, in 1969 King
became the first blues artist
to perform in concert with a major classical orchestra
when he appeared live with the St. Louis Symphony
Orchestra.

Like several notable lefties, King played his right-
handed Flying V backward and strung "upside down"
(that is, the way a left-hander would approach a right-
handed guitar, by flipping it over but not restringing

BLUES GUITARIST:
"ALBERT KING"

it). He usually used an alternate tuning that he steadfastly refused to reveal, although it is known to have started with a low C on the E string, and possibly ran C-B-E-G-B-E or C-F-C-F-A-D, low to high. After retiring his original '59 V, King plied his trade on a newer, custom-made, left-handed Flying V with the more traditional three-a-side Gibson headstock and his initials inlaid in abalone along the fingerboard.

King performed his final show in Los Angeles on December 19, 1992, and died two days later in Memphis of a heart attack. ♥

Albert King christened this left-handed Flying V "Lucy." It was built by master luthier Dan Erlewine for King in 1971, and King used it on many of his later albums. *Collection Steven Seagal/Photograph Rick Gould*

GIBSON "LUCILLE"

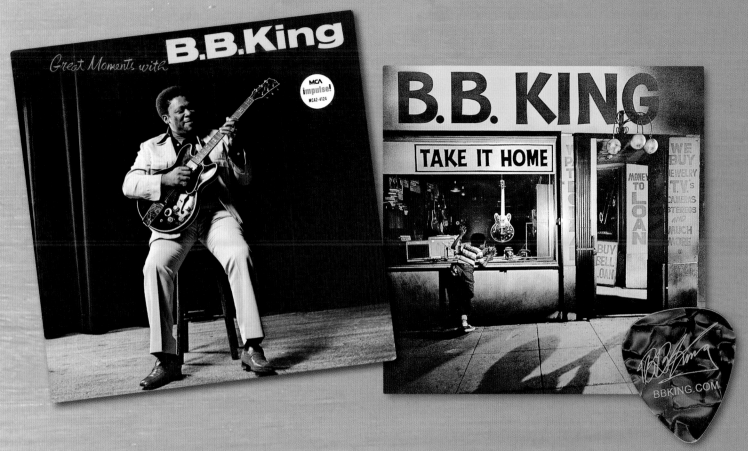

WHEN THE "GUITARS WITH NAMES" category pops up over a few cold malted beverages, it is often declared that there's none more famous than the late B. B. King's "Lucille". The qualifying statement often absent from this truism is that there really isn't just *one* Lucille, in the physical sense—or, at least there hasn't been for a long, long time. King famously landed upon the name Lucille in 1949 after he rushed back into a burning dancehall in Twist, Arkansas, to save his Gibson acoustic guitar after two attendees knocked over a barrel of kerosene while brawling over a woman by that name. Having nearly perished in the endeavor, King told *Ebony* magazine in 1992 that he decided to give his guitar, and all that would follow it, the name Lucille "to remind myself never to do anything that foolish again."

B. B. was born Riley B. King in 1925 in a small town outside Indianola, Mississippi, where a guitar-playing

preacher first pricked his interest in the instrument. After making the transition from sanctified music to "the Devil's music"—the blues—he made his way to Memphis in the late '40s, where he roomed with his cousin Booker "Bukka" White for a time and landed his own spot on WDIA radio in West Memphis via an audition with one of his musical heroes: harmonica player Sonny Boy Williamson, a regular on the station. For promotional purposes, King was given the moniker "Beale Street Blues Boy," which was eventually amended to "Blues Boy" and finally "B. B." As he evolved from local radio personality to regional recording artist to, eventually, national blues artist and even sometime crossover success, King went through a lot of guitars, all of them named Lucille after that fire in Twist.

Early on King played several full-depth Gibson archtop electrics, picked up a Les Paul Goldtop with P-90s for a time, and was even photographed cradling a Fender Telecaster, but by the early '60s he had become if not a one-guitar man, a one-model man, and that model was a Gibson ES-355.

Facing page: The Lucille that King used for years was the prototype that he was given by Gibson. After being stolen, it was subsequently returned to him by a fan who found it in a pawnshop in Las Vegas. *Rick Gould*

Some of the many Lucilles through the years. Top left: Memphis, Tennessee, circa 1948. *Colin Escott/Michael Ochs Archives/Getty Images.* Top right: Apollo Theatre, Harlem, New York, 1963. *Michael Ochs Archives/Getty Images.* Bottom left: Newport, Rhode Island, 1969. *David Redfern/Redferns/Getty Images.* Bottom right: Circa 1970. *Michael Ochs Archives/Getty Images*

This Lucille is part of actor Steven Seagal's collection. It was given to Seagal after a show and signed by King. In fact, it still has King's dried sweat on it from that evening's performance. *Rick Gould*

The ES-355 was the up-market sibling of the seminal ES-335 and ES-345. In addition to its upgraded electronics with added six-position Varitone switch and stereo outputs to split the signals from its two humbuckers, it also featured cosmetic refinements, such as an ebony fingerboard with pearl block markers, multi-ply body and fingerboard binding, and gold-plated hardware. Beginning in 1980, King played Gibson's contemporary renditions of this guitar offered in the form of the B. B. King Lucille, which uses the ES-355 design with some minor changes, including a top with no f-holes to reveal its hollow wings and extra ornamentation befitting a signature model.

"Lucille don't want to play anything but the blues," King noted in the liner to the 1968 album named for his guitar. "Lucille is real, when I play her it's almost like hearing words, and of course, naturally I hear cries. I'd be playing sometimes and as I'd play, it seems like it almost has a conversation with me." ♦

New Orleans Jazz and Heritage Festival, April 28, 2005. *Chris Graythen/Getty Images*

King and goldtop in a 1961 press photo.
Gilles Petard/Redferns/Getty Images

ARAGON MUSIC COMPANY presents:

FREDDIE KING!! IF

AZTECA!! and CLOUDBUR

at the aragon

1106 LAWH
561-9500

ALL TICKETS: $4⁰⁰ TICKETS AVAILABLE AT: ARAGON
TICKET OU

FRIDAY MAY!! TH

Let's Hide Away and Dance Away with FREDDY KING (strictly instrumental)

HIDE AWAY
SEN-SA-SHUN
SAN-HO-ZAY
SIDE TRACKED
WASH OUT
IN THE OPEN
HEADS UP
JUST PICKIN'
SWOOSHY
THE STUMBLE
OUT FRONT
BUTTERSCOTCH

ALTHOUGH HE WAS BORN IN TEXAS, Freddie King became synonymous with hard-driving electric Chicago blues. He was grounded in his trade while combing the Southside clubs and catching the great blues artists of the late '40s and early '50s after his family moved to the Windy City in 1949 when he was just thirteen. He always retained a certain Texas twist to his playing, though, and that might partly be credited with his originality in a crowded blues field. King had started learning guitar at the age of six, and by the early '50s he was trying hard to forge a career in his own right, while also working a "day job" in Chicago's steel mills. Having been born Frederick Christian, Freddie is thought to have changed his stage name to "King" to benefit from associations with B. B. King (oddly, he also spelled his name "Freddy" up until 1968, and "Freddie" after that). By the time King was experiencing some success in his own right, he was doing it with a '54 Les Paul goldtop, and although he eventually moved over to an ES-335-type Gibson, he is most closely associated with the seminal P-90–loaded Les Paul.

False starts and failed attempts to launch a recording career throughout much of the '50s found King finally logging his first two proper studio albums in 1961, and he sported his goldtop on the covers of both of them: *Freddy King Sings the Original*

Hits and *Let's Hide Away and Dance Away with Freddy King*. It was the latter that inspired young English guitarist Eric Clapton to seek out a Les Paul of his own, and, as a result, arguably spawned the British blues-rock boom. Later, King would help initiate successive generations of bluesmen and blues-rockers to the craft, touring with fellow Texans ZZ Top and offering advice to a young Stevie Ray Vaughan. Throughout the middle and latter parts of his career, King made good inroads with young, white audiences more often associated with the rock and blues-rock scenes. He performed alongside Led Zeppelin in 1969 at the Texas Pop Festival, and around the same time was signed to Leon Russell's label, Shelter Records.

With his aggressive playing style, hybrid fingers-and-thumbpick technique, and eviscerating tone, Freddie King's guitar work was always hard to miss. He was a big man and put plenty of weight behind his touch—a momentum that translated viscerally through his Les Paul goldtop and into the amplifier. The rigors of touring—and, perhaps, King's tendency to drink a Bloody Mary rather than eat a square meal while setting up for the show—took their toll on the guitarist's health, and he died of complications from chronic ulcers and pancreatitis in 1976, at the age of just forty-two. At his posthumous induction into the Rock and Roll Hall of Fame in 2012, King's daughter Wanda talked about having broken her father's Les Paul goldtop while running around the house with her siblings—perhaps the event that inspired his move to Gibson semi-acoustic electrics. ★

FREDDIE KING
TAKING CARE OF BUSINESS
1956-1973

AMID THE PUNKS, early new wavers, and stadium rockers that ruled the airwaves of the late 1970s, Dire Straits burst onto the scene sounding like nothing else around. The outfit's first two albums, driven by a classic stripped-down four-piece lineup, gave the impression of rootsy pub rockers captured in the throes of a heated last set, with Knopfler's red pre-CBS Stratocaster leading the charge through the melee to beat the throng to the bar for last call. Yet, as much as these releases—their debut, *Dire Straits* (1978), and *Communique* (1979)—contained, alongside the guitar acrobatics, a wealth of musical subtlety that revealed Knopfler and company as more than just a bar band, Dire Straits' third LP unveiled not only the musical maturity that would make them megastars, but also an enticing new voice—an instrumental voice, that is. Following the incendiary electric licks of its epic opener, "Tunnel of Love," *Making Movies*' second track, "Romeo and Juliet," sashayed onto the scene via the now legendary arpeggio chords played on a guitar that has garnered as much "What the hell is *that*?" factor as any put to vinyl.

Mark Knopfler's famous National Style O.
Rick Gould

Facing page: Dire Straits' Mark Knopfler plays his National Style O on stage alongside guitarist Hal Lindes in 1982.
Phil Dent/Redferns/Getty Images

MARK KNOPFLER AND EMMYLOU HARRIS
REAL LIVE ROADRUNNING

DIRE STRAITS   WALK OF LIFE

DIRE STRAITS   MONEY FOR NOTHING

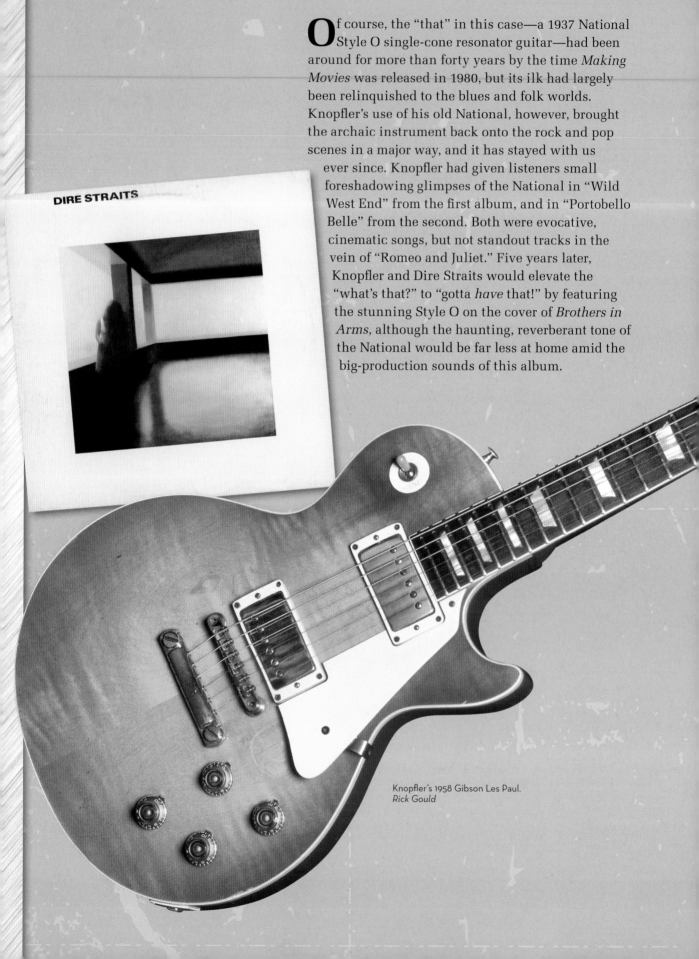

Of course, the "that" in this case—a 1937 National Style O single-cone resonator guitar—had been around for more than forty years by the time *Making Movies* was released in 1980, but its ilk had largely been relinquished to the blues and folk worlds. Knopfler's use of his old National, however, brought the archaic instrument back onto the rock and pop scenes in a major way, and it has stayed with us ever since. Knopfler had given listeners small foreshadowing glimpses of the National in "Wild West End" from the first album, and in "Portobello Belle" from the second. Both were evocative, cinematic songs, but not standout tracks in the vein of "Romeo and Juliet." Five years later, Knopfler and Dire Straits would elevate the "what's that?" to "gotta *have* that!" by featuring the stunning Style O on the cover of *Brothers in Arms*, although the haunting, reverberant tone of the National would be far less at home amid the big-production sounds of this album.

DIRE STRAITS

Knopfler's 1958 Gibson Les Paul.
Rick Gould

THE NOTTING HILLBILLIES

missing...

Knopfler has owned his Style O (the letter *O*, not the numeral *0*) since before Dire Straits' first release, and it's a stunning example of the form. These guitars were introduced in the late 1920s after a collaborative design effort between National co-owner John Dopyera and guitarist/inventor George Beauchamp, with help from Adolph Rickenbacker's manufacturing company (Beauchamp and Rickenbacker would later partner again to bring out some of the first electric guitars, which aimed to make the loud, punchy National resonator guitars somewhat redundant). The Style O's tone came from a single resonator cone made of spun aluminum (much like an inverted speaker cone within the body of the guitar) that contacted the strings at its peak via a "biscuit" bridge. The guitar's stunning looks were imparted by a cast bell-brass body with highly polished nickel plating that was etched with Hawaiian scenes, as seen on the *Brothers in Arms* cover. Unparalleled either in look or in tone, great vintage Nationals are fully deserving of all the lust that has been heaped upon them since Knopfler brought his into the public eye some thirty years ago and, in the process, possibly saved the instrument from oblivion.

Knopfler has long been partial to red Stratocasters. One of his modern red Strats awaits on stage at Olympiahalle, Munich, in 2008. *Stefan M. Prager/Redferns/Getty Images*

Lennon's 1958 Rickenbacker 325, procured in a Hamburg guitar shop in 1960. It was the first American guitar owned by a Beatle. *Courtesy Nigel Osborne/Jawbone Press*

John and his 325, Hamburg, 1960. *Astrid Kirchherr–K & K/Redferns/ Getty Images*

PARLOPHONE

DICK JAMES MUSIC LTD.

'A' SIDE

PRODUCED BY
GEORGE MARTIN

TRADE MARK

MADE IN GT. BRITAIN

45-R 4983
(7XCE.17217)
MONO

PLEASE PLEASE ME
(McCartney–Lennon)
THE BEATLES

Harrison and his Duo Jet onstage with the pre-Ringo Beatles, circa May 1962, at the Star Club in Hamburg. *Bert Kaempfert Music—K & K/Redferns/Getty Images*

Harrison's '57 Duo Jet, purchased for £75 in Liverpool. *Courtesy Nigel Osborne/Jawbone Press*

WHILE MANY THINK OF THE BEATLES as the forward guard of the British Invasion, before they stormed across the Atlantic, the Fab Four were all about American rock 'n' roll. This meant that back in the era of Hamburg's Reeperbahn and Liverpool's Cavern, the ultimate badge of honor for John Lennon and George Harrison was an American-made electric guitar. In 1959, in the pre-Beatle days, both played Hofner Club 40 models for a time, each with a single pickup mounted in the neck position. Later that year, Harrison moved over to a fancier Selmer Futurama with three pickups. It was a guitar that, for many British players, stood in lieu of the hallowed and virtually unobtainable Fender Stratocaster. Toward the end of 1960, however, Lennon acquired the first American-made guitar owned by a Beatle: a 1958 Rickenbacker 325 that was actually a "new" guitar that had been in stock for about two years. As Harrison told BBC Radio in 1987, "We walked into this shop . . . in Hamburg. John bought that little Rickenbacker that became very well known through the Beatle concerts, with a scaled-down neck. . . . You have to imagine that in those days, when we were first out of Liverpool, any good American guitar looked sensational to us. We only had beat-up, crummy guitars at that stage."

4 BIG NIGHTS
at
LIVERPOOL'S FIRST AND FOREMOST BEAT MUSIC CENTRE
THE CAVERN
10 MATHEW STREET, (off North John Street) Tel: CENtral 1591

WEDNESDAY, 27th MARCH, 1963   7-15 p.m. to 11-15 p.m.
THE FABULOUS
1   KARL DENVER TRIO
Plus

Decca's Great New Disc Stars   Return of Manchester's "Beatles"
THE BIG THREE   THE HOLLIES
EARL PRESTON & THE TT's   THE SAPPHIRES
Members 5/-   Visitors 6/-   Please be Early

FRIDAY, 29th MARCH, 1963   7-30 p.m. to 11-15 p.m.
Liverpool's One and Only
2   Gerry & The Pacemakers
Plus Three Other Top Line Groups
Members 4/6 · Visitors 5/6

SUNDAY, 7th APRIL, 1963   7-30 p.m. to 11-15 p.m.
"TWIST 'N' TRAD" SPECIAL
Return Visit of the Sensational
3   Alan Elsdon Jazz Band
Plus   The Four Mosts   The Swinging Bluegenes
    The Flintstones   The Zenith Six Jazz Band
Members 5/6 · Visitors 6/6

GOOD FRIDAY, 12th APRIL, 1963   4 p.m. to Midnight
A Shot of Rhythm & Blues
R & B MARATHON No. 2 STARRING
4 # THE BEATLES
PLUS 8 OTHER GREAT MERSEYSIDE R & B GROUPS
Members 7/6   Visitors 8/6   Pass Outs Available
Please, Please be Early · 4 o'clock Start

Evening Sessions Sun., Tues., Wed., Fri., & Sat. Every Week
Don't Forget! There are Swinging Lunchtime Sessions
Featuring Top Rock Groups each Mon., Tues., Wed., Thurs. & Friday
12 noon to 2-15 p.m. Members 1/- Visitors 1/6
AT THE CAVERN CLUB

The "scaled-down neck" Harrison mentions refers to the 325's 20.75-inch scale length. Often referred to as a "three-quarter-sized" guitar—as are instruments such as Fender's 22.5-inch Duo-Sonic and some Gibson Melody Makers and Les Paul Juniors made to a shorter scale—the Rickenbacker 325, though extremely short for an "adult" guitar, is actually closer to five-sixths the size of a full 25.5-inch scale guitar, such as a Stratocaster. These stats made the diminutive electric fairly unpopular in the late '50s, and relatively few were produced, but Lennon adored his own 325. It became the sound of the Beatles' rhythm guitar for the first five years of the group's existence (replaced in 1964 by a second 325, a black one given to him by Rickenbacker), and it found its way into the annals of guitar idolatry as a result.

Cavern Club, Liverpool, August 1962. *Michael Ochs Archives/Getty Images*

Harrison's Rickenbacker 360/12, famous for the opening chord of "A Hard Day's Night" and as the guitar that inspired Roger McGuinn of the Byrds to pick up a 360/12. *Courtesy Nigel Osborne/Jawbone Press*

NEMS ENTERPRISES PRESENT AT
NEW BRIGHTON TOWER
FOR ONE NIGHT ONLY 7·30 to 11·30
FRIDAY, JUNE 14th.
"Merseyside's Greatest..."
THE BEATLES
AND
GERRY and PACEMA...

TICKETS
6/. * AT DOOR ON NIGHT **7/.**
IN ADVANCE
A BOB WOOLER PRODUCTION

DON'T MISS FRIDAY, JU...
JET HARRIS...

I'M A
Beatles
BOOSTER

MEMBER
BeaTles
FAN CLUB

LEACH ENTERTAINMENTS PRESENT
OPERATION BiG BEAT - 5TH
AT THE
TOWER BALLROOM
NEW BRIGHTON
FRI. 14TH SEPT. 7·30 - 1·0 A.M.
FEATURING AN ALL STAR 6 GROUP LINE UP · STARRING
THE NORTH'S TOP ROCK COMBO, APPEARING AT 10·30 PROMPT
The BEATLES
RORY STORM with the Hurricanes
GERRY and the PACEMAKERS
THE 4 JAYS
BILLY KRAMER with the COASTERS
THE MERSEY BEATS

TICKETS **5/.**

* LICENSED BARS (UNTIL 12·15 A.M.)
* LATE TRANSPORT (ALL AREAS L'POOL & WIRRAL)
COACHES LEAVE ST. JOHN'S LANE/LIME ST. 7·00-8·30 P.M.
FROM
RUSHWORTHS · NEMS · CRANES · STROTHERS
LEWIS'S · TOP HAT RECORD BAR · TOWER BALLROOM

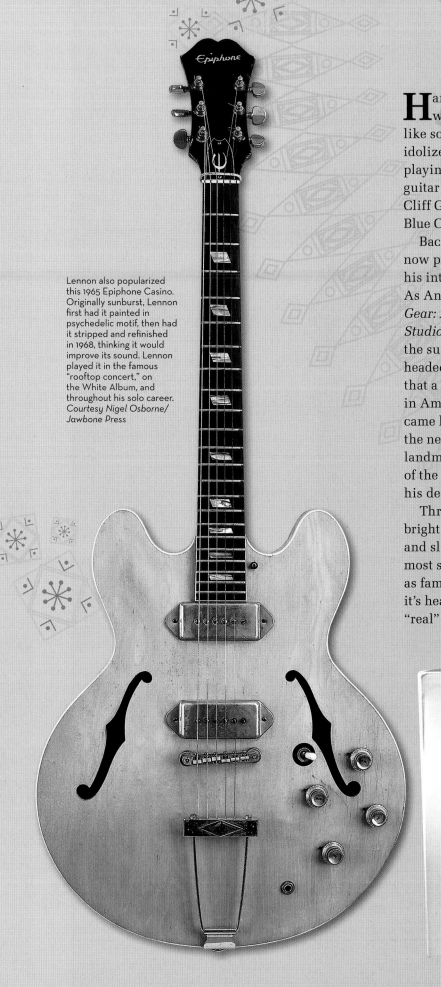

Lennon also popularized this 1965 Epiphone Casino. Originally sunburst, Lennon first had it painted in psychedelic motif, then had it stripped and refinished in 1968, thinking it would improve its sound. Lennon played it in the famous "rooftop concert," on the White Album, and throughout his solo career. *Courtesy Nigel Osborne/ Jawbone Press*

Harrison's first decent electric, on the other hand, was a genuine classic from the get-go. Although, like so many British youth of the day, he had first idolized a Strat like the one he had seen Buddy Holly playing in photographs, Harrison eventually landed a guitar played by another American rock 'n' roll hero, Cliff Gallup, lead guitarist with Gene Vincent and the Blue Caps.

Back in Liverpool in 1961 (with Paul McCartney now playing his famous Hofner bass), Harrison had his interest piqued by an ad in the *Liverpool Echo*. As Andy Babiuk writes in his 2001 book, *Beatles Gear: All the Fab Four's Instruments, from Stage to Studio*, Harrison scraped together the £75 that was the sum total of his savings from Beatles gigs and headed to the address given to check out a guitar that a British sailor had picked up at a port of call in America. The black '57 Gretsch Duo Jet that he came home with became his main guitar throughout the next three years, including on all of the Beatles' landmark early recordings and the band's 1964 tour of the United States. Harrison kept it right up until his death in 2001.

Throughout the early '60s, the Rickenbacker's bright, meaty rhythm jangle and the Gretsch's thick and slightly gritty lead lines defined the sound of the most successful dual-guitar band of all time. And, as famous—and wealthy—as their players became, it's heartening to know that they treasured these first "real" guitars until the very end. ★

THROUGHOUT HIS PLAYING with Canadian rockers Rush, Alex Lifeson has redefined the boundaries of progressive-rock guitar. Embodying far more than that genre label often implies, Lifeson's playing soars beyond the drama and the bluster to reveal truly stunning virtuosity that has been praised and admired by fans—and players—of all stripes, and it has landed him in the upper echelon of performance artists as a result. As much as his playing can't be pigeonholed, his status as a god of the Les Paul also remains atypical: Lifeson's tone and attack might be pure high-gain, high-sustain LP territory, but his frequent use of a Floyd Rose vibrato unit on this otherwise hard-tail standard takes it all into another dimension.

Lifeson was born Aleksandar Zivojinovic to Serbian parents in Toronto in 1953, changing his last name to the literal translation of his family name upon launching his career as a musician. Factually speaking, he is the only remaining founding member of Rush, having begun the band with two other musicians in 1968, but the Rush as we know it only took shape after Geddy Lee took over on bass and vocals just a few weeks later—and even more so, following the band's first album, when drummer Neil Peart joined in 1974. The band's first single was

Facing page: Alex Lifeson and Rush perform in San Antonio, Texas, November 30, 2012. *Gary Miller/ FilmMagic/Getty Images*

a cover of Buddy Holly's "Not Fade Away," and the early direction coalesced around a style that followed in the footsteps of world-dominant Led Zeppelin, but by the mid-'70s Rush was forging a bold new musical direction. The 1975 album *Fly by Night* found Rush stretching out along five extended, cinematic tracks. While not a commercial success by any means, it somewhat foretold their 1976 breakthrough, *2112*.

Curious listeners who lack the intestinal fortitude for extended prog-rock motifs can sample a taste of Lifeson's abilities by dipping into the poppier songs, such as "The Spirit of Radio" or "Freewill" from 1980's *Permanent Waves*, or "Tom Sawyer" or "Red Barchetta" from 1981's *Moving Pictures*, each among the band's more radio-friendly tracks. To hear him really stretch out, though, venture into any of several sidelong, multi-movement pieces that define the real Rush for hardcore fans, and discover a guitarist of immense talents and tone. ★

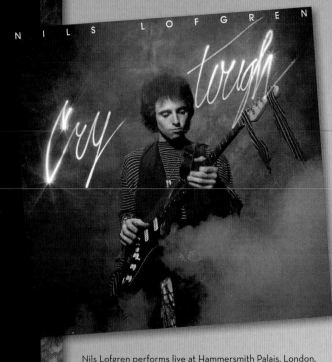

Nils Lofgren performs live at Hammersmith Palais, London, 1977. *Estate of Keith Morris/Redferns/Getty Images*

THOUGH HE RELEASED FOUR STELLAR ALBUMS in the early 1970s with his band Grin, Nils Lofgren got his foot in the door thanks to sessions with Neil Young, who famously drafted the teenaged guitar-slinger to play piano on Young's 1970 solo album, *After the Gold Rush*, despite Lofgren's lack of experience on the instrument. After Grin dissolved in 1974, Lofgren released a string of solo LPs before replacing Steve Van Vandt in Bruce Springsteen's E Street Band in 1984 for the massive *Born in the U.S.A.* tour.

It's through his appearances with Springsteen over three decades that Lofgren's become best known for a particular natural-finish 1961 Stratocaster. As the guitarist explained to *Fender News*, "My first guitar, in the mid-'60s, was a Tele; I got it because Jeff Beck played one. Soon after that, I saw Jimi Hendrix live . . . and the

Lofgren hits a high note in Denmark.
Jorgen Angel/Redferns/Getty Images

Strat soon became to me—even more than the Tele—the instrument that I was most comfortable with, as far as having different sounds."

Lofgren has actually owned two 1961 models. The first was acquired from a friend in a trade for a twelve-string acoustic. The more recognizable Strat, however, came into the Lofgren's hands a bit later. "The other '61 I found in a pawn shop in Berkeley when I was on the road in the late '60s," he told interviewer Peter Walker. "It was this ugly purple thing, but I bought it because it sounded great. I gave it to my brother, Michael, who is a master carpenter, to restore it. He stripped it and dyed it natural wood, and made a beautiful oak pickguard."

This "oakguard" Strat is also notable for its Alembic Blaster preamp unit, visible where the stock recessed output is usually located. When toggled on, the Blaster allows the player to increase volume without affecting tone. A rubber effects pedal knob in place of the traditional skirted Strat volume knob gives Lofgren better control of the volume to use the Blaster to create swirling effects.

Finally, the guitar is outfitted with Bill Lawrence double-blade pickup in the neck position (Lofgren is known to use the pickups, as well as Joe Barden double-blades in other guitars as well). Also noteworthy is Lofgren's technique, which involves a downstroked thumbpick and harmonic-inducing upstrokes with his second and third fingers.

Despite a penchant for aftermarket modifications, Lofgren is an enthusiastic Fender user through and through (on the road, he also uses a Jazzmaster, numerous other Stratocasters, and Fender amps). "I've found that with a Fender, you can lose your finesse and not totally lose it on the instrument, if you can understand that," he told *Premier Guitar* in 2009. "I like to lean into the guitar and use those five settings you can get out of a Strat. I like playing lots of different guitars, but I'll always reach for a Strat. It's the most beautiful electric guitar ever made." ✪

—*Dennis Pernu*

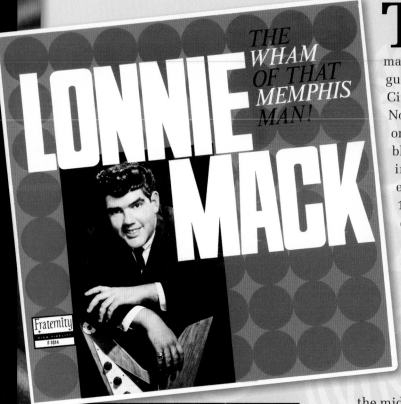

THE WHAM OF THAT MEMPHIS MAN!

LONNIE MACK

Fraternity
HIGH FIDELITY
F-1014

LONNIE MACK

ROADHOUSES & DANCE HALLS

ON TOUR

TOO OFTEN FORGOTTEN in the pantheon of great originators, Lonnie Mack was considered by many to be the first genuine blues-rock guitarist, and like his hometown of Cincinnati, Ohio—a crossroads between North and South, East and West—was a one-man melting plot of guitar stylings, blending rock 'n' roll, country, and blues into something inimitably his own. And ever since ordering the instrument in 1957 after seeing it in a promotional drawing, Mack was more dedicated than most to a single guitar: a 1958 Gibson Flying V.

Born to farming parents in a rural community in southern Indiana, not far from Cincinnati, Mack followed the family's propensity for music, performing in country and rockabilly bands around southern Ohio, southern Indiana, and northern Kentucky in the mid- to late '50s before he was even old enough to legally drink in the establishments where he was earning his pay.

With cash in his pocket, the young Mack went on the prowl for a new guitar that would be worthy of his devotion to the music, and he was told of a prototype that Cincinnati music store owner Glen Hughes had seen on a recent visit to the Gibson factory in Kalamazoo, Michigan. "I think I paid pretty much the list price," Mack told Sean McDevitt for gibson.com in 2007. "It was either $340 or $360, with the case. . . . It was a lot of money for a seventeen-year-old kid to come up with, but I was working, you know. I was a working musician, and I had lots of jobs. We was working ten days a week— seven days and three matinees!" In 1958 Mack's order finally arrived—purportedly the seventh Flying V off the Gibson line. He soon modified it by adding a "cross bar" between the points of the V, to which he bolted a Bigsby vibrato tailpiece and proceeded to ply his trade.

Working as part of the house band for Cincinnati's King Records, Mack recorded with James Brown, Freddie King, Hank Ballard, and several other early R&B stars, but he made his mark as a solo artist during some spare time in a 1962 session backing the Charmaines for Fraternity Records, cutting a rousing instrumental rendition of Chuck Berry's "Memphis, Tennessee" that was released as a single in the following year. The 1964 single "Wham!" consolidated his status and featured more of that frenetic, tremulous tone (often aided by the simultaneous use of both a Bigsby tailpiece and the lush vibrato on his Magnatone amplifier) that gave Mack a unique voice in guitardom right from the start. His 1958 Flying V was broken at both neck and headstock and refinished twice (ultimately sticking at cherry), but it never failed to help Mack stand large in the tonal stakes. ★

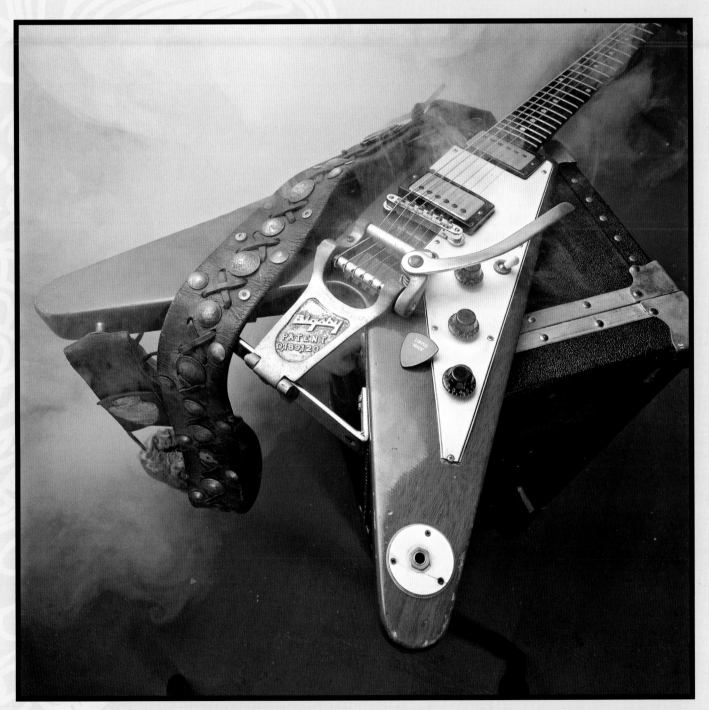

Lonnie Mack's 1958 Gibson Flying V with custom Bigsby tailpiece bracket.
Peter Amft/blues interactions, inc./courtesy Alligator Records & Artist Management, Inc.

LIKE THE BIRTH CHILD of some cloning experiment that accidentally melded the DNA of Eddie Van Halen, Ritchie Blackmore, and Niccolo Paganini, Yngwie Malmsteen brought a distinctive new voice to the shred-rock arena when he arrived on the scene in the early 1980s. Rather than indulging in the tapping and hammer-ons of Van Halen and others, Malmsteen displayed a fluid, legato-like alternate picking technique and an impressively vocal vibrato that enabled him to roll out neoclassical runs at breathtaking speeds and found him hailed as the single-handed founder of a new classical-metal genre. And while his early work with the bands Steeler and Alcatrazz, as well as his 1984 solo debut *Rising Force*, helped him ascend the ranks of poodle-haired, Superstrat-toting virtuosi, Malmsteen did it all on a plain old (if uniquely modified) 1972 Fender Stratocaster, the first serious guitar he ever acquired as an aspiring teenage guitar hero in Stockholm, Sweden.

Malmsteen at the Culture Room, Fort Lauderdale, Florida, May 28, 2006. © *Larry Marano/Retna Ltd.*

A brace of Malmsteen's CBS-era Strats. His most famous 1972, "The Duck," is second from right. *Rick Gould*

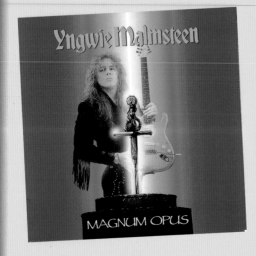

MAGNUM OPUS

In 2005, Malmsteen told Hugh Ochoa of stratcollector.com that he first decided the course of his life at the age of seven in 1970, while watching a documentary on the death of Jimi Hendrix. The show ran a clip of Hendrix burning his Stratocaster at Monterey, and although the young Malmsteen couldn't even see just what kind of guitar was aflame, he knew he had to have it. A year later, on his eighth birthday, Yngwie's sister gave him Deep Purple's *Fireball* album and he discovered that Ritchie Blackmore played a Stratocaster, the same guitar Hendrix had played and burned. American-made guitars were rare and prohibitively expensive in Sweden in the 1970s, but Malmsteen eventually acquired a white 1972 Strat, and the instrument clicked for him right from the start.

Malmsteen created the famous "scalloped" divots in his Strat's fingerboard himself, after observing such construction on an old lute that had come in for work at a repair shop where he apprenticed as a teenager. He tried the technique on a few of his own cheaper guitars, then, finding it appealed to him, took the file to his prized "Duck." The Swede wasn't the

first to perform on a scalloped fingerboard (his hero Ritchie Blackmore had been using the technique for some time), but his pyrotechnics on the instrument helped popularize the mod among the shred crowd. Although Malmsteen now has a large collection that includes many pre-CBS '50s and early-'60s Strats and several Gibsons, he has always expressed a preference for Stratocasters made between 1968 and 1972, largely because he feels the bigger headstock improves the resonance on those models. Unlike his colleagues in the genre during the early '80s, Malmsteen eschewed Floyd Rose vibrato systems (again for tonal reasons) and has always retained his stock Fender vibrato units. Other than the scalloped neck and jumbo frets, his '72 Strat, and the Fender signature models based upon it, are largely stock, with other minor modifications, including a DiMarzio HS-3 pickup in the bridge position (alongside standard Stratocaster pickups in the neck and middle positions) and a brass nut. None of these are the high-gain accoutrements one might expect from a shredder like Malmsteen, but ram these clean single-coils through upward of twenty Marshall JMP 50s, and the setup apparently gets the job done. ✪

Rick Gould

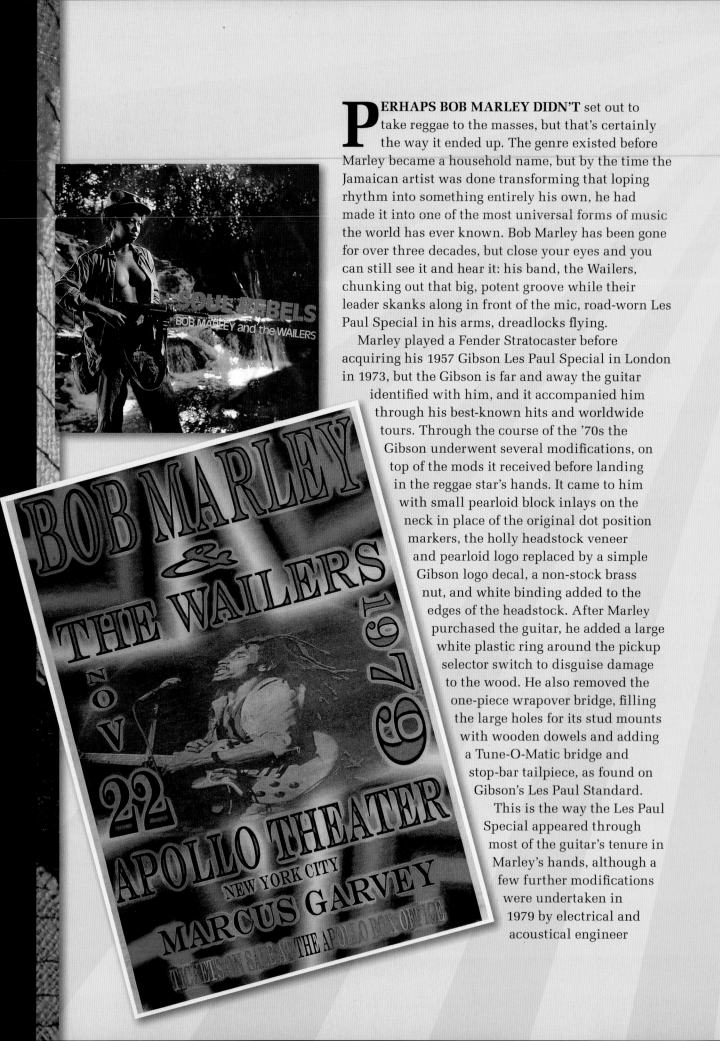

PERHAPS BOB MARLEY DIDN'T set out to take reggae to the masses, but that's certainly the way it ended up. The genre existed before Marley became a household name, but by the time the Jamaican artist was done transforming that loping rhythm into something entirely his own, he had made it into one of the most universal forms of music the world has ever known. Bob Marley has been gone for over three decades, but close your eyes and you can still see it and hear it: his band, the Wailers, chunking out that big, potent groove while their leader skanks along in front of the mic, road-worn Les Paul Special in his arms, dreadlocks flying.

Marley played a Fender Stratocaster before acquiring his 1957 Gibson Les Paul Special in London in 1973, but the Gibson is far and away the guitar identified with him, and it accompanied him through his best-known hits and worldwide tours. Through the course of the '70s the Gibson underwent several modifications, on top of the mods it received before landing in the reggae star's hands. It came to him with small pearloid block inlays on the neck in place of the original dot position markers, the holly headstock veneer and pearloid logo replaced by a simple Gibson logo decal, a non-stock brass nut, and white binding added to the edges of the headstock. After Marley purchased the guitar, he added a large white plastic ring around the pickup selector switch to disguise damage to the wood. He also removed the one-piece wrapover bridge, filling the large holes for its stud mounts with wooden dowels and adding a Tune-O-Matic bridge and stop-bar tailpiece, as found on Gibson's Les Paul Standard. This is the way the Les Paul Special appeared through most of the guitar's tenure in Marley's hands, although a few further modifications were undertaken in 1979 by electrical and acoustical engineer and effects pedal innovator Roger Mayer, who replaced the original black plastic pickguard with an aluminum one and replaced the large white plastic switch ring with an eyeball-shaped aluminum ring held in place with two screws. Mayer had also set up the guitars of both Marley and Wailers guitarist Junior Marvin, dressing their frets and setting their intonation prior to the recording of *Exodus* in 1977. "If you listen to *Exodus* and compare it with previous albums, you can hear that both Bob's and Junior's guitars resonate and sustain better and are in perfect harmony with each other," Mayer told this writer in 2004. Despite these modifications, Marley's Les Paul Special retained its formative parts—namely its original P-90 pickups and solid mahogany body and neck—and, therefore, it's thick, juicy tone, as can be heard driving almost every tune the star recorded on electric guitar from 1973 onward.

Marley's Les Paul Special is now on display, in its final form, in the Bob Marley Museum in Kingston, Jamaica. ★

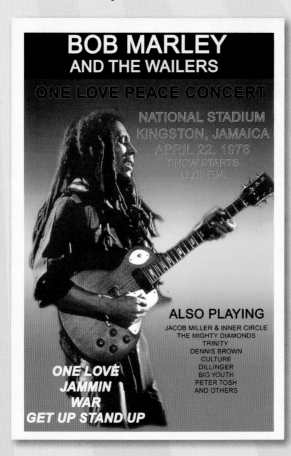

Armed with his 1957 Gibson Les Paul Special, Bob Marley performs at the New York Academy of Music in Brooklyn, New York, in May 1976. *Richard E. Aaron/ Redferns/Getty Images*

Singer Cliff Richard performs with the Shadows, including bassist Brian Locking and Hank Marvin with his famous red Strat, on the *Sunday Night at the Palladium* TV show in London in 1960. *Popperfoto/Getty Images*

Hank Marvin's 1959 Fender Stratocaster with gold hardware, the first Strat imported directly into England. *Courtesy Nigel Osborne/Jawbone Press*

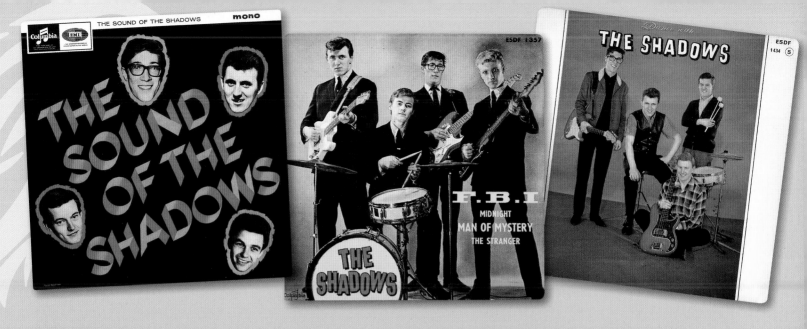

MOST OF THE EARLY STARS of the electric guitar were American musicians, an understandable phenomenon given rock 'n' roll's birth on the left side of the Atlantic *and* a ban on US imports to the UK through much of the 1950s that deprived British musicians of American-made guitars. Shortly before this embargo was lifted in 1960 though, Hank Marvin received a guitar that would become famous as the first Stratocaster owned by an English guitarist. It was brought into the country by singer Cliff Richard, whom Marvin backed in The Shadows.

Marvin was already on his way to stardom by this time, thanks to the early instrumental hits The Shadows had logged, in addition to the band's hits with Richard, but with red Strat in hand the lanky, bespectacled guitarist forged a more recognizable identity on both sides of the pond and went on to become one of the most influential early British rock 'n' rollers. With hits split nearly fifty-fifty between Shadows instrumental releases and vocal numbers recorded as Cliff Richard and The Shadows, Marvin was at the forefront of a total of sixty-nine British Top 40 chart singles, a number that includes a whopping twelve No. 1 hits. The most seminal of these, the classic "Apache" among them, were laid down with his '59 Stratocaster.

Marvin's acquisition of said Strat involves a now-famous case of mistaken identity. Ironically, Buddy Holly was an early influence, and Marvin says that hearing one of Holly's songs on the radio inspired him to drop the banjo in favor of the guitar, but American rock 'n' rollers were near-mythical creatures at the time, and Marvin had no idea what guitar Holly played. A fan of James Burton's work with Ricky Nelson, Marvin discovered that Burton played a Fender, but he didn't know precisely what model. While perusing a catalog in 1959 with his frontman Richards, Marvin spotted a red Stratocaster with gold-plated hardware. "I decided that had to be the model he played," Marvin told this writer in a 1994 interview for Teletext, "because it was the most expensive one, and I figured James Burton must play the top model." An upcoming trip that Richards was making to the US afforded Marvin the chance to acquire a guitar just like the one in the catalog with which he had become besotted. Weeks later the singer returned with red Strat in hand. Marvin didn't discover until a short while later that James Burton in fact played a Telecaster, but by this time it mattered not—the Strat was the guitar for him.

And what a fortuitous error it was. The Stratocaster's bright, well-defined sound, and its versatile vibrato system in particular, became a major part of Marvin's playing style. He utilized the vibrato bar on just about everything he played, applying it to subtle tremulous wiggles and deeper, emotive bends that evoked a rich, atmospheric tone through the tape echo unit he used between guitar and Vox AC15 amplifier (later an AC30). All told, this setup established a sound that Pete Townshend, Mark Knopfler, and even Frank Zappa have acknowledged as a major influence.

Marvin's original '59 Stratocaster is now in the possession of Shadows bandmate Bruce Welch, although Hank has continued to play Strats—alongside the occasional Burns guitar—throughout his career. ◆

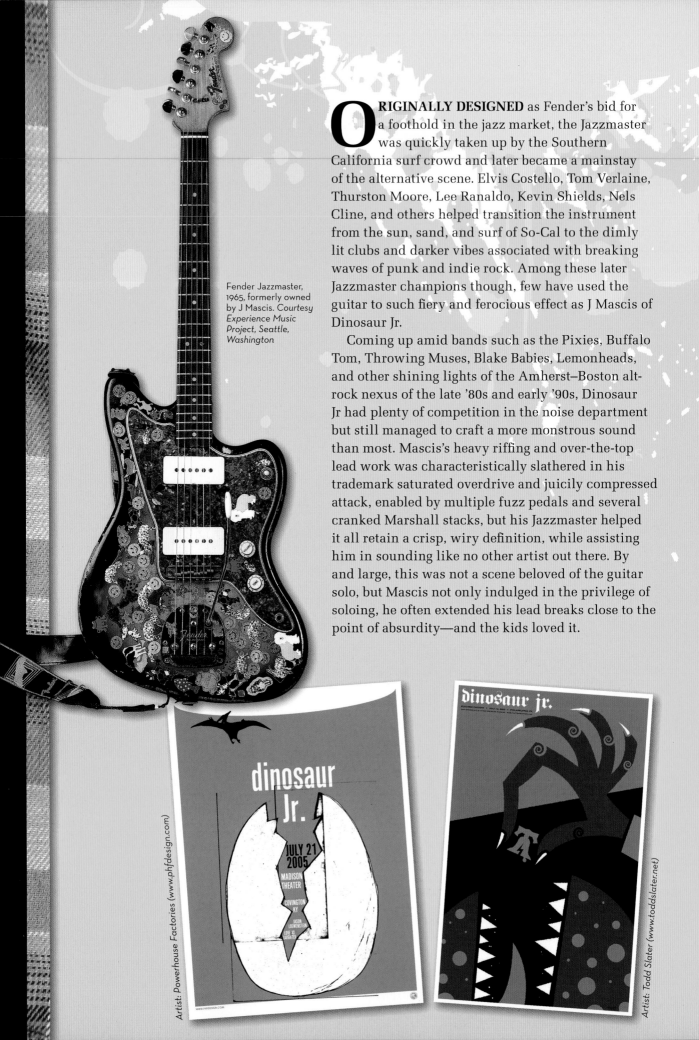

ORIGINALLY DESIGNED as Fender's bid for a foothold in the jazz market, the Jazzmaster was quickly taken up by the Southern California surf crowd and later became a mainstay of the alternative scene. Elvis Costello, Tom Verlaine, Thurston Moore, Lee Ranaldo, Kevin Shields, Nels Cline, and others helped transition the instrument from the sun, sand, and surf of So-Cal to the dimly lit clubs and darker vibes associated with breaking waves of punk and indie rock. Among these later Jazzmaster champions though, few have used the guitar to such fiery and ferocious effect as J Mascis of Dinosaur Jr.

Coming up amid bands such as the Pixies, Buffalo Tom, Throwing Muses, Blake Babies, Lemonheads, and other shining lights of the Amherst–Boston alt-rock nexus of the late '80s and early '90s, Dinosaur Jr had plenty of competition in the noise department but still managed to craft a more monstrous sound than most. Mascis's heavy riffing and over-the-top lead work was characteristically slathered in his trademark saturated overdrive and juicily compressed attack, enabled by multiple fuzz pedals and several cranked Marshall stacks, but his Jazzmaster helped it all retain a crisp, wiry definition, while assisting him in sounding like no other artist out there. By and large, this was not a scene beloved of the guitar solo, but Mascis not only indulged in the privilege of soloing, he often extended his lead breaks close to the point of absurdity—and the kids loved it.

Fender Jazzmaster, 1965, formerly owned by J Mascis. *Courtesy Experience Music Project, Seattle, Washington*

Artist: Powerhouse Factories (www.phfdesign.com)

Artist: Todd Slater (www.toddslater.net)

Mascis has owned and played a number of Jazzmasters, and has also turned to Fender Telecasters and Gibson Les Pauls in the studio, but the most distinctive of his guitars are a 1959 model with a gold anodized pickguard and a 1965 example with a tortoiseshell guard often seen in the early 1990s and now in the Experience Music Project collection. Both guitars have been modified with Gibson-style Tune-O-Matic bridges to improve their stability (Mascis finds the original "rocking" bridges unsuitable for his playing style), and each has been refinished, possibly several times: the '59 displays a mostly black finish with some metallic bluish purple showing through, while the later model retains the Mascis-certified purple. Fender took the purple theme to heart with an Artist Series J Mascis Jazzmaster, which also carries the artist's Tune-O-Matic mod in the form of an Adjusto-Matic bridge and a reinforced vibrato system. For the sound of a semi-beat Jazzmaster pushed to extremes, check out early Dinosaur Jr tracks like "Feel the Pain," "The Wagon," and "Out There," or even newer standouts like "Almost Ready". ★

Mascis and Dinosaur Jr, Variety Playhouse, Atlanta, July 8, 2005.
© Robb D. Cohen/Retna Ltd.

THE RED SPECIAL

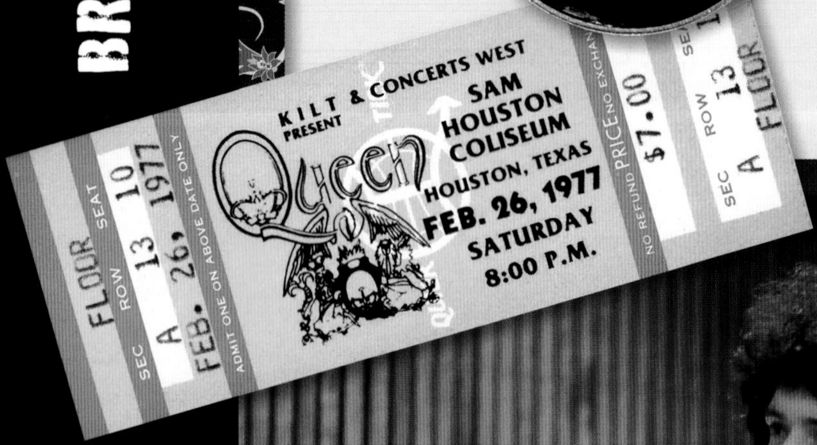

A HANDFUL OF NAME ARTISTS can talk of making their own first guitars as kids—impoverished Delta-bred blues players or would-be rock 'n' rollers who couldn't save up the pennies to purchase a production model in the early days of the electric guitar, perhaps, but there are few prominent guitar heroes who built the instrument that they also used throughout the heights of their careers, and which they continue to play to this day.

KILT & CONCERTS WEST PRESENT

Queen

SAM HOUSTON COLISEUM
HOUSTON, TEXAS
FEB. 26, 1977
SATURDAY
8:00 P.M.

FLOOR SEAT 10
SEC 13 ROW A
FEB. 26, 1977
ADMIT ONE ON ABOVE DATE ONLY

PRICE $7.00 NO REFUND NO EXCHANGE

SEC 13 ROW A FLOOR SEAT

In this regard, Brian May stands alone. And he's a unique player in several other respects too.

May rose to stardom with his band, Queen, in an era when Gibson Les Pauls and SGs, along with belting Marshall and Hiwatt stacks, ruled the day. Amid this rock environment, his use of a homebrewed axe with three single-coil pickups and a backline of Vox AC30s stood out as something entirely different and helped his tone to stand out from the crowd too. May's sound is utterly unmistakable, yet it is as fiery, hot, and aggressive as that of any rocker of the '70s and early '80s.

Geoff Dann/Redferns Collection/Getty Images

Facing page: Brian May at Musicland Studios, Munich, spring 1980. © *Peter Hince*

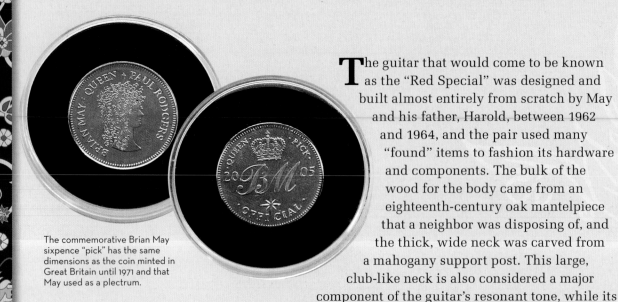

The commemorative Brian May sixpence "pick" has the same dimensions as the coin minted in Great Britain until 1971 and that May used as a plectrum.

The guitar that would come to be known as the "Red Special" was designed and built almost entirely from scratch by May and his father, Harold, between 1962 and 1964, and the pair used many "found" items to fashion its hardware and components. The bulk of the wood for the body came from an eighteenth-century oak mantelpiece that a neighbor was disposing of, and the thick, wide neck was carved from a mahogany support post. This large, club-like neck is also considered a major component of the guitar's resonant tone, while its dimensions provided the kind of playability that the large-handed May demanded. Outwardly appearing solid, the Red Special's body is actually what is referred to today as a chambered or semi-solid construction: block-board wings carved to form the outer bouts of the guitar were glued to the oak core, and the entirety was covered with a mahogany veneer front and back to hide the hollow chambers (one of which is still visible when the large scratch plate is removed). The twenty-four-fret fingerboard was also cut from oak, and the neck, body, and fingerboard were finished in Rustin's Plastic Coating, a popular British paint. May's ingenious vibrato tailpiece was crafted from a hardened-steel knife-edge fulcrum tensioned by two motorcycle-engine valve springs,

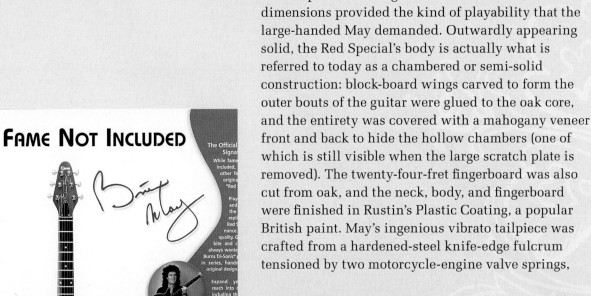

2002 ad for the Brian May Signature guitar produced by Burns.

Circa 1967 photo of May with the Red Special and his pre-Queen outfit, 1984.

with a tremolo arm fashioned from a knitting needle. The bridge is handmade from six individual blocks of aluminum, each of which carries an adjustable roller saddle.

The only significant pre-manufactured components are the tuners and the pickups, the latter being a trio of Burns Tri-Sonics that May potted with Araldite epoxy (a thick glue) to reduce microphony. The Tri-Sonics are routed through a switching array of May's own devising, with individual on/off and phase switches for each pickup. From the individual pickup selections heard on some solos to the bridge/middle combo used both for the round, jangly, clean tones on the hits "Under Pressure" and "We Are the Champions" and the heavy tones on "We Will Rock You" and "Tie Your Mother Down," to the honking, out-of-phase bridge/neck pairing heard on "Keep Yourself Alive," "Ogre Battle," and the solo to "Bohemian Rhapsody," this simple but effective switching array contributes greatly to the Red Special's sonic versatility. ♦

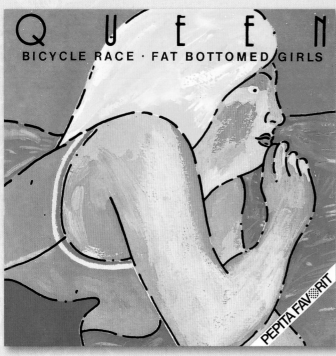

John Mayer swears by his Signature Stratocaster backstage at the Hard Rock Calling festival in London on June 28, 2008. *Joby Sessions/Guitarist Magazine/Getty Images*

ONE OF THE LEADING LIGHTS of a new breed of popular guitar hero, emerging just when it seemed that maybe guitar heroes had forever fallen from popular music, John Mayer has proven he can hang with the likes of Eric Clapton, Buddy Guy, and Robert Cray on stage at the Crossroads Festival and still make adolescent fans swoon with his next chart-topping hit. Peel away the tabloid stories about the latest heartbroken starlet left in the heartthrob's wake, and Mayer, at his core, is really just a guitar player and one that has long favored Fender's seminal Stratocaster.

Mayer's star ascended so swiftly that Fender recognized him while he was still just in his mid-twenties. In 2005 the company issued a John Mayer Stratocaster in three-tone sunburst, black, and Olympic White, as well as a heavy-relic black rendition from the Custom Shop, but Mayer launched his own career on the back of an earlier Artist Series guitar from the hallowed California maker, a Stevie Ray Vaughan Stratocaster that he purchased with money saved from his job at a gas station. He boasts an extensive guitar

HOUSE OF BLUES
PRESENTS

08 SEPTEMBER ◇ PORTLAND, OR
10 SEPTEMBER ◇ LAS VEGAS, NV
11 SEPTEMBER ◇ SAN DIEGO, CA
13 SEPTEMBER ◇ ANAHEIM, CA
14 SEPTEMBER ◇ LOS ANGELES, CA
15 SEPTEMBER ◇ LOS ANGELES, CA
21 SEPTEMBER ◇ CHICAGO, IL
22 SEPTEMBER ◇ CHICAGO, IL
27 SEPTEMBER ◇ NEW ORLEANS, LA
30 SEPTEMBER ◇ ORLANDO, FL
OCTOBER ◇ MYRTLE BEACH, SC
4 OCTOBER ◇ CLEVELAND, OH
05 OCTOBER ◇ TORONTO, ON

THE JOHN MAYER TRIO

2005

DESIGN & HAND PRINTED LETTERPRESS BY YEEHAWINDUSTRIES.COM

collection today, but still takes his signature models and contemporary Strats out on the road, alongside other newer gems such as a Custom Shop rosewood Stratocaster.

John Mayer was born in Bridgeport, Connecticut, in 1977 and was raised in nearby Fairfield. His early musical skills were given a bump at Boston's Berklee College of Music, although he left that estimable institution after just two semesters, moved to Atlanta, and set about igniting his musical career. After a notable performance at Austin's SXSW music festival in March 2000, Mayer signed first to Aware Records and then to Columbia, which rereleased his previously Internet-only debut album *Room for Squares* to major commercial and critical success. Alongside the singles "No Such Thing" and "Why Georgia," the album track "Your Body Is a Wonderland" earned Mayer a Grammy Award in 2003, his first of seven Grammies earned from nineteen nominations.

When fully amped with Strat in hand, John Mayer has a playing style that exhibits classic blues tendencies, laced with a versatility that signals his contemporary pop sensibilities. At other times, though, he can be far more adventurous than this mélange might imply. Check out, for example, his use of an AdrenaLinn sequencer pedal to create the stirring arpeggiated guitar part in "Bigger than My Body," along with his collaborations with everyone from jazzer Herbie Hancock to hip hop artist Kanye West. For some tabloid-minded fans, John Mayer might be a household name more for his romances with Jessica Simpson or Jennifer Aniston, but music clearly fuels his fire, and he has certainly helped to bring the Stratocaster back into the Top Forty nearly sixty years after it first hit the scene. ◆

2006 John Mayer Signature Cypress Mica Stratocaster. *Fender Musical Instruments Corporation*

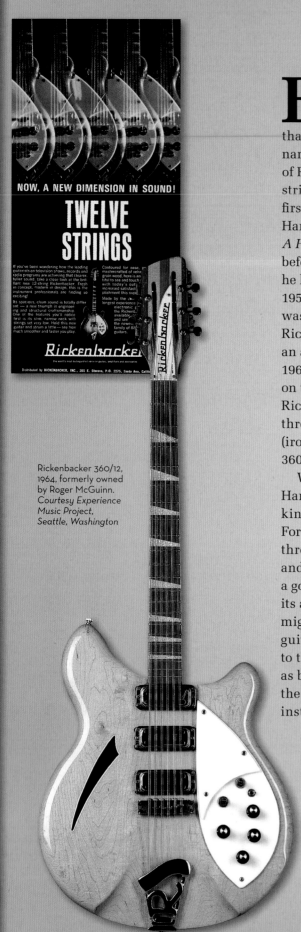

Rickenbacker 360/12, 1964, formerly owned by Roger McGuinn. *Courtesy Experience Music Project, Seattle, Washington*

BOB DYLAN IS OFTEN CREDITED with taking folk music electric, but as for the enduring *sound* of electric folk music, well, that honor has to go to The Byrds—and if we want to narrow it down to a single sonic moment, the chime of Roger McGuinn's Rickenbacker 360/12 twelve-string takes it hands down. McGuinn acquired his first Rickenbacker twelve-string after seeing George Harrison play a similar model in the Beatles' movie *A Hard Day's Night*, but, as a devoted acoustic folky before forming The Byrds with Gene Clark in 1964, he had played an acoustic Martin twelve-string since 1957. From around 1965 on, however, if McGuinn was playing electric, it was more often than not on a Rick 12. He used his first Rickenbacker, a 360/12 with an added third pickup, to record the hit title track to 1965's *Mr. Tambourine Man* and several other songs on the album, but he was forced to order a second Rickenbacker—this time a 370/12, distinguished by its three pickups—when his first was stolen in England (ironically, George Harrison's second Rickenbacker 360/12, a 1965 model, was stolen in the US in 1966).

While the 360/12 first hit its mark in the hands of Harrison, the guitar was conceived for exactly the kind of player that Roger McGuinn turned out to be. For a time in the early '60s the acoustic folk boom threatened the burgeoning electric guitar market, and Rickenbacker owner Francis Hall figured that a good electric twelve-string—a format popular in its acoustic format on the folk and blues scenes— might lure some crossover players. In designing the guitar, Rickenbacker brought a few real brainstorms to the fold to give the new electric twelve-string as broad an appeal as possible. Designers kept the neck dimensions as narrow as possible so the instrument would feel less cumbersome than most

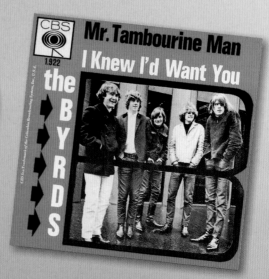

acoustic twelves and thereby appeal to a wider range of players. They also ingeniously foreshortened the headstock by positioning every other tuner on the six-per-side headstock at a 90-degree angle, thereby avoiding the ungainly look of the traditional elongated twelve-string headstock. Prototypes were received enthusiastically by the players Rickenbacker tested them on, and the 360/12 went into production by the end of 1963. Just a couple of months later, in February 1964, The Beatles came to the US for three concerts and two appearances on *The Ed Sullivan Show*. Hall presented a 360/12 to George Harrison in his hotel room in New York City, The Beatle loved it, and the instrument's success was secured.

While the Rickenbacker electric twelve-string was at the center of The Byrds' signature sound, it had a little help in producing the ringing, chiming tones for which it is remembered. To contain the sonic assault of all those jangling strings, engineer Ray Gerhardt at Columbia Studios in Los Angeles recorded McGuinn direct through the board, adding copious amounts of outboard tube compression. McGuinn recalls that for many years, this technique made it impossible for him to accurately re-create his studio sound live on stage in the absence of good compressor pedals in the '60s. Rickenbacker's signature-model 360/12/RM (now deleted) contained a high-quality onboard compressor circuit, and McGuinn told Bob Cianci in *Premier Guitar* magazine that he now uses a JangleBox compressor on stage. ⬧

McGuinn onstage with The Byrds, circa 1967. *Sony BMG Music Entertainment/Getty Images*

IN A STYLE SO SMOOTH AND EFFORTLESS that it almost underplayed the immense skill required to achieve it, Wes Montgomery laid down fleet, swinging, octave-based runs and single-note melodic lines that set a new standard for jazz guitar in the late 1950s and early 1960s. His playing influenced everyone from George Benson to Pat Metheny and paved the way for what we might call the modern era of electric jazz guitar. And thanks to Montgomery's Gibson L-5CES, his tone was every bit as smooth and dynamic as his chops.

Montgomery played a number of Gibson archtops early on, including a standard two-pickup L-5CES with a pair of Alnico V single-coils in the mid- to late '50s, but we know him best for his later use

Plucking the strings with his double-jointed thumb, Wes Montgomery plays his Gibson L-5CES with rounded Venetian cutaway at the Newport Jazz Festival on July 3, 1967. *David Redfern/Getty Images*

of the custom-made versions supplied to him by Gibson. The better-known of these had a single humbucking pickup mounted in the neck position and a heart-shaped mother-of-pearl inlay in the body just below the pickguard, where Montgomery's fingertips would wear down the finish on other guitars because of the way he braced his hand while playing. This is the guitar we hear from around the time of the seminal 1963 set *Boss Guitar* and onward, and the one that can be seen in the many surviving films and photographs of Montgomery's live performances. Montgomery also frequently used another custom L-5CES with two humbuckers.

Gibson's L-5CES, alongside the Super 400, is one of the most lauded of all archtop electric jazz guitars. A descendant of the seminal Lloyd Loar–designed L-5 archtop acoustics of the early '20s, the L-5CES (for "Cutaway Electric Spanish") retained the carved, arched, solid spruce top and carved, arched, maple back of the high-end acoustic archtops, when so many other archtop electrics employed laminated tops (notably Gibson's own ES-175, released in 1949 and a true standard of jazz boxes by the mid-'50s). The L-5CES also features the 25.5-inch scale length traditional to the breed. On a big, 17-inch-wide, full-depth archtop like this, both humbucking pickups and the Alnico V single-coils sound fat, rich, and warm, and the difference wouldn't necessarily be easily distinguished in Montgomery's recordings (particularly amid other variables, such as the amplifier and microphone used for any given session).

Suffice it to say that Montgomery sounded *rich* on all of it, while his own unique playing style has to be seen to be believed. The guitarist used only his bare thumb, which contributes to his warm, fat tone, and swiped at the strings with down strokes only for his single-note lines, attacking chords and his signature octave runs with both down- and upstrokes. And, as none other than George Benson noted in the liner notes to PolyGram's *Ultimate Wes Montgomery* (1998), "his thumb was double-jointed. He could bend it all the way back to touch his wrist, which he would do to shock people." For groove, tone, and sheer melodic genius, Montgomery remains difficult to beat, decades after he left this planet in 1968 at the age of forty-five. And that gorgeous L-5CES is just icing on the cake. ★

Wes Montgomery's later Gibson L-5CES with sharp Florentine cutaway, used on his classic album *Movin' Wes*. *Courtesy Skinner, Boston and Marlborough, Massachusetts*

ALTHOUGH THE SOLID-BODY electric guitar came about largely as a prediction of the kind of hardware that this new, rockin' form of music bubbling under the surface circa 1950 was likely to require, the players who ushered in rock 'n' roll just a few years later more often did it on hollow-body archtop electrics. Elvis Presley's lead guitarist, Scotty Moore, is a case in point. Having adopted

Scotty Moore picks his golden Gibson ES-295 alongside Elvis Presley and bassist Bill Black at a show in 1955–1956.

Fender's adventurous new Esquire around 1951 or '52 for his early work with country outfit the Starlite Wranglers, he traded up in 1953 for an instrument that would have been considered a bit classier at the time: a Gibson ES-295. Thus Moore, who would soon become a formative force in rockabilly and rock 'n' roll guitar, seemed to be swimming against the tide—not that that tide noticed or cared. With gold ES-295 in hand, the guitarist laid down the lead guitar tracks on all of Presley's classic, early Sun recordings up until July 1955.

The ES-295 was a new model for Gibson at the time, born just a year before in 1952, and was essentially just a gold-finished, two-pickup rendition of the ES-175 that debuted in 1949. It shared the ES-175's laminated-maple construction, but departed in its use of a trapeze-like wraparound bridge and tailpiece. The same piece of hardware was used on the first Les Paul, released the same year, though it was wrongly adopted on that seminal solid-body, partnered with a flat neck pitch that required loading the strings *under* the bridge bar rather than over it. Even when mounted correctly, this bridge was still a cumbersome device that afforded barely any scope for intonation adjustment. Soon after purchasing his '53 ES-295 from the O. K. Houck Piano Company in Memphis, Tennessee, Moore modified it with the addition of a simple trapeze tailpiece and a Gretsch Melita Synchrosonic bridge, which had six independent, fully adjustable saddles and represented a mammoth step forward in tweakability.

Writing at scottymoore.net, James V. Roy notes that, after playing the ES-295 on Elvis's "That's All Right" and "Good Rockin' Tonight" in 1954, and "Milkcow Blues Boogie" and "Baby Let's Play House" in 1955 (among others), Moore traded it toward a new L-5CES on July 7, 1955, again at Houck's music store. The L-5CES, which retained the carved, solid spruce top of Gibson's big archtops of the jazz age, was considered another step up the ladder, and Moore climbed yet another rung in October 1956 when an endorsement deal with Gibson landed him a new Super 400CESN. His original ES-295 was purchased by Elvis memorabilia collector Jimmy Velvet, who sold it to an undisclosed collector in the early '90s for $125,000, its aftermarket Melita bridge still intact. Other guitars that have occasionally been (wrongly) rumored to be "Scotty Moore's ES-295" are a pair of signed examples hanging in the Hard Rock Cafés in Dallas and Nashville, a third in the Memphis Music Hall of Fame, and a fourth that was owned for a time by the late guitar phenomenon Danny Gatton. ★

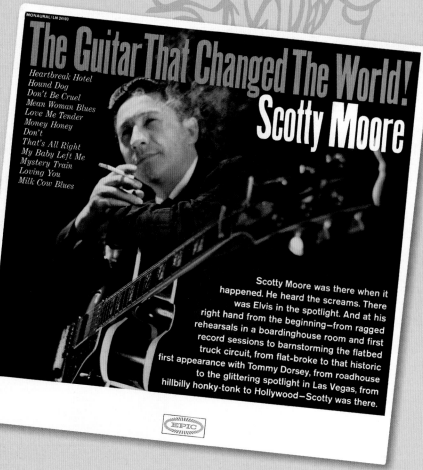

THURSTON MOORE & LEE RANALDO

FENDER JAZZMASTERS

THE WARFIELD — S.F.
982 MARKET STREET
LIMITED SEATS ON MAIN FL
SONIC YOUTH
DOORS @ 7PM / NO CAMERAS
THU SEP 24 1992 8:00PM

17SEP92 ZBP452 ADULT
GEN ADM 16.50

FLIP TO A PHOTO OF SONIC YOUTH'S Thurston Moore and Lee Ranaldo playing their oh-so-hip modified Fender Jazzmasters and you're more than likely to fire up the old "Why the Jazzmaster?" debate among guitar fiends. A disproportionate number of alternative-minded performers have chosen Jazzmasters throughout the years—a list that includes Robert Smith of The Cure, J Mascis of Dinosaur Jr, Kevin Shields and Bilinda Butcher of My Bloody Valentine, Tom Verlaine of Television, Ira Kaplan of Yo La Tengo, Nels Cline of Wilco, and of course Elvis Costello—but perhaps none have made more out-there noises on the things than Moore and Ranaldo. Yet the pundits continue to ask, *why?*

Artist: Raymond Pettibon

Above: Ranaldo with Sonic Youth, Roundhouse, London, August 31, 2007. *Marc Broussely/Redferns/Getty Images*

Facing page: Moore with Sonic Youth, Shepherd's Bush Empire, London, June 24, 2002. *Hayley Madden/Redferns/Getty Images*

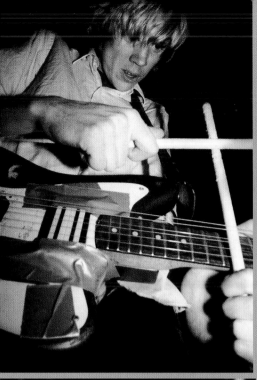

Just a few be-stickered Sonic Youth Jazzmasters. Top left: That can't be good for the neck. New York City, circa 1986. *Monica Dee/Retna Ltd.* Top center: Jazzmaster fiftieth anniversary, the Knitting Factory, New York City, September 12, 2008. *Roger Kisby/Getty Images.* Top right, bottom left, and bottom center: Jazzmaster 50th anniversary. *Thos Robinson/Getty Images.* Bottom right: Voodoo Music Festival, New Orleans, October 16, 2004. *Chris Graythen/Getty Images*

For many avant-garde players, the Jazzmaster's design quirks are a big part of its appeal. Its vibrato unit is a little smoother and subtler than the Stratocaster's seminal synchronized tremolo that preceded it, and the low, wide coils of its pickups are prone to be a little more microphonic and therefore more easily provide feedback than the narrower single-coils of the Strat and Tele. The two most likely reasons for its popularity among the alternative set, however, are that it was simply *different* than the pre-CBS Stratocasters and Telecasters that more mainstream rock, blues, and country artists were playing, and, more importantly, *cheaper*.

& LEE RANALDO

Artist: Jim Altieri (www.altieriart.com)

Lee Ranaldo, Jimmy Rip, Tom Verlaine, Nels Cline, J Mascis, and Thurston Moore at the Jazzmaster 50th anniversary concert, The Knitting Factory, New York City, September 12, 2008. *Thos Robinson/Getty Images*

In the early days of Sonic Youth, Moore and Ranaldo both played Fender Jaguars, younger siblings to the Jazzmaster, but their use of heavy strings and lower alternate tunings made the move to the Jazzmaster's longer, 25.5-inch scale length a logical step (the Jaguar was built on a shorter 24-inch scale). Both players have owned several examples of the model, most of which they have modified to their own tastes for ease of function and improved performance. On their mainstay gigging Jazzmasters, Moore and Ranaldo disconnected the independent "rhythm setting" tone and volume controls and switch that lurk above the neck pickup, removed the standard tone control below the bridge pickup, and replaced the original pickguards with items that carry just a single volume control and three-way toggle switch. Moore replaced his guitar's original rocker bridge with a Gibson-style Tune-O-Matic, while Ranaldo swapped his for a Fender Mustang bridge, which differs from the Jazzmaster bridge mainly in its use of solid-steel saddles rather than threaded steel. Finally, Ranaldo swapped the pickups in his Jazzmaster—a guitar he has dubbed the "JazzBlaster"—for a pair of Fender Wide Range Humbuckers taken from a '70s Telecaster Deluxe, while Moore retained his guitar's original wide single-coils. Other than Ranaldo's pickup swap, the modifications don't radically change the nature of these famous Jazzmasters, but mainly result in more hot-rodded, streamlined guitars that were less likely to be whacked into an undesirable tone setting mid-flight during any of the pair's famed noise-art solo excursions. All that remained was to apply random stickers and graphics to taste, and you're ready to make 'em squeal. ✪

“TRIGGER”

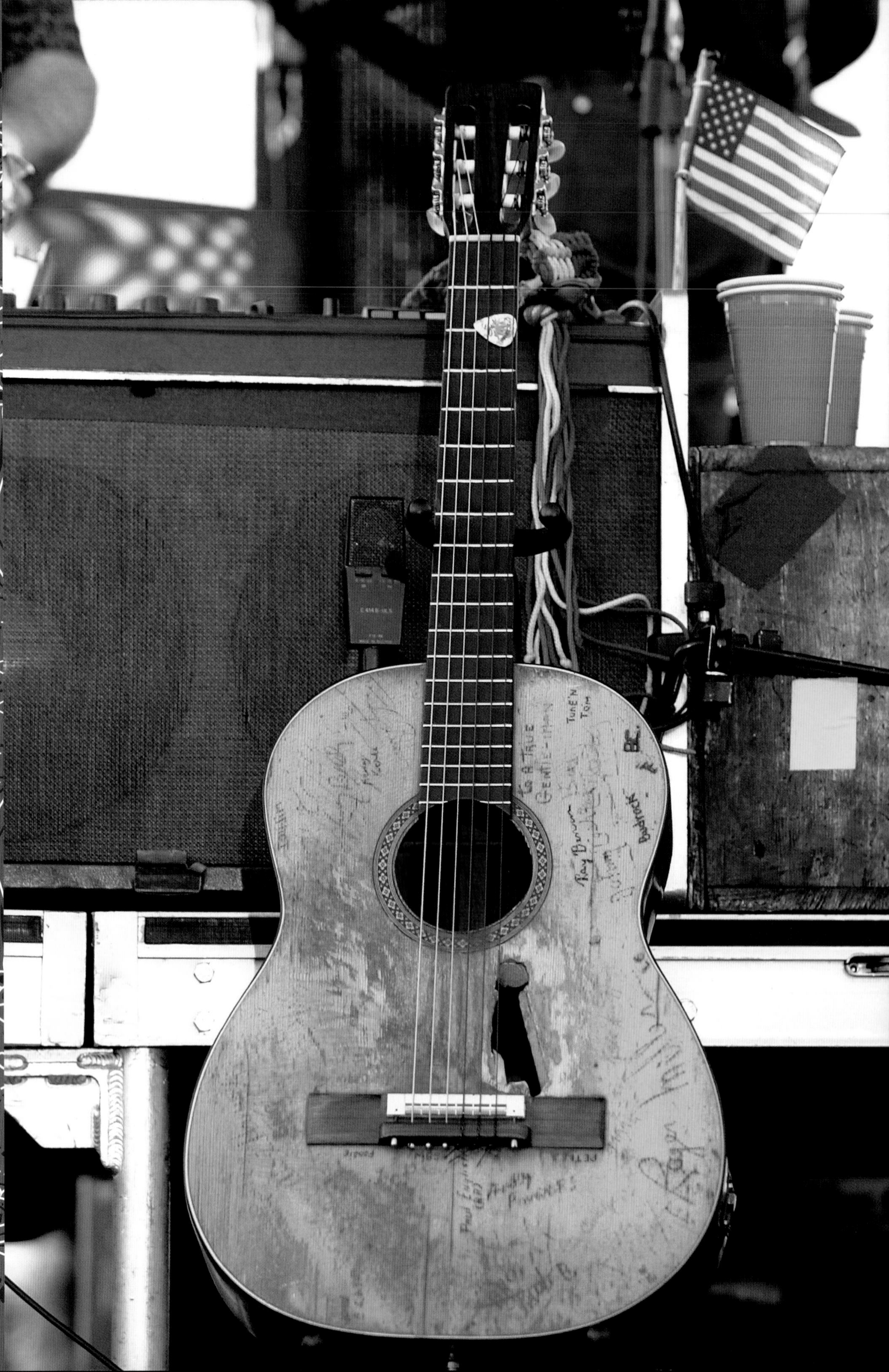

WHENEVER HIS PROLIFIC musical output is analyzed, the traits typically first noted of the great Willie Nelson are the voice that trickles over the listener like sun-warmed honey, followed by the eclectic songcraft. Less often praised, though equally deserving of attention, are his guitar playing and guitar tone. Both are expressions of this artist's muse, and both are as instantly recognizable as his singing and songwriting. Fans of the Redheaded Stranger need only hear a half-dozen notes to recognize an intro hailing another tune played on Nelson's old faithful, a late-'60s Martin N-20 classical guitar known affectionately as "Trigger." The guitar is a major part of the Willie Nelson lore and has been with him on the road and in the studio since 1969.

Stephanie Chernikowski/WireImage/Getty Images

★★★★★★★★★★★★★★
WILLIE NELSON'S
ANNUAL 4th of JULY
PICNIC—1985
★★★★★★★★★★★★★★
SOUTH PARK MEADOWS—AUSTIN, TEXAS
JULY 4, 1985—THURSDAY
PARKING—8:00 AM • GATES OPEN—10:00 AM
SHOW—12 NOON—RAIN OR SHINE
Est. Price-$16.75 • CC-$1.25 • TOTAL-$18.00 Tax Included

LAWN 28976
LAWN 28976

WILLIE NELSON
FEB. SUNDAY — 8:00 P.M.
17 THE UNIVERSITY OF TOLEDO
CENTENNIAL HALL
NO DRUGS AND/OR ALCOHOL ALLOWED
1985 ALL SEATS RESERVED — NO REFUND
ADMIT ONE — $13.50

ENTRY
21 28
SEC. ROW

WILLIE NELSON

FEBRUARY 15TH AT THE PALACE THEATRE

Above: Artist: Rob Servo (www.robservo.com)

Facing page: Jordan Strauss/WireImage/Getty Images

215

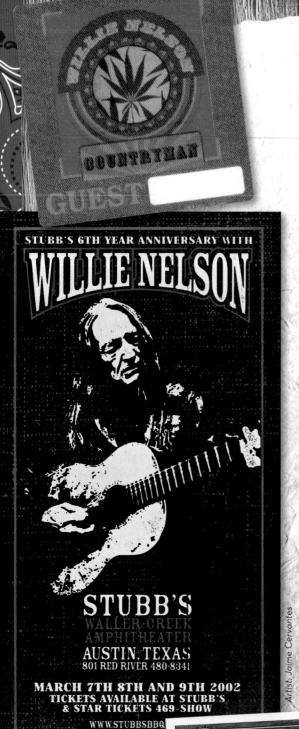

Nelson acquired Trigger sight unseen in a time of need, after dropping and fatally damaging a nylon-string Baldwin electro-acoustic that he had been playing previous to this legendary Martin's arrival into his life. Having sent the Baldwin to Shot Jackson's guitar shop in Nashville for repair only to be informed it was a write-off, Nelson bought the Martin N-20 over the phone for $750 after being told it was the only similar instrument in the place. Nelson stipulated that Jackson should put the Baldwin's Prismatone pickup into the Martin before shipping it to him (this being one of the few truly successful acoustic guitar pickups of the day). This is how the artist received the guitar just a few days later and how it has remained ever since.

Like so many notable stars' guitars, Trigger's look is as recognizable as its sound. Built for finger-style classical playing, the N-20 model required no pickguard, but years of flatpicking have worn a hole that runs from beneath the bridge almost to the sound hole through the instrument's thin spruce top. Inspired by Leon Russell to give the guitar a little extra mojo by collecting the signatures of friends and fellow musicians, Nelson has had more than one hundred people adorn Trigger with their autographs, including Johnny Cash, Waylon Jennings, Gene Autrey, Roger Miller, Kris Kristofferson, and even football coaches and lawyers whom Nelson has befriended. Nelson has occasionally stated that he will retire when the wear on Trigger finally makes the guitar unplayable. Fans of this incomparable artist undoubtedly hope and pray that this distinctive concoction of spruce and mahogany continues to prove surprisingly resilient. ✪

Artist: Jaime Cervantes

Facing page: Willie and Trigger at the Palomino Club, Los Angeles, 1970. *Michael Ochs Archives/Getty Images*

Nichols plays his 1953 Tele with Merle Haggard and the Strangers at Civic Center Hall in Philadelphia, February 14, 1970. This was the same show later immortalized in the live LP, *The Fightin' Side of Me*. John Cerami via Terry Downs

NOT UNLIKE BUCK OWENS and Don Rich, Merle Haggard and his trusty sideman, Roy Nichols, formed a Tele-wielding duo that will forever be interlinked in the annals of country music, tagged as the "Outlaw" kin to the hard-twanging Bakersfield sound. Although Merle Haggard's name would achieve wider fame, and would give Roy Nichols his own greatest fame by association, Nichols was an established guitarist with a good reputation on the country scene long before Haggard had even begun to make a name for himself, and he even gave his would-be boss a leg up in the industry shortly after his release from prison.

Born in Chandler, Arizona, in 1932, Nichols grew up mainly in Fresno, California, where his family owned a camp for migrant workers who had made their way west during the Great Depression and the difficult years that followed. He learned to play the guitar at the age of eleven, and, just three years later, began playing at local dancehalls just to supplement the family income. Shortly before his sixteenth birthday, Nichols hit the road with the hillbilly band, the Maddox Brothers and Rose—the first truly professional gig in an early career that would land him jobs with Johnny Cash, Cliffie Stone,

Wynn Stewart, Lefty Frizzell, and other significant names on the country circuit in the 1950s and early '60s. From the late '50s onward, Nichols was best associated with a whiteguard '57 Telecaster, although he played several others throughout the years.

Merle Haggard was born in 1937 in Oildale, California, a suburb of Bakersfield, to parents who had come west from Oklahoma looking to escape the dust bowl during the Great Depression. The death of his father in the mid-'40s seemed to tip Haggard toward delinquency, and the start of a life of petty crime that landed him in one juvenile facility after another until early adulthood. During one stint on the outside, Haggard attended a Lefty Frizzell show and, after singing along to several numbers from his seat, was asked to join the artist on stage. This taste of the limelight launched his efforts to make it in the music business, and Haggard was soon performing at venues around Bakersfield. In 1957, however, Haggard was arrested for attempted robbery of a bar in Bakersfield, and was sentenced to three years in San Quentin Prison.

On this occasion the hard time in the notorious adult facility seemed to show Haggard the error of his ways. After his release in 1960 he set about walking the straight and narrow, and got to work on forging a

career as an artist, while wiring houses and digging ditches to earn a living. A trip to Las Vegas, Nevada, later that year took Haggard to a show featuring Wynn Stewart and Roy Nichols, and what would be a life-changing meeting. "Roy wanted to get off and go to the restroom or something," Haggard told the Associated Press in 2001, "He said, 'Here, play this thing,' and handed me his guitar. I sung 'Devil Woman' and Wynn Stewart saw me and hired me on the spot. . . . Because of Roy, my career commenced. He was the stylist that set the pace." Haggard played bass with Stewart for a time, with Nichols on guitar, while also working on his dream of a solo career. In the early years of this effort, he scored a minor hit with Wynn Stewart's "Sing a Sad Song" in 1964, and a Top 10 the following year with Lynn Anderson's "(My Friends Are Gonna Be) Strangers," a song that established a theme for Haggard's career. In 1965 he formed the band Merle Haggard and the Strangers for his first US tour, hired Nichols on guitar, and hit the ground running. The Tele-totin' outlaws would work together until 1987, scoring thirty-eight No. 1 songs on the *Billboard* Country Chart, including "I'm a Lonesome Fugitive," "Mama Tried," "Okie from Muskogee," and "The Fightin' Side of Me."

While Haggard was no mean picker himself, his role on Telecaster more often covered rhythm duties (which he frequently handled on an acoustic guitar, too). Nichols, on the other hand, was a consummate twang artist, and one of the early pioneers of hybrid picking, a style that employs both a flat pick and the middle and ring fingers of the right hand. He was also adept at slick faux-steel bends, licks that have become staples of the country guitar style, often pre-bending notes before picking them to create effective pedal-steel sounds. Nichols suffered a stroke in 1996 that left him unable to play the guitar. He died in 2001 of an apparent heart attack while being admitted to a hospital in Bakersfield for treatment of an infection. Haggard passed away in April 2016, though he continued to perform until February of that year. ★

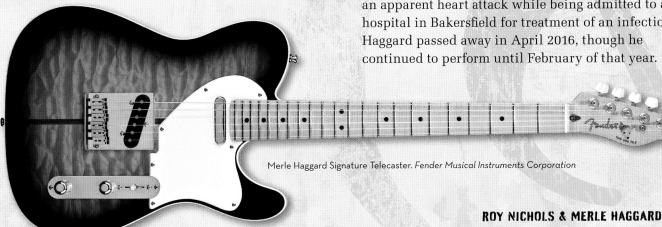

Merle Haggard Signature Telecaster. *Fender Musical Instruments Corporation*

WHAT DO YOU CHOOSE AS the archetypal instrument of an artist who has owned more than two thousand guitars over the past thirty-five years and routinely plays dozens in the course of a single show, often strapping on several at a time? Well, the one that packs the most guitars into a single instrument, obviously. Cheap Trick guitarist Rick Nielsen is known for his collection of custom-made guitars, many of them built for him by the Hamer company. And few guitars anywhere are

Nielsen's first-ever appearance with the first-ever five-neck. © Robert Alford

quite as custom—or anywhere near as outrageous—as
Nielsen's original five-neck instrument. The guitarist
actually owns three Hamer five-necks, although the
first, custom made in 1980, is the most recognizable.
It sports a bright-orange finish and has been seen in
thousands of live performances in the nearly thirty
years since the artist acquired it. In 1990 Nielsen
added to his collection with a checkered black-and-
yellow five-neck, and in 2004 Hamer built him a
korina-bodied five-neck with a thinline-style
f-hole above the topmost neck.

Steve Pitkin/Pitkin Studio

Of the five necks, two are entirely nonstandard (the fretless at the bottom and the twelve-string at the top). The center three necks are standard six-strings, the middle of those with a vibrato tailpiece. Clearly Nielsen, however, the archetypal rock 'n' roll clown, uses his Hamer five-neck just for kicks and as a showpiece—and undoubtedly to poke a little fun at the original symbol of rock 'n' roll excess: the double-neck guitar. Word has it that all five necks are fully functional, although the bottom three are rarely tuned up. Certainly the bottom two necks are extremely difficult, if not impossible, to reach for any kind of useful playing. Still, there they all are, and they certainly cut a dashing figure.

As far as sheer numbers go, Nielsen has tamed his urge toward excess ever so slightly in recent years and whittled his collection down to around 250 guitars. Many of these are other custom-made Hamers with his own image or those of bandmates or other artists finished into the bodies, as well as other themes, such as a Miller Beer guitar and several finished with renditions of his signature checkerboard pattern. In addition to these more whimsical instruments, Nielsen's collection includes a number of valuable vintage pieces too, including a 1954 Gretsch 6130 Round Up, an entirely un-ironic 1961 Gibson ES-1235 double-neck, and a pair of 1958 Gibson Explorers. Unlike many artists, Nielsen frequently takes any or all of these on tour to give paying fans a look at, and listen to, their rare charms. That said, if you want to hear the crowd go wild, just wait for Nielsen to strap on one of those Hamer five-necks and strut it round the stage. ★

Artist: Travis Bone (www.furturtle.com)

THE SELF-PROCLAIMED "loudest guitarist in history," Ted Nugent plays guitars that would seem totally unfit for high-decibel rock: hollow-bodied Gibson Byrdland archtop electrics. The model was co-designed by two first-call '50s session players, Billy Byrd and Hank Garland, and was aimed primarily at jazz, country, and dance-band guitarists of the day. In addition to being fully hollow rather than semi-hollow like an ES-335, the Byrdland is also a short-scale design at 23.5 inches, which takes a significant chunk out of the standard Gibson 24.75 inches (or 25.5 inches for many full-sized jazz guitars of the day); it also has a slimmer, narrower neck than usual.

Facing page: The Motor City Madman at home with a brace of Byrdlands and then some.
© Robert Alford

Rick Gould

As if foretelling the high-volume rock that some Motor City–based Byrdlands would be used for a decade and a half later, the guitar was one of Gibson's early efforts to combat the feedback that traditional archtops were prone to. It was also one of the company's first two "thinline" models when released in 1955 alongside the ES-350T, also a short-scale guitar for the first twenty-two years of its existence. Both guitars were only 2.25 inches deep, although a full 17 inches wide, but while the ES-350T was made with a laminated maple top, as first seen on the ES-175 of 1949, the Byrdland had a carved solid spruce top, just like the big-boy jazz boxes of old. The Byrdland debuted with a rounded Venetian cutaway and a pair of Gibson's then-new Alnico V pickups, which were similar to P-90s but had pole pieces made from alnico bar magnets rather than steel bolts. It took on two humbuckers in 1957 and a sharper Florentine cutaway in 1960. The rounded Venetian cutaway returned some years later (both variations are available today), but by that time Nugent had already selected his Byrdland with a deep, pointed cutaway, and was ready to make some noise.

Despite the seeming incongruities in the guitar's design, the Nuge applied his '60s Byrdlands to an unholy maelstrom of metalesque exploits. In the late '60s and early '70s the Detroit rocker ramped up the fury with the Amboy Dukes and launched his solo career proper with the *Ted Nugent* album of 1975. Far and away his best-known hit, "Cat Scratch Fever," appeared on the 1977 album of the same name. Although Nugent used a little early-'60s tan Tolex Fender Deluxe amp, cranked to the max, to record the single, as Aspen Pittman notes in his *The Tube Amp Book,* he is known for playing through massive stacks on the live stage, piling up Twin Reverbs in the early days, then Marshalls, and, most recently, Peavey 5150s.

Except for a dalliance with PRS, the Gibson Byrdland has remained a constant with Nugent—and if we can't find any documentation for the claim of "loudest guitarist on earth," we can probably concede the Motor City Madman the title of "loudest guitarist on a hollow-body archtop" with few reservations. ✪

There's no doubt when Ted Nugent whips it out.

He's the prime manipulator of high energy rock 'n' roll. He's a bristling bundle of electrified nerve ends plugged into gut-rending guitartechnics. His sell-out concerts leave audiences blissfully drained and amazed. And now he's unleashed a blistering new album, "Free-For-All," that unequivocably answers the question, "Just how far can Ted Nugent go?" Grab ahold of a live wire. "Free-For-All." Ted Nugent. Raw. On Epic Records and Tapes.

TED NUGENT FREE-FOR-ALL

Facing page: Spirit of the Wild Tour, Cobo Hall, Detroit, Michigan, December 31, 1994.

© Robert Alford

ALTHOUGH HE ATTAINED SOME SUCCESS as a professional musician before either Eric Clapton or Jeff Beck, particularly as a working session guitarist on London's busy studio scene, Jimmy Page arrives third in our trilogy of London Tele slingers, being the last of the three to take up guitar duties with the Yardbirds. As would come to pass, however, Page would make more significant use of a Telecaster throughout his career than either Clapton or Beck, and would never entirely discard the model, even while becoming more commonly associated with the Gibson Les Paul (see following spread) and, occasionally, the EDS-1275 double-neck (see pages 232–233).

Born in Heston in West London in 1944, and raised mainly in Epsom, Surrey, essentially another London suburb, Jimmy Page found much the same path to the guitar as his fellow London six-stringers, listening to records by bluesers such as Buddy Guy, Hubert Sumlin, B. B. King, and Otis Rush, but was

Jimmy Page's heavily decorated Telecaster, seen here in Copenhagen in 1968 (along with Robert Plant and the New Yardbirds), was perhaps most famously employed on the solo in "Stairway to Heaven" in 1971—a solo which no doubt sent countless would-be guitar heroes mistakenly in search of Gibson Les Pauls. *Jorgen Angel/Redferns/Getty Images*

arguably more influenced by rock 'n' rollers like Elvis sidemen James Burton and Scotty Moore. Page's early fluency on the instrument landed him in several up-and-coming cover bands, which transitioned to a burgeoning studio career. By the mid-1960s he was one of the first-call session aces on London's pop and blues-rock scene—or, arguably, second-call guitarist behind Big Jim Sullivan, another early proponent of the fuzz box (and for whom effects pioneer Roger Mayer also designed a prototype unit like the one he built for Page). The first time the Yardbirds knocked on the door to ask him to join the band (replacing the departed Eric Clapton), Page declined, and passed the job along to friend Jeff Beck. Less than a year later, however, in the summer of 1966, he was again approached, this time to fill the shoes of departing bassist Paul Samwell-Smith until rhythm guitarist Chris Dreja could learn the instrument. This time, Page agreed, and took up the bass for upcoming Yardbirds dates, segueing to guitar once Dreja had come to grips with the four-string.

The Telecaster Page played for much of his tenure in the Yardbirds was one given him by Jeff Beck, the '59 whiteguard model with rosewood fingerboard that Beck had acquired from a pre-Yardbirds bandmate. Page soon covered the guitar in reflective metal discs, perhaps an homage to the Esquire played by Syd Barrett of the Pink Floyd, then repainted the guitar in psychedelic colors with a large dragon graphic to match the mood of the times. He used this Tele alongside Beck's guitar work on the only real Yardbirds hit of the Page/Beck era, "Happenings Ten Years Time Ago," as well as on the song "Stroll On," recorded for the Yardbirds' appearance on the seminal Michelangelo Antonioni film *Blowup*. After Beck's firing from the band midway through a US tour in October 1966, Page was the sole Yardbirds guitarist until the demise of the band, and more and more he used it as a test lab for musical ideas that he would explore further with his next venture. When two more original Yardbirds, singer Keith Relf and drummer Jim McCarty, departed in 1968, he soldiered on as the New Yardbirds, hiring singer Robert Plant and drummer John Bonham to avoid reneging on contractual obligations for a Scandinavian tour. Growing further and further from what The Yardbirds had been just a year before—

with more intensive adventures into its own blend of psychedelic rock mixed with heavy electric blues and some acoustic folk, and the musicianship to pull it off—this lineup was clearly an entirely different band. The addition of bassist John Paul Jones, who had occasionally sat in for Dreja as a session player in the past, calcified the new direction. Page dropped the New Yardbirds name and dubbed the outfit Led Zeppelin.

The heavily decorated rosewood-'board Tele remained a major part of Page's arsenal in Led Zeppelin. He employed it heavily on the band's first album, *Led Zeppelin*, but perhaps most famously pulled it out for the seminal solo to "Stairway to Heaven" in 1971, a performance that no doubt sends countless thousands of wannabe guitar heroes mistakenly in search of the Gibson Les Pauls that Page was often seen playing on stage by that time, or the double-neck that he used to perform the song live, playing the intro on the upper twelve-string neck, and the solo on the lower six-string neck. During the remainder of the Led Zeppelin years Page would acquire and play a handful of other Telecasters, but the '59 or '60 Tele with the dragon graphics would always be considered "the one" in the minds of Zeppelin fanatics. ◆

1959 GIBSON LES PAULS "NUMBER ONE" & "NUMBER TWO"

Jimmy Page finds bliss in 1972. *Robert Knight Archive/Redferns/Getty Images*

IN LES PAUL CIRCLES, Jimmy Page needs no introduction. His "Number One" '59 Les Paul might be considered *the* primo 'burst in the minds of many fans, and although many early landmark Zep recordings were done on a Telecaster, Page himself is often deemed the consummate Les Paul artist when any discussion of this vaunted axe arises. Purchased from Joe Walsh in 1969 for the then-princely sum of $1,200, the guitar replaced Page's famous 1959 "Dragon" Telecaster, a holdover from his Yardbirds days.

"Jimmy . . . was looking for a Les Paul and asked if I knew of any, 'cause he couldn't find any that he liked, and I had two," Walsh told *Guitar World* magazine in 2012. "So I kept the one I liked the most and flew . . . with the other one. I laid it on him and said, 'Try this out.' He really liked it. So whatever my expenses were, that's what I charged him . . . I just thought he should have a Les Paul for godsakes!"

"Number One" arguably went on to become his most iconic Zeppelin-era guitar, and even served Page in good stead during the band's celebrated December 2007 reunion show at London's O2 Arena. Of course, "Number One" got its name for a reason: Page also had a "Number Two" (another '59 Standard 'burst) and "Number Three" (a '69 Les Paul Deluxe).

Walsh had had "Number One's" neck shaved down to the thinner profile of a '60 Les Paul Standard, so it was already modified when Page received it. The Zep guitarist added his preferred Grover tuners, and, over the years, changed out a broken original double-cream bridge pickup for a later T-top Gibson humbucker, which was in turn changed to a custom-wound Seymour Duncan humbucker years later. After this, the neck pickup was eventually swapped for another original PAF. Page also installed a phase-reverse switch, activated by push-pull potentiometers, in an effort to achieve the "Peter Green" out-of-phase tone.

Page bought "Number Two" at a music store in London's Charing Cross Road early on in the days of Led Zeppelin, mainly as a backup for "Number One." Of this second Les Paul, Pat Foley, head of Gibson's artist relations, said, "When I first saw it at his home, I was knocked out—I thought it was a better looking guitar than his 'Number One.' The neck is still very slim, but not quite as extreme as the reshaping of the neck on LP Number One. The finish had a little bit more of a sunburst pattern remaining, and you could see where the original red had faded and left a gray-brown sunburst." Over the years, this Les Paul was modified even more dramatically than "Number One," with individual coil-split switches on the tone controls, series-parallel switching on the volume controls, and two pushbutton switches beneath the pickguard, for universal phase and universal series/parallel switching.

And Page's Les Paul "Number Two." *Backbeat UK/Outline Press*

JIMMY PAGE STANDING STRADDLE-LEGGED before a raging Marshall stack while strangling three shades of fury out of a Gibson double-neck has got to be one of the most iconic rock images of all time. Was there any aspiring teen rocker of the '70s, on either side of the Atlantic, who didn't at one time dream of owning one of these things? Known to most simply as "a double-neck," the Gibson model in question is actually the EDS-1275 Double 12 (EDS for "Electric Double Spanish," one up on Gibson's traditional ES "Electric Spanish" designation). And although it wasn't designed with heavy rock in mind, it proved to be exactly what Page needed to get the job done.

Facing Page: Olympia Stadium, Detroit, Michigan, January 31, 1975.
© Robert Alford

GIBSON EDS-1275

Upon its introduction in 1958, the EDS-1275 was constructed as a semi-hollow-bodied guitar, with very few examples ever made using this original design. Around 1962, the model evolved to the SG-style body that is far more familiar, and it remained in production with that format until around 1968. Each type carried two humbucking pickups for each neck, but the control layout changed as the body construction evolved. The SG-shaped rendition had one three-way pickup selector and Gibson's traditional four-knob control section, all positioned beneath the lower (six-string) neck, with a neck-selector switch between the two "guitars." Unlike the twenty-two-fret necks on most Gibson solid and semi-hollow electrics, both versions of the EDS-1275 carried twenty-fret necks that were set deeper into the body than those of an SG, a feature necessary to provide adequate strength and good balance. Gibson's production records indicate that only 110 of both types were produced in the first ten years of the EDS-1275's run, and it's a fair guess that a high proportion of those ended up in the hands of stadium rockers of the late '60s and early '70s. Steve Howe of Yes, Charlie Whitney of Family, and Alex Lifeson of Rush all strutted across the stage with an EDS-1275 at some point in their careers, but Page's use of the instrument with Led Zeppelin is by far the most famous example of this guitar in action.

Page acquired his EDS-1275—serial number 911117, believed to have been made in 1966—shortly after the recording of "Stairway to Heaven" in 1971, specifically to play that song live on stage. "I needed something that would be able to reflect the pacing of 'Stairway'," Page said in an interview on German radio in 2006, "and would still be able to use the electric twelve-string and the six-string neck, without swapping guitars. The double-neck was the one instrument that was going to fulfill it." Although the legendary introduction to "Stairway to Heaven" on Led Zeppelin's untitled fourth album was originally recorded on an acoustic guitar, Page's performance of that solo instrumental segment on an electric twelve-string became a major feature of the band's live performances—and the ability to switch instantly to the six-string neck for the incendiary solo that followed really helped to ramp up the "pacing" that Page refers to.

For all his noteworthy work on a Les Paul, and his dalliances with Telecasters and even a Danelectro, Page and his EDS-1275 will always stand tall in rock's annals. ✪

Facing page: Civic Auditorium, Honolulu, Hawaii, September 1971. *Robert Knight Archive/Getty Images*

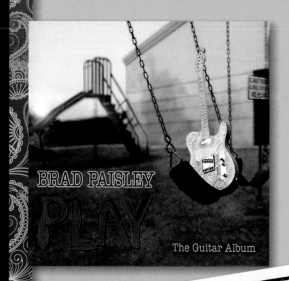

BRAD PAISLEY

PLAY

The Guitar Album

THE GRAND OLE OPRY
WELCOMES
Its Newest Member
BRAD PAISLEY
February 17, 2001

© 2002 HATCH SHOW PRINT - NASHVILLE, TN

Hatch Print poster announcing Brad Paisley's induction into the Grand Ole Opry on February 17, 2001.

MOST ICONIC FENDER GUITARS, and Telecasters in particular, are pre-CBS models—the "blackguard" Teles made from 1950 to 1954 and the "whiteguard" models that followed until CBS's acquisition of Fender at the end of 1964. If you're born with the name Brad Paisley, however, and are destined to become a country guitar hero, you've really got no choice other than to seek out an original Paisley Telecaster from the late '60s. Regarded for many years, by many players at least, as looking rather like some marketing man's rendition of a hippie acid trip, the Paisley Tele was first given some respectability by James Burton and has recently been raised to new heights by Brad Paisley, acknowledged savior of traditional country Tele picking. He has used an original '68 Paisley Red Telecaster that's older than him on all of his significant recordings and most live tours (where it is supplemented by four Tele reproductions made by luthier Bill Crook).

While pre-CBS Fender guitars still remain most prized, the Paisley Tele is one of a handful of CBS-era models that has attained collectible status over the years, thanks in part to its limited production numbers. Although Paisley Red by name, the effects of the paisley stick-on graphics on the top of the guitar, as well as the aging of the finish, give it a much lighter look, and it's often referred to as a "Pink Paisley" model. Paisley (the guitarist) says it's more than just the eye-catching looks that make these instruments desirable. "I feel the maple-capped neck is one of the factors that makes those such good instruments," he told *Vintage Guitar* magazine's Ward Meeker in 2005. "Also, some of the lightest guitars Fender ever made were from the late '60s. A lot of people think of early-'50s Teles as being these really light, perfect guitars. But they were very inconsistent. Most of them had a magic all their own, but some of them weren't as light as late-'60s Telecasters. Those two factors— a great piece of wood and a great neck . . . and quality control hadn't yet gone downhill in the late '60s."

Paisley himself is often credited with bringing authentic Tele twang back to Nashville in an era when overpolished, rack-processed tones threatened to take over Guitar Town. For archetypal examples of the Brad Paisley—and Paisley Telecaster—tone, listen to tunes such as "The World" or "Alcohol" from *Time Well Wasted*, or "Throttleneck," an instrumental track from *5th Gear* that won him his first Grammy Award. Paisley is the first to acknowledge that it takes more than a good guitar to create a hit sound, and he gives his amps credit for a big part of the winning formula. Long enamored of a 1962 Vox AC30, which he still often uses in the studio, Paisley is also a fan of several Dr. Z models, often playing a Stingray (prototype of the production model Stang Ray), a Z-Wreck, and others. Paisley also uses amps by Trainwreck and Tony Bruno, usually running through several together both live and in the studio. ✪

Brad Paisley and his 1968 Paisley Fender Telecaster. *Robert Knight Archive/ Redferns/Getty Images*

Les Paul displays the body sections of his homemade guitar nicknamed "The Log." Jon Sievert/Michael Ochs Archives/ Getty Images

THE MOST FAMOUS ARTIST ever to become synonymous with a guitar model, Les Paul was the consummate do-it-yourselfer. Although he helped usher in the era of the solid-body electric guitar, he was not one for colluding with off-the-shelf instruments. Paul had started the entire ball rolling, of course, way back in 1940 or so, with a contraption that appears very little like a Les Paul today but prefigured the future solid-body more than many guitars that preceded it, thanks to its solid-body core. Given free rein to develop his inventions in the Epiphone factory on weekends, Paul sawed the body wings and neck from a full-depth Epiphone archtop and attached them to a pine four-by-four that formed the center of a guitar he called "the Log." Equipped with a pair of home-wound pickups and a vibrato tailpiece of his devising, the instrument was ready to go. However ungainly it looked, Paul played it on several professional recording and performance dates throughout the '40s and into the early '50s. Unable to see the future of the music world in this Frankenstein of a guitar, however, both Epiphone and future Epiphone owner Gibson declined to put Paul's ideas into production—until Fender's plank-bodied guitars hit the scene in 1950 and gave the competition a kick in the seat of the pants.

Even after Gibson adapted the principles embodied in the Log and ran with them, Paul was rarely entirely satisfied with the results and never quite jibed with the Standard versions of Les Pauls that the company produced and sold throughout the years. He was famously irate that a semi-trapeze tailpiece of his own design was employed with too flat a neck angle on the very first goldtop Les Paul Models of 1952 and early '53, forcing a far less playable setup that involved wrapping the strings under the bridge bar rather than over it as intended. Paul also commented several times that Gibson transposed his original visions for the Standard and Custom models, giving the former the complex mahogany and maple body construction and the

latter the simple mahogany-only body. When Les Paul returned to Gibson as an endorsee in the late '60s, the company saw it as an important opportunity to bring the original carved-top, single-cutaway design back to the fold after nearly eight years of the SG's reign as the company's flagship solid-body. For Les Paul, the artist and inventor, this was an opportunity to get another raft of advancements through the door in Kalamazoo and into production. ★

Les Paul and Mary Ford vamp for a newspaper promotional poster in 1951. Paul plays a heavily modified Gibson L-12 archtop, while Ford picks Les's "Clunker" special.

IN ADDITION TO THE RETURN of the Les Paul Model (soon known as the Les Paul Deluxe) and Les Paul Custom to the market in 1968, another result of Les Paul's re-upping with Gibson arrived in 1969 in the form of the Les Paul Personal and Les Paul Professional, both of which carried his beloved low-impedance pickups. These quirky models never sold well (the Personal, based on Paul's own home-tweaked guitar, even carried the arguably whacky addition of an XLR mic input on its top edge for a "mobile" vocal microphone), and in 1971 the pair evolved into the single Les Paul Recording Model, which retained the same low-impedance pickups with an added high/low switch that converted the signal to high-impedance for use with standard amplifiers, a phase switch, and an eleven-position "Decade" tone switch. The Recording Model also offered a slightly more acceptable layout. All three models featured all-mahogany bodies that were slightly larger, and therefore generally heavier, than those of the traditional Les Paul Standard and Custom. The Les

Paul Recording became Paul's model of choice, and he frequently played one live (alternating with his own, personally modified Personal-like Les Paul) right up until his death in 2009.

Although he was an enthusiastic live performer, Paul's greatest innovations were in the studio—where he pioneered multi-track recording, close-mic'ing of vocals, and other techniques that remain popular today—and his guitars were designed specifically to excel in the studio environment. The low-impedance pickups made it possible to plug these guitars directly into the board to record a linear, high-fidelity signal that could be EQ'd and effected with outboard equipment or later in the mix. Although the technique has caught on with some guitarists, it never became the revolution that Paul obviously intended and expected. It's ironic that Les Paul remained devoted to the more oddball models among the range that bore his name, while the Les Paul Standard became one of the most desirable, and expensive, electric guitars of all time. ✦

Facing page: Les Paul plays his own heavily modified Les Paul Personal Model, the prototype for the Les Paul Recording Model. Note the nutty microphone jack on the upper edge of the body, added controls for mic volume, high/low pickup impedance selection, and EQ—and the further addition of Paul's own black-box preamp for enhanced tone shaping.
Richard E. Aaron/Redferns/Getty Images

"PERRY BURST"

AEROSMITH COFOUNDER JOE PERRY has been associated with a number of specific guitars throughout his career, from a pair of workhorse Stratocasters in the band's earliest years to a selection of B. C. Riches in the late '70s, and, later, the "Bullet and Bones" custom. As was the wont of blues-based rockers in the 1970s, both Perry and his guitar foil in Aerosmith, Brad Whitford, began partaking of Les Pauls as the band gained more recognition.

While Whitford was often seen (and heard) slinging '50s-vintage goldtops, one of the mainstays in Perry's road case was a guard-less "Black Beauty" Custom acquired around the time that the band released their third LP, *Toys in the Attic* (1975). But the Les Paul with the more interesting story would prove to be a tobacco 'burst Standard (serial number 9-0663) of the much-coveted 1959 vintage that Perry picked up in 1976 for $2,500 from storied Nashville guitar broker George Gruhn. The '59 was heavily gigged throughout the late 1970s, but in the early '80s Perry, who by this time had split from the band, sold it off to help ease financial difficulties.

In the years that followed, Perry's tobacco 'burst apparently passed through several hands (including those of Texas bluesman Eric Johnson, according to Gibson, and Derek St. Holmes, according to other sources) before coming into the possession of Guns N' Roses guitarist Slash, a huge Perry fan. Slash has recalled that the guitar came to his attention circa 1989 while it was owned by Tut Campbell, a Georgia-based guitar dealer. After verifying that it was indeed the Perry 'burst by comparing photos he had sent to him to an old poster of Perry, Slash struck a deal to purchase the instrument. While Slash told *Vintage Guitar* magazine in 2001 that he paid $800 for the guitar, other reports that the price was $8,000 (a princely sum even for a '59 'burst in those days) seem much more likely. Slash later used the Les Paul in the filming of GN'R's epic 1992 "November Rain" video. By some accounts, Perry tried to purchase back the guitar over the years, but Slash demurred, eventually giving it to Perry in 2000 as a surprise gift on the occasion of Perry's fiftieth birthday.

As an interesting side note, the late luthier Kris Derrig, perhaps most renowned for building the Les Paul replica that Slash used to record much of GN'R's 1987 debut LP, *Appetite for Destruction*, had extensive access to the Perry Burst while it was in Campbell's possession.

As for the original, Perry told Gibson.com, "It's got everything a great Les Paul is supposed to have. The neck isn't quite as fat as, say, a '54 goldtop, but it's still got a good, meaty neck. It's not a high-output guitar, so it's got a lot of tone.... And it's got all the natural sustain and warmth, and when you turn it up it growls." ✪

—*Dennis Pernu*

The Joe Perry 1959 Les Paul signature model. *Gibson Musical Instruments*

Facing page: Perry works his tobacco 'burst and talkbox at the 1977 Reading Festival. *Peter Still/Redferns/Getty Images*

243

Original 1956 sheet music for Carl Perkins's hit "Blue Suede Shoes," featuring Perkins playing one of his Gibson Les Paul goldtops.

AFTER SUCCESS BROUGHT IN ENOUGH MONEY for him to splurge on a guitar, Carl Perkins splashed out on a new 1956 Gibson ES-5 Switchmaster. Ironically, the move found him going in the opposite direction from that in which Gibson had intended to push the growing number of guitarists on the rock 'n' roll scene. At Sun Records, Perkins had recorded the hits that earned him this spending cash on a pair of '50s Les Paul goldtops, and these solid-bodies are responsible for the sound that we still most associate him with to this day.

The move was symptomatic, however, of the general way in which Gibson's fledgling solid-body failed to catch fire with early rock 'n' rollers, who were still more likely to proceed with the archtop electrics they had used to create the new genre in the first place (witness Scotty Moore, Danny Cedrone, and Chuck Berry) or to adopt Gretsch's flashier entrants into the arena. Plenty of '50s bluesmen strapped on Les Pauls, sure, but Perkins's use of a 1952 or early 1953 goldtop with a cumbersome "wrap-under" tailpiece to record "Honey Don't" toward the end of 1955, and a '55 goldtop with a Bigsby tailpiece to record "Blue Suede Shoes" in January 1956, signaled the most prominent adoption of the model by an early rockabilly or rock 'n' roll artist.

With fifty years of musical hindsight fogging the rearview mirror, it's too easy to forget what a groundbreaking star and enormous influence Perkins actually was. Sun labelmates Elvis Presley and Johnny Cash went on to greater fame throughout their careers, but Perkins was regarded by musicians as one of the founding fathers of rock 'n' roll. In Carl Perkins, one can truly hear the blend of country and blues that formed the genre (a dash of Hank Williams's vocal yelps, a pinch of Muddy Waters's instrumental attitude), while a closer listen to many other major mid- and late-'50s rock 'n' roll stars who came later tends to reveal a series of artists who mainly seemed to be trying hard to sound like Carl Perkins. All in all, Perkins's sound was one that might strictly be categorized more as pure rockabilly—although rockabilly itself was a way station on the road to rock 'n' roll anyway.

Perkins differed from many early rock 'n' roll idols in that he wrote his own songs. His first major single, "Blue Suede Shoes," is perhaps better remembered today for Elvis Presley's cover of the tune, but Perkins's original recording was actually a bigger hit, peaking at No. 2 on the Billboard pop and R&B charts and No. 1 on the country chart, and scoring Sun Records' first gold disc with more than one million copies sold by late spring of 1956. Sometime after this, Perkins painted his Les Paul blue in celebration of the hit record, and he retained the guitar even after buying his ES-5. The former goldtop remains in the possession of the Perkins family in Jackson, Tennessee. ✪

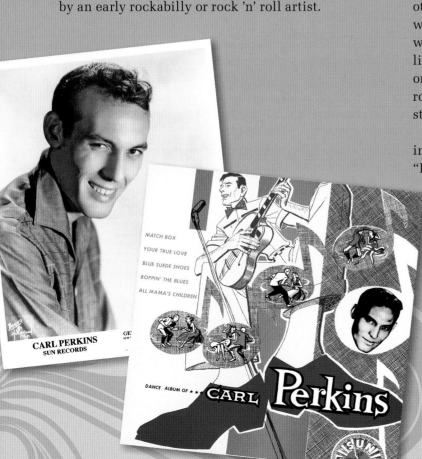

LUTHER PERKINS

FENDER ESQUIRES

246

LP 1220

DOIN' MY TIME

FOLSOM PRISON BLUES

SO DOGGONE LONESOME

ROCK ISLAND LINE

I HEARD THAT LONESOME WHISTLE

Johnny CASH

REMEMBER ME

COUNTRY BOY

I WALK THE LINE

WITH HIS

HOT

AND

BLUE

GUITAR!

CRY! CRY! CRY!

WRECK OF THE OLD '97

IF THE GOOD LORD'S WILLING

I WAS THERE WHEN IT HAPPENED

ANOTHER ALBUM OF Great SUN Hits

NOT QUITE TRAVIS PICKING, you could instead call it "Perkins picking," the alternating *boom-chicka-boom-chicka-boom-chicka-boom* riff that Luther Perkins laid down behind so many Johnny Cash songs and which became an instant tell that the Man in Black was about to strut his stuff on your radio. Upon hearing the twangy opening strains of "Folsom Prison Blues," "Get Rhythm," or "Cry, Cry, Cry," anyone who knows the remotest little thing about the guitar will nail Perkins's tone as coming from a Telecaster. But Perkins was a simple player, and his choice of guitar was even simpler than that. Throughout his career, Luther Perkins never played a Fender Telecaster, but instead preferred its single-pickup sibling, the Esquire.

Perkins went through several Esquires in his early days with Cash, trading up to acquire guitars whose condition, looks, or tone he preferred. The first, bought used in 1954, was a blackguard Esquire with some body damage and a volume control that was stuck on full. In 1956 Perkins obtained first a new whiteguard Esquire with a red custom finish (the instrument believed to have been used on "I Walk the Line") and later purchased a whiteguard Esquire finished in black that he customized with

Luther Perkins's favorite Esquire: the standard blonde whiteguard heard on just about everything he did with Johnny Cash up until the mid-'60s. *Courtesy Allen St. John*

the initials "L. P." on the upper bout. In 1958, though, he stepped up to his favorite Esquire of the bunch, and the most archetypal example of its kind: a standard blonde whiteguard model with a maple neck. Heard on just about everything he did with Johnny Cash up until the mid-'60s, this late-'50s Esquire remained Perkins's number-one guitar, despite Fender's gift of an early Jazzmaster (which Perkins did use on the famous *Live from Folsom Prison* concert and other mid- to late-'60s performances).

While the Esquire is essentially a Telecaster without a neck pickup, the manner in which Fender incorporated this component change into the instrument gives the guitar two subtle but important character differences. First, the absence of a neck pickup means there's no magnet at that position in the body to pull on the strings and possibly dampen their vibration, however slightly. Many players feel this gives an Esquire a more open, ringing tone and great sustain (qualities no good Tele is short of in the first place). Second, retaining the three-way switch in a single-pickup guitar necessitated some nifty wiring tricks that give the Esquire three distinct voicings: (1) the tone control is bypassed by placing the switch in the bridge position, resulting in a brighter, hotter tone than with the tone control in circuit; (2) the tone control is put back in circuit with the switch in the middle position; and (3) a preset "bassy" sound is achieved by a small network of capacitors with the switch in the forward position. The first position is likely the sound heard on twangier phrases like the guitar break in "Get Rhythm," while the third position can be heard laying down the chunky *chicka-boom* in "Hey Porter" and "I Walk the Line."

Classically simple, deceptively infectious, both Perkins and Esquire are a match made in rockabilly heaven. ★

Facing page: Perkins backs Johnny Cash with his favorite Esquire of the bunch: a standard blonde whiteguard model with a maple neck. It was heard on just about everything he did with Johnny Cash up until the mid-1960s. *GAB Archive/Getty Images*

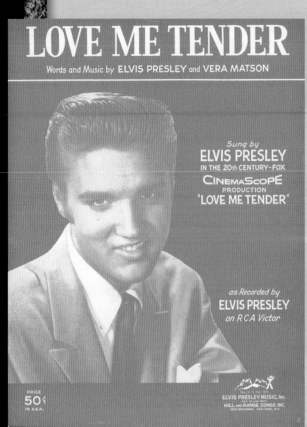

IN THE BEGINNING, Elvis Presley played a series of Martin guitars, moving up the range as fortune and finances allowed. Having begun on a 000-18, late in 1954 he traded this toward the best known of these, a 1942 Martin D-18, a guitar he used for recording and performances. He stepped up once again, to a Martin D-28, later in 1955.

Although the D-18 already had twelve years of playing under its belt by the time Presley acquired it, the budding star, known for his heavy-handed rhythm style, put further wear and tear on it quickly. He added stick-on letters to the guitar that once spelled out "ELVIS" but was shortened to "ELVI" after losing its "S" somewhere along the way. This D-18 is also notable for its sloppily re-glued bridge (a repair apparently undertaken during Presley's tenure), and several scuffs and scratches, including plenty of "belt buckle rash" on its mahogany back. ★

Elvis Presley's 1942 Martin D-18, which he played on many of his Sun recordings from 1954 through 1955. *Courtesy Nigel Osborne/ Jawbone Press*

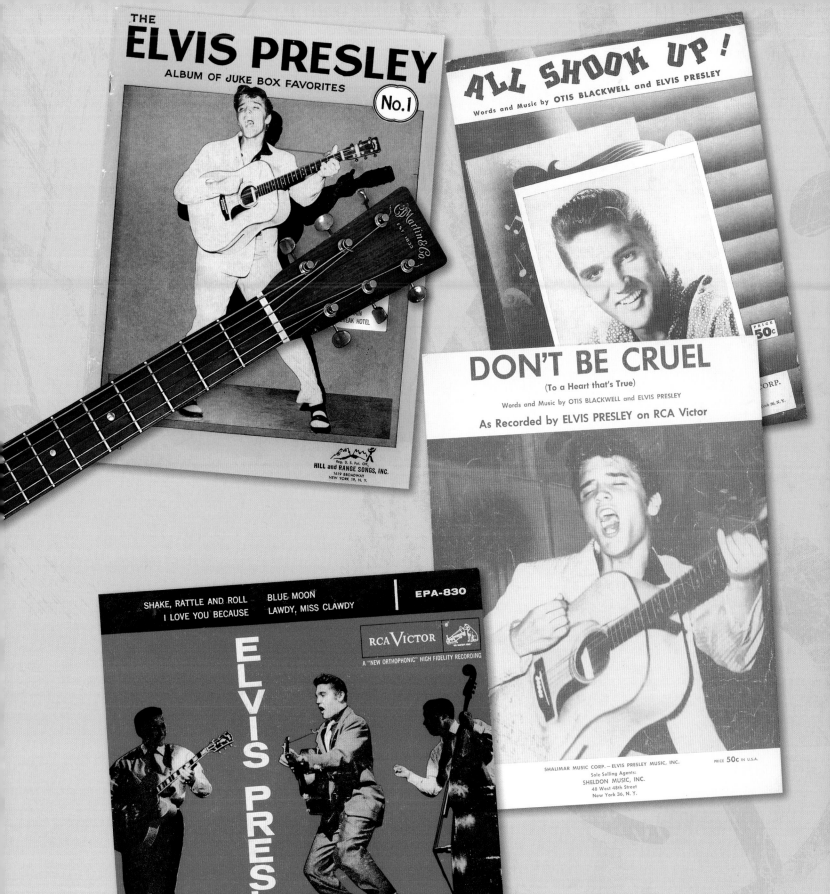

THE STATEMENT "Born out of a marriage of rhythm-and-blues and country, [fill in the blank] evolved into a major force in popular music," could describe any number of genres, instruments, or people. The description certainly fits Elvis Presley and his music to a T. It also accurately describes one of Presley's favorite acoustic guitars, the Gibson J-200, which propelled the star's driving rhythm chops through much of his career peak. Developed as the ultimate punchy, cutting rhythm machine for country stars of the late 1930s, the J-200 offered the maximum volume and clarity available from

RCA VICTOR

45 RPM
"NEW ORTHOPHONIC"
HIGH FIDELITY

47-7035
Elvis Presley
Music Inc., BMI
H2WW-0779

2:10

JAILHOUSE ROCK
(from the Avon prod., on M-G-M release
"Jailhouse Rock")
(Jerry Leiber-Mike Stoller)
ELVIS PRESLEY

Elvis Presley Enterprises, Inc.

an acoustic guitar in its day, as well as the bold, flashy looks that helped a performer stand out on stage. These qualities translated perfectly to rock 'n' roll, and Elvis embraced his Gibson J-200 with a passion that the King rarely, if ever, displayed for a musical instrument.

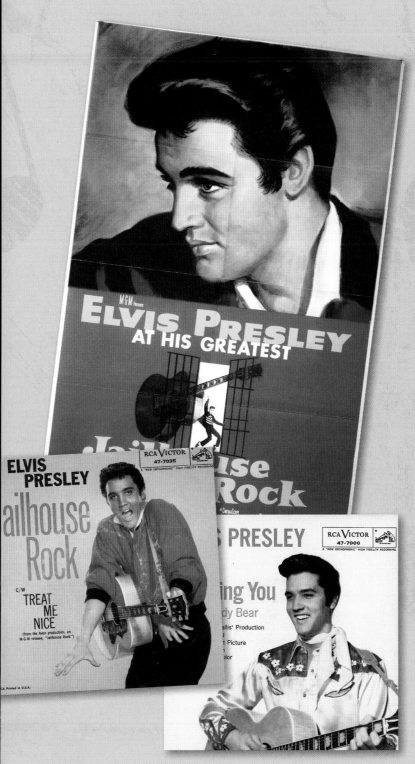

As enormous a star as Presley was, it's interesting to consider that he very likely came to this instrument out of his admiration for those who had played it before him and who had already established it as the pinnacle of its breed. The forefather of the J-200 hit the scene in 1937 when "Singing Cowboy" Ray Whitley ordered a 17-inch-wide flat-top from Gibson with a unique rounded profile and deluxe cosmetic appointments. The original one-off was labeled "L-5 Special" for the similarity of its neck and body proportions to those of Gibson's L-5 archtop. Other early examples of the design were made on a custom-order-only basis. Country-and-western crooners Gene Autrey, Tex Ritter, Roy Rogers, and Ray "Crash" Corrigan commissioned their own versions of the instrument. The guitar appeared in the Gibson catalog a year later as the Super Jumbo and was soon known simply as the SJ-200 (some historians believe Corrigan's to have been the first SJ-200 built), then the J-200. Gibson uses the SJ-200 designation again today.

According to Presley's lead guitarist, Scotty Moore, the King was given a J-200N (the "N" denoting a natural finish) in October 1956, thanks to Moore's own endorsement deal to play a Gibson Super 400CESN archtop electric. Ever tight on the reins, however, Presley manager Colonel Tom Parker wouldn't let his star accept endorsements. According to Moore's recollections, documented at scottymoore.com, Parker requested an invoice from Gibson, which Elvis paid in full. The J-200 quickly became Presley's favorite instrument, and a year later he commissioned a custom-made tooled-leather cover, which the guitar is frequently seen wearing in live concert photos and film footage.

Originally a stock factory model, the guitar received the custom appointments that it was later known for after being sent out for restoration upon Elvis's return from army service in 1960. At this time, the famous "ELVIS PRESLEY" inlay was added to the fingerboard, and the original pickguard was swapped out for a pointy black custom affair. You can see—and hear—Elvis's blonde J-200 in the movies *Jailhouse Rock*, *King Creole*, *G.I. Blues*, and, with new pointy pickguard, *Wild in the Country*. ★

HOHNER HG490

AFTER FIRST GLIMPSING A HOT young R&B artist in the early '80s, Hohner HG490 in hand, we might have been forgiven for assuming the thing was just a prop. Who plays a Hohner Telecaster copy, anyway? Who plays *any* Hohner electric guitar, for that matter? The late Prince did, that's who, and when we learned he was one scorching-hot guitarist, we had to figure he knew what he was doing. For examples of his Hohner at work, listen to the incendiary lead on "Purple Rain" and the slinky chops of "When You Were Mine" from *Dirty Mind*. For that matter, witness the reams of live film footage left of Prince with his T-style guitar.

A "Tele-style" guitar in the broad sense, the HG490 was really not much of a copy, strictly speaking, given that few of its features truly aped the classic Telecaster template. The guitar features a book-matched flame-maple top and back with a walnut center strip, a tortoiseshell pickguard, bridge-plate surround, black binding, and Strat-style pickups, to name just a few details. A handful of these items already help it depart from the classic Nashville Tele twang, and its bridge construction—with through-body stringing, but with the pickup suspended in the plastic tortoiseshell guard plate rather than hanging from a steel plate—takes it even further from the seminal design. Manufactured at the Moridaira Musical Instruments factory in Japan throughout its original run, the guitar began life in the early '70s as the H. S. Anderson Mad Cat. Hohner bought the rights to the design and continued its Japanese production with its own brand on the headstock and the HG490 model designation.

Generally accorded the limited respect of Japanese copies and pawnshop prizes in the '70s and early '80s, the HG490 received a considerable status boost thanks to Prince's adoption of the guitar, which led several fans, and others looking for a bargain, to pick one up and discover that it really was quite a well-made instrument. In fact, Prince's use of the instrument helped to keep the model alive, and Hohner reissued it several times over the years, as the TE and Prinz models early on and recently as the affordable, Chinese-made HTA490 The Artist and the more expensive, Czech-made The Artist Elite.

Said artist's own original HG490 (he had several backups) has underwent some changes over the years,

including the replacement of its original pickups with, first, Kinman noiseless T-style pickups and then, later, the Fender Stratocaster Noiseless set that remains in it today. As for original late-'70s Hohners of the same model, they can now fetch upward of $2,000 on the used (dare we say "vintage"?) market. ◆

Facing page: Prince birthday show, Cobo Hall, Detroit, Michigan, June 7, 1986. © Robert Alford

BORN IN CALIFORNIA to a musical family, Bonnie Raitt began exploring the blues at an early age and set out to perform on her own in the late '60s and early '70s, doing acoustic coffee house gigs in and around Cambridge, Massachusetts, while enrolled as a student at Harvard/Radcliffe. The blues soon bit her good though, and she left her dual major in social relations and African studies to amp up and hit the road full time. She has never looked back. The electric Bonnie Raitt that we know today

Bonnie Raitt plays slide on her 1965 Fender Stratocaster on "I'm in the Mood" with John Lee Hooker, promoting their duet on Hooker's 1989 album *The Healer*.
Richard E. Aaron/Redferns/Getty Images

is one of the blues' most respected slide players, and her instrument of choice is the Fender Stratocaster, specifically a rag-tag and road-weary 1965 Strat, a guitar from a turning point in Fender's history.

Raitt acquired her stripped and heavily gigged example, which wasn't going to be anyone's prize, back before "vintage" Strats had much cache even in the best condition. The body and headstock had lost their paint and logos respectively, as if awaiting a refinish, and the former had taken on a ruddy, natural brown stain. The pickups remained though, and the guitar was otherwise functional and, it would seem, a tonally superior example of the breed, as Raitt has proven over the course of many years and nine Grammy Awards. Other than its scruffy looks, this Stratocaster is exemplary of the "transition period" represented by early post-CBS Strats. It carries the large headstock that CBS execs purportedly introduced so the iconic electric guitar would be more recognizable on TV, the pearloid dots that were seen as an upgrade of the former clay dots in the rosewood fingerboard, and the three-ply white plastic pickguard characteristic of the era. Otherwise, the '65 Stratocaster differs little from its pre-CBS predecessors of at least a couple years before.

Raitt's fluid style and sweet yet biting tone helped to make her playing instantly recognizable among myriad slide guitarists. She tunes her Strat in open G (D-G-D-G-B-D low to high) and uses a custom-cut glass wine bottle neck on her middle finger while attacking the strings with a clear plastic thumb pick and the bare (though fingernail-aided) fingers of her right hand. The seeming simplicity of many of her lead lines belies an innate melodic sensibility and an ability to hit straight at the hook of the tune, qualities that have helped her become one of few hardcore blues-slide players to cross over into mainstream success. Even on the major hits, songs like "Love Sneaking up on You" and "Something to Talk About," that slinky, sweet slide oozes in and stamps Raitt's signature all over the tune just as assuredly as do her distinctive vocals. ★

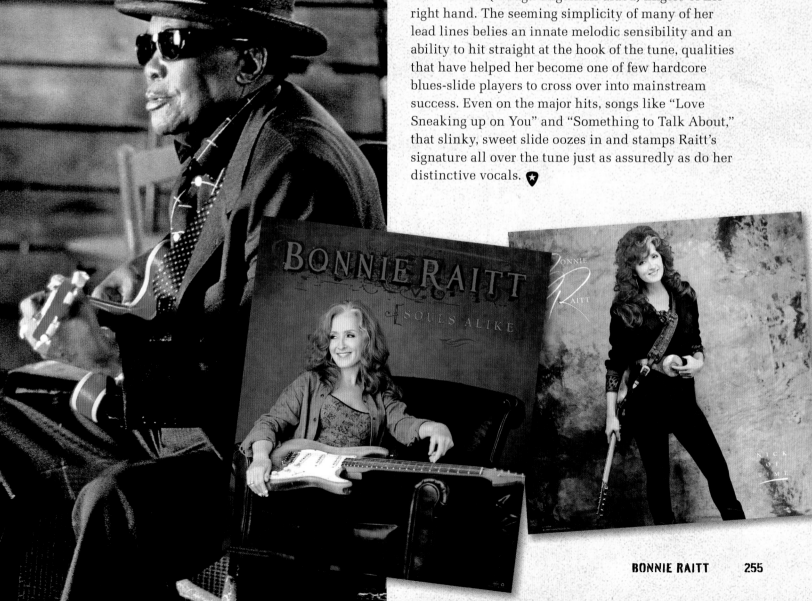

MOSRITE VENTURES II

Johnny Ramone, Masonic Auditorium,
Detroit, January 14, 1978. © Robert Matheu

A GUITAR THAT WAS ORIGINALLY
DESIGNED as a signature model for an
instrumental surf band of the early '60s might
seem an odd choice for the guitarist at the center
of one of the world's most seminal punk bands, but
Johnny Ramone's use of a Mosrite Ventures II makes
a lot of sense when you put aside what "punk" has
come to mean and listen more closely to how the
Ramones actually sounded. This band didn't set out
to invent punk rock per se—they wanted to *reinvent*
rock 'n' roll, period. Songs like "Rock 'n' Roll High
School," "Rockaway Beach," and "Blitzkrieg Bop"
copped a lot more from the Beach Boys and Chuck
Berry than they did from the heavier rock styles that
populated clubs in the years between the birth of
rock 'n' roll and its reinvention at the hands of four
leather-jacketed hoods from Queens, New York.

The white Mosrite that became Johnny Ramone's (born John Cummings) longstanding number-one guitar was actually his second, purchased around 1976 after his first, a blue Ventures II, was stolen. Johnny played the second Mosrite on the vast majority of the band's recordings and live appearances from the time of its acquisition to the Ramones' split in 1996. As might be expected, two decades of punk guitar fury took its toll on the instrument, but Johnny wasn't a gear smasher. That would require some form of artifice, posturing even, and the Ramones were all about the serious business of making punk rock music. Johnny's Mosrite Ventures II was worn down to the bare wood from twenty years of being played, and played *hard*. Forget your rhythm guitar/lead guitar distinctions: for Johnny, there was only one kind of guitar playing and it involved hammering out the power chords through a flurry of down strokes exclusively. Solos? Pah! (I think we can even excuse the indulgent driving one-note break in "I Wanna Be Sedated.")

Throughout his use of the guitar, Johnny Ramone modified his Ventures II to suit his requirements. He retained the original Mosrite roller bridge but he added a more solid Gibson stopbar to firm up the tail end, and he replaced the stock tuners with Grovers. He also swapped out the pickups over the course of time, eventually replacing the originals with a Seymour Duncan SM-1 Firebird-style humbucker in the neck position and a Seymour Duncan FS-1 Fat Strat single-coil in the bridge position. Pedals and effects? No, no, no. Ram it straight into a Marshall stack, and you're ready to bop 'til you drop. ◆

Dave Rawlings performs with Gillian Welch at Newport, Rhode Island, August 3, 2008. © *Erika Goldring/Retna Ltd.*

KGNU & Outback Concerts Present
An Evening With...

Gillian Welch

& David Rawlings

Boulder Theater
June 15th 2005
All Ages 8pm
www.bouldertheater.com

Artist: *Jefferson Holland (www.cryptographics.com)*

BEST KNOWN FOR HIS WORK with Gillian Welch, Dave Rawlings has moved to the fore of Americana over the course of the past decade-plus, and rightly so. His nimble, inventive guitar work is never short of superb (not to mention his songwriting and harmony and lead vocal capabilities), and his ability to shine both as an accompanist and a frontman is equaled by few others in the genre, as variously displayed in his work with Bright Eyes, Old Crow Medicine Show, his own Dave Rawlings Machine, and, of course, Welch (who has always noted that the pair "are a band called 'Gillian Welch'"). And fascinating to guitar fans, of course, is his devotion to a hard-traveled 1935 Epiphone Olympic archtop acoustic guitar, an instrument made during the height of the jazz age and resurrected to perform at the center of some of the most progressive playing of the Americana or alt-country movement.

Rawlings found his Olympic in a friend's workshop in the mid-'90s. Covered in sawdust, missing its bridge, and generally rather beat, it clearly needed some work, but apparently gave off a vibe that told the guitarist the effort would be worth it. After a partial rebuild and the construction of a custom, one-piece mahogany bridge, Rawlings put the '35 Epi into action, notably on Welch's 1996 debut, *Revival.* It has remained his main guitar for the past fifteen years, and he continues to play it straight into a mic—even live onstage—without added pickup or amplification.

Epiphone introduced the Olympic in 1931 as a 13-inch-wide student-grade model with a carved solid spruce top; mahogany back, sides, and neck; a rosewood fingerboard with simple dot inlays; and segmented f-holes. In 1933 it gained another ⅜ inch in width, and in 1934 it was adopted into Epiphone's Masterbuilt series, although it remained more of an entry-level instrument compared to its partners in that lineup, such as the larger Triumph and Blackstone models. These are the specs that Rawlings's guitar was born with in 1935, when it was offered with a $35 price tag. In 1937, amid the craze for "advancing" archtop sizes in the quest for volume, the Olympic gained another 2 inches in body width. It was discontinued in 1950.

For many years 1930s Olympics remained reasonable buys among vintage small-bodied archtops, usually fetching no more than three figures in average condition, but Rawlings's use of the Olympic has put those days behind us, as does any notable artist's adoption of just about any interesting, previously under-appreciated vintage guitar. It's worth noting that—as with any star/guitar pairing—acquiring a similar mid-'30s Olympic isn't necessarily a guarantee of achieving Rawlings-like tone, or, certainly, chops. In addition to the work done to bring this Olympic back to life, there's every indication that it might be an unusual example of the breed. Regarding the custom one-piece bridge, one of the keys to its tone, Rawlings told Simon Solondz of *Acoustic Guitar Magazine,* "I think with a top this small it really behooves you to get as much stuff touching the top as you can, because the top doesn't have that much flex to it." Rawlings has also praised the unusually balanced tone and volume that this guitar emits: "It doesn't have any dead spots or any high spots—which is very, very strange. It makes it fun to play lead, because you don't have to worry where you're at." ♠

Artist: Chris Williams (www.plasticflame.com)

Artist: Michael DeKay (www.imagemadedesign.com)

DISQUES SWING

ANDRÉ♭

DJANGO
REINHARDT

Imp. A. KARCHER, Paris

GRANDE SALLE PLEYEL
Salle chauffée   252, Rue du Faubourg Saint-Honoré, 252   Salle chauffée

Dimanche 2 Février, 15 heures

LE HOT CLUB DE FRANCE
présente pour la première fois à Paris :

GRAND GALA
de
DJANGO REINHARDT

comme
COMPOSITEUR, CHEF D'ORCHESTRE
VIRTUOSE - GUITARISTE

avec son nouveau
GRAND ORCHESTRE SWING
(15 EXECUTANTS)

et le
QUINTETTE DU HOT CLUB DE FRANCE
avec
DJANGO REINHARDT
VEDETTE DES DISQUES "SWING"

PLACES de 10 à 45 frs (Loges 60 frs)
on chez PLEYEL - SALLE GAVEAU - DURAND - "LA BOITE A MUSIQUE"
Boulevard Raspail - "BROADWAY" - 79, Champs-Elysées - "MUSIC-SHOP" -
rue Pierre-Charron - HAMM, 139, rue de Rennes - "LE DISCOBOLE" - Galerie des
Arcades, Gare Saint-Lazare - et au Siège du HOT CLUB DE FRANCE 14, rue Chaptal.
Eugène GRUNBERG, Impresario - 252, rue du Faub. St-Honoré

Django Reinhardt's 1940
Selmer Modèle Django
Reinhardt, serial number
503. The guitar was donated
to Paris's Musée de la
Musique by Django's widow,
Naguine, in later years.
*Jean-Marc Anglès/Musée de
la Musique*

FEW GUITARISTS OF THE FIRST HALF of the twentieth century were as influential as Django Reinhardt, and his groundbreaking playing had repercussions that continue to ripple to this day. He had a direct and major influence on jazz guitar, and an indirect—though entirely discernible—effect on playing styles in several other popular genres. Reinhardt achieved all this on a guitar that would seem to be very much against type for any jazz guitarist in the broad sense, if not for that fact that his use of this big-bodied, flat-top acoustic helped establish it as *the* Gypsy jazz instrument of choice, a status the design continues to enjoy more than fifty years after his death.

The designs that would eventually make up the Selmer Modèle Django Reinhardt Series were originally the brainchild of Italian-born guitarist and luthier Mario Maccaferri, who conceived the instruments while performing and teaching in London in the late '20s. Manufactured by the French saxaphone maker in a corner of Selmer's Paris factory and first offered for sale in the company's London retail outlet, these were truly groundbreaking instruments, but also rather quirky in their first incarnations. To the former point, these flat-topped guitars employed unusual D-shaped and oval sound holes, cutaways when such designs were still unheard of, and advanced enclosed tuners on slotted headstocks. Most were made with laminated backs and sides too, to partner their solid tops, though for reasons thought be tonally and structurally beneficial rather than to save costs on wood stocks. Among their oddities, on the other hand, was a built-in resonator of sorts—described by Maccaferri in his British patent as an "auxiliary sounding box"—that was attached under the soundboard or top. Never popular (nor successful in performance), these internal resonators were removed by many players and soon

Django Reinhardt with his violinist foil, Stéphane Grappelli, the two soloists in the Quintette du Hot Club de France.

dropped from the design altogether.

Reinhardt only took up his Selmer shortly after Maccaferri had left the company in 1933 (in the early '50s the Italian designer would put his name on distinctive injection-molded plastic guitars made in similar shapes), but his patronage of the design helped to secure it as an all-time classic. The example most associated with Reinhardt, a guitar believed to have been the last he owned and played, was a Selmer Modèle Django Reinhardt made in 1940, bearing serial number 503. Speaking of his love for the instrument, in reference to the supposed inferiority of traditional American-made archtop acoustics that most jazz players of the day were using—guitars made by Gibson, Epiphone, Gretsch, and others—Reinhardt said, "Mon frère, all the Americans will wish they could play on this guitar! At least it's got tone, you can hear the chords like you can on the piano. Don't talk to me any more about their tinpot guitars! Listen to this, it speaks like a cathedral!"

Nine years after Reinhardt's death in 1953, his widow, Naguine, donated the Selmer Modèle Django Reinhardt to the Musée du Conservatoire de Paris, and it was subsequently displayed in the Musée de la Musique de Paris. ✪

Django Reinhardt's Busato jazz guitar, made by Parisian luthier Bernabe "Pablo" Busato, in the 1940. *Collection Alain Antonietto*

WITH AN IMPRESSIVE *two* songs in *Guitar World* magazine's "100 Greatest Guitar Solos" readers poll ("Crazy Train" and "Mr. Crowley") and a legion of fans still worshiping his unparalleled shredding abilities more than three decades after his blazing career was cut short, Randy Rhoads is firmly established as one of the brightest stars in the metal-guitar heavens. After forming Quiet Riot while still in his teens, Rhoads stepped up his game when Ozzy Osbourne asked him to audition for his band in 1979. Along came Rhoads—practice amp in one hand, beloved white 1974 Les Paul Custom in the other—and before the young guitarist had even finished his warmup licks, Osborne had told him, "You've got the gig." What followed was an incendiary ascent—and a too-swift ending—that burned Randy Rhoads indelibly into the pages of rock history.

Like Lindsey Buckingham's similar Custom, Rhoads's was a Les Paul of the oft-derided Norlin era, but these are guitars that made classic-rock records and helped fill arenas around the world when wielded by decibel-pushing stars of the day. With his Custom slung low, the young guitarist forged a sound and style that have remained touchstones for the more popular breed of metal, and a reference point for heavy-rock guitarists to this day.

Rhoads was born in Santa Monica, California, to a pair of music teachers, and music was a primary way of life in the Rhoads family right from the start. Randy formed the band that would become Quiet Riot while still just sixteen years old, and he quickly became a central figure on the West Coast metal scene.

Amid copious tales of rockers who have died too young, the story of Rhoads's death is a particularly tragic one. Neither a heavy drinker nor a drug abuser, he was killed when riding in a small Beechcraft plane in which Ozzy Osbourne's tour-bus driver, Andrew Aycock, was attempting a low pass over the bus to wake sleeping crewmembers. A wing clipped the top of the bus, and the plane crashed into a nearby garage, bursting into flames upon impact. Aycock, who was also killed in the crash along with tour makeup artist Rachel Youngblood, was later found to have been taking cocaine through the night. An image of the white Les Paul Custom is engraved into the marble of Randy Rhoads's tomb in San Bernardino, California. ★

Above: The Randy Rhoads Les Paul Custom model. *Gibson Musical Instruments*

Facing page: Rhoads pushes his Norlin-era Custom to the limit during the Blizzard of Oz sessions at Ridge Farm Studios, May 1980. *Fin Costello/Redferns/Getty Images*

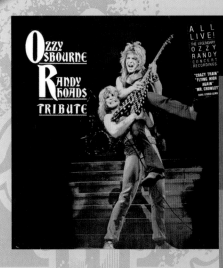

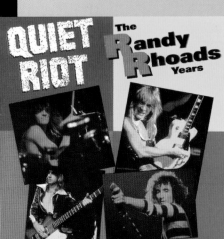

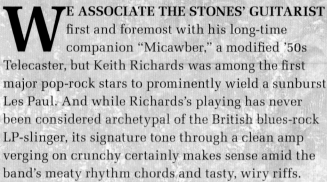

WE ASSOCIATE THE STONES' GUITARIST first and foremost with his long-time companion "Micawber," a modified '50s Telecaster, but Keith Richards was among the first major pop-rock stars to prominently wield a sunburst Les Paul. And while Richards's playing has never been considered archetypal of the British blues-rock LP-slinger, its signature tone through a clean amp verging on crunchy certainly makes sense amid the band's meaty rhythm chords and tasty, wiry riffs.

According to information provided by high-end guitar brokerage Richard Henry, the "Keith Burst" is a 1959 Les Paul that first arrived at Farmers Music Store in Luton, England, in 1961, and was played for a time by John Bowen of Mike Dean & the Kingsmen. Bowen had a Bigsby added to the guitar at Selmer's Music—a

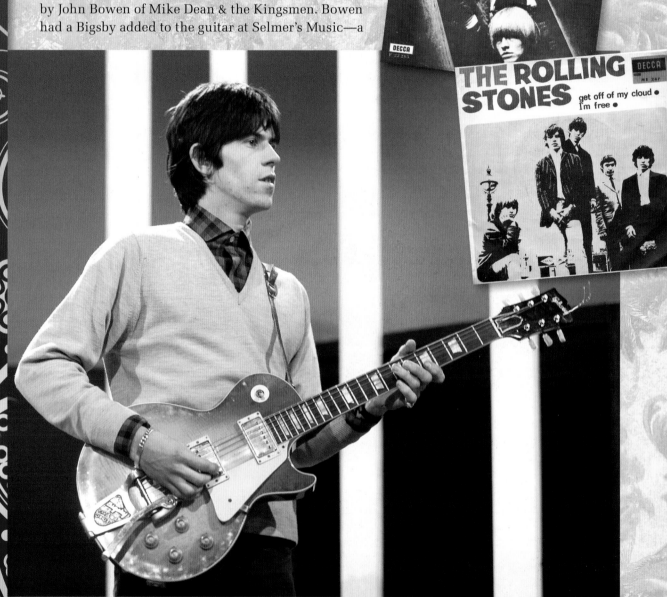

Keef and the Bigsby-equipped "Keith Burst" appear on *Thank Your Lucky Stars*, March 21, 1965. *David Redfern/Getty Images*

Mick gives the Keith Burst some sympathy while Keef bangs away on his Dan Armstrong Plexi at London's Olympic Studios in June 1968. *Mark and Colleen Hayward/ Redferns/Getty Images*

regular haunt for musicians on the booming London music scene of the day—before trading it in there in late 1962. A young Keith Richards would occasionally visit the store, and on one of those occasions he purchased the Les Paul with Bigsby there.

Throughout the early days of the Stones, the Les Paul was one of Richards's most prominent guitars. The best-known photos of the era show him playing it during a 1964 performance on the TV show *Ready Steady Go!*, and he also played it on tour in the United States that same year, when it popped up during the Stones' performance on *The Ed Sullivan Show*. Early Rolling Stones hits purportedly recorded with the Les Paul include "Satisfaction," "Get Off My Cloud," "Let's Spend the Night Together," and "Little Red Rooster." As seen in color photos from the time, just five years after it left the factory, the guitar had already faded to a deep amber 'burst with a little iced-tea shading around the body edges.

Accounts of the guitar's travels from this point onward tend to differ. The best-corroborated rendition, again from Richard Henry, recounts that Richards sold it to Mick Taylor in 1967 when Taylor (a future Stones guitarist) replaced Peter Green in John Mayall & the Blues Breakers, but not before another former Blues Breaker—one Eric Clapton—

borrowed it for a live show with the band in 1966. Following this path, the "Keith Burst" returned to the Rolling Stones fold when Taylor replaced the late Brian Jones, playing it prominently during the band's Hyde Park concert in July 1969. Both Taylor and Richards then played the Les Paul on a tour of the States later that year.

In 1971, the "Keith Burst" surrendered its Stones-hood once again, and forever after, when it was either stolen from the mansion Nellcote in southern France, where the band was recording *Exile on Main Street*; stolen from the Marquee Club during a Stones performance; or given (or sold) to Heavy Metal Kids guitarist Cosmo Verrico to replace a guitar of his that was stolen. In any case, Verrico sold the Les Paul to Bernie Marsden of Whitesnake, who finally concluded the "Keith Burst's" star ownership by flipping it to private collector Mike Jopp a week later. The guitar remained in Jopp's ownership until 2003 and was last sold at auction in 2004 by Christie's in New York, going to a private collector in Europe. Richards has played other Les Pauls now and then throughout his career—most notably, perhaps, a three-pickup black Custom that appeared in some Norlin-era Gibson ads—but that original '59 with post-factory Bigsby will always be remembered as the "Keith Burst." ★

KEITH RICHARDS HAS BANDIED PLENTY of guitars about the stage through the years—Les Pauls, ES-335s, ES-345s, ES-355s, Stratocasters, Ernie Ball/Music Man Silhouettes, a Dan Armstrong Lucite guitar, and a Zemaitis—but he is far and away most associated with the modified early-'50s blackguard Telelecaster that has remained his signature instrument since 1972's *Exile on Main St.* Indeed, Richards was one of the players who took the Tele from country and blues into mainstream rock, where it had rarely been used since the '50s and where it has remained a major player ever since.

Named "Micawber" by Richards, after the beloved rascal and hero Wilkins Micawber character from Charles Dickens's novel *David Copperfield*, this Telecaster is understood to be a 1952 or '53 model that retains its original body and neck (with their original, heavily road-worn finishes) and knurled knobs and control plate, but it has been modified in many other

Rolling Stone Keith Richards strums a power chord on "Micawber" during a concert in Munich, Germany, on June 6, 2003. *Joerg Koch/AFP/Getty Images*

ways. Most notable among these alterations is the Gibson PAF humbucking pickup that Richards installed in the neck position early in his ownership of the guitar ("backward," with the adjustable pole pieces toward the bridge). The neck pickup is often considered the "weak link" of the Telecaster, tonally speaking, and players have sought to improve this setting in several ways, a humbucker modification being one of the more popular options, although it, of course, requires routing a considerable amount of wood from the body. Micawber was also updated with a latter-day, six-saddle brass bridge, from which Richards removed the block-style saddle from the low E position to better accommodate his preference for using only five strings when playing in open-G tuning, as he always does with this Tele. Other notable details include modern, diecast tuners and the white Strat-style switch tip in place of the original black barrel switch tip. Known for its cutting yet meaty tone, Micawber can be heard on too many classic

Stones recordings to mention, and it is also habitually used for specific songs in live performances, usually "Brown Sugar" and "Honky Tonk Women," two of the band's most popular tunes.

On tour, Richards carts several backup Telecasters that are also usually used on specific songs. Most distinctive among these are "Malcolm," a blonde 1954, and "Sonny," a sunburst 1966. Both also have humbuckers added in the neck position and six-saddle brass bridges with the low E saddle removed. Although countless guitarists happily maintain six strings when playing in open G (which, as such, runs D-G-D-G-B-D, low to high), Richards has often mentioned that the low D in fact gets in the way of his own playing, and the bassist's parts too. To complete his rich, gnarly, rock 'n' roll tone on stage, Richards habitually rams his Teles and other guitars through a pair of vintage late-'50s "high-powered" (80-watt) tweed Fender Twin amplifiers, while frequently blending large and small amps in the studio. ★

Robbie Robertson and the bronzed '58 in his Santa Monica recording studio during a 1987 photo session to promote his first solo album. *George Rose/Getty Images*

MUSIC FANS WHO ARE UNFAMILIAR with the intricacies of Robbie Robertson's career tend to know him primarily as the guitarist with the Band and Bob Dylan, and to picture him, if at all, with the odd monster of a Stratocaster that he wielded in much of the concert documentary *The Last Waltz*. Dig just a little deeper, though, and you quickly find that this understated artist boasts a career that stretches virtually from the roots of rock 'n' roll to span many of the high points in the history of popular music. The guitarist was born Jaime Royal Robertson in Toronto, Canada, in 1943 to a Canadian father and a mother of Mohawk descent. He learned the guitar at an early age during visits to his mother's relations on the Six Nations Reserve, and he was an active professional musician around the Toronto scene while still in his teens.

Robertson joined formative rock 'n' roller Ronnie Hawkins and his band, the Hawks, in 1960 and toured the United States and Canada with the outfit until 1964. After a brief stint on their own, Robertson and the Hawks—which included Levon Helm, Garth Hudson, Rick Danko, and Richard Manuel—signed on as Bob Dylan's backup band in 1965, and upon signing to Capitol Records in 1967 as a band in their

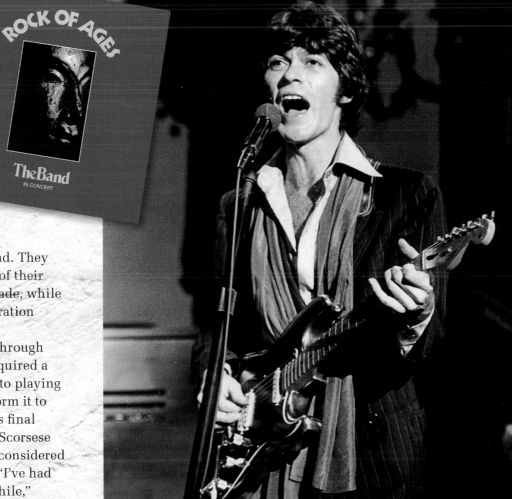

own right, changed their name to the Band. They would release several successful albums of their own into the middle of the following decade, while returning time and again to their collaboration with Dylan.

Known as more of a Telecaster player through the early years of the Band, Robertson acquired a pre-CBS Stratocaster along the way, took to playing it more frequently, and decided to transform it to a sort of monument in honor of the Band's final concert together, documented by Martin Scorsese in the film *The Last Waltz*, which is still considered among the best concert films ever made. "I've had this souped-up old Stratocaster quite a while," Robertson told *Musician* magazine in 1987. "It has number 0254 on the back. You can tell it's old 'cause the neck's a little thick. Before I used it in *Last Waltz*, I had it bronzed, like baby shoes." To clear up some picking space for the fingerpicks he habitually used, Robertson also had the Strat's middle pickup moved back alongside the bridge pickup, a mode that makes the guitar look like it carries a humbucking pickup, but it's actually the two single-coil Strat pickups. Robertson has often said this guitar was a 1958 Stratocaster, although the thicker neck profile, the round string guide on the headstock, and its 254 serial number might suggest an older guitar from 1954, although the interchangeability of Fender parts makes this virtually impossible to determine without disassembling the guitar. While he used this freshly bronzed pre-CBS Stratocaster throughout much of *The Last Waltz*, the bronze shell, in addition to giving it "a very thick, sturdy sound," also added considerable weight to the guitar. At times, Roberts lightened the load by switching to what appears to be a '57 Stratocaster in two-tone sunburst, although it's unclear whether this was his guitar or Bob Dylan's (certainly Dylan plays it on the finale, "I Shall Be

The '58 Strat's most famous appearance came in the Band's concert documentary, *The Last Waltz*, filmed November 25, 1976, in San Francisco. *Larry Hulst/Michael Ochs Archives/Getty Images*

Released"). Robertson later added a "double-locking" Washburn vibrato unit to the Stratocaster, taking it even further from its Leo-certified origins.

Bronze Strats aside, Robertson's wry, spare playing style has made him a true guitarist of note, and he has been admired by many prominent names in the music industry, in addition to legions of fans, for his rootsy tone and tasteful fills. Turning once again to the live documentary film, there are few better examples of his sound, or his musicality, than the performances on "The Night They Drove Old Dixie Down," "Ophelia," and "The Weight," the latter a Band classic written by Robertson himself. Fender issued a Custom Shop Robbie Robertson Stratocaster available in the artist's preferred Moonburst finish as well as a lacquer-based bronze, and he has been seen playing one of two Fender Custom Shop Strats decorated by the Apache artist Darren Vigil Gray. ★

Ronson with Ziggy
Stardust and the
Spiders from Mars.
© Chris Foster/Retna Ltd.

PLAY DON'T WORRY
MICK RONSON

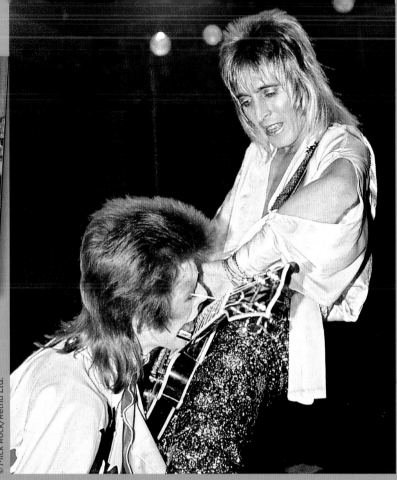

© Mick Rock/Retna Ltd.

DAVID BOWIE MIGHT HAVE embodied the Ziggy persona, but Mick Ronson's incendiary guitar tone and fluid, infectious licks drove the musical experience behind Ziggy Stardust and the Spiders from Mars. Although his name is raised less frequently than those of several other late-'60s and earlier-'70s Les Paul–toting Brit-rock masters, this humble artist from Hull, Yorkshire, in the north of England wielded one of the most instantly recognizable tones in the history of cranked guitar. Cue up the start of "Ziggy Stardust" and the eyes of every guitarist in the room will light up, while most non-players will break into enthusiastic displays of air guitar.

Ronson's power and tonal appeal derived from simple yet mighty ingredients. The Gibson Les Paul reigned supreme with top British rock guitarists of the era, and Ronson's choice followed suit. His was a 1968 Les Paul Custom, the first "real" Les Paul with humbuckers in the eight years since the demise of the single-cutaway Standard and Custom in 1960. Although Ronson's guitar had emerged from the factory with the traditional "Black Beauty" finish, the guitarist had the top stripped back to natural. He reported in interviews having been told by a fellow musician that stripping the top of an acoustic increased its high-end response, so he applied the same logic to his electric, although the results aren't likely to have been nearly as significant with a solid-body guitar. Slightly more effective, perhaps, and another trend of the day, Ronson also removed the gold-plated metal covers from his pickups, a mod long considered to help boost highs.

In addition to being the age of the Les Paul, this was also an era of *monstrous* amplifiers, and Ronson's 200-watt Marshall Major—which he nicknamed "The Pig"—was as gargantuan as any out there. As with many great tonesmiths, Ronson didn't throw a whole lot more into the brew. He used a Vox Tone Bender pedal on occasions when fuzz was required more than pure tube-amp overdrive, and he also employed a wah-wah pedal, which he occasionally used as designed, but also sometimes left at set positions to act as a tone filter to notch his midrange sound (as heard in the slightly nasal guitar tone on "Ziggy Stardust").

The Ronson/Bowie catalog is rife with other timeless examples of rock power. From the early years of their association, the pre-Ziggy "The Man Who Sold the World" (from the album of the same name) offers a relentless, addictive, slightly eastern-tinged signature riff. More upbeat, both in tempo and mood, "Suffragette City," "The Jean Genie," and "Panic in Detroit"—all unexpected frat-rockers of a sort—display trenchant tones, playful musicianship, and surprising staying power. After notably assisting other artists such as Mott the Hoople, Lou Reed, and even John Mellencamp (whose hit "Jack and Diane" he co-wrote), Mick Ronson died in April 1993 of inoperable liver cancer. ♦

Carlos Santana's own first PRS Santana prototype model. *Rick Gould*

A NOTORIOUS TONE-SEEKER from the earliest days of his playing career, Carlos Santana has been on a quest for the ultimate guitar, which fortuitously collided with that of a young man whose own quest in life seemed to be to *build* just such an instrument for him. From his 1969 Woodstock appearance until the early '80s, Santana played a number of Gibson SGs and Les Pauls, and notably endorsed Yamaha's SG2000 for a while, but he was never entirely satisfied with any of these instruments. Meanwhile, a young guitarist from Annapolis, Maryland, by the name of Paul Reed Smith was making his first guitar in college, and by the mid-'70s he was setting up his own business to custom-build instruments that he eventually hoped he would sell to the stars. Smith landed one of his early efforts with rocker Ted Nugent, then received an order for a twelve-string from fusion supremo Al DiMeola, followed by an order from Heart's Howard Leese for a more standard six-string. But the real turning point in his career, and in the success of PRS Guitars, arrived when he slipped his own personal instrument backstage at a Santana concert in 1981.

Artist: Jay Michael (www.flyrightstudios.com)

Santana was impressed with the craftsmanship that Smith's guitar exhibited and decided to try it out on stage that night. The early PRS played well, but its version of the P-90 single-coil pickup didn't jibe with Santana's rig, which was set up for the humbuckers that gave him his trademark singing sustain. The pair parted ways with Santana agreeing to try another model in the future. The occasion of making repairs to Leese's early PRS provided Smith with an opportunity, and he shipped it to Santana—who was out on the road—for a test-drive before sending it back to Leese. This time, the format clicked. Santana loved the guitar and even used it on his 1981 album, *Zebop!*. He ordered his own custom-build from Smith, requesting a vibrato unit "that would stay in tune" and a few other modifications. A longstanding partnership between maker and artist was born.

Santana's own guitars, and the Santana II and Santana MD production models they have spawned, have gone through several iterations but retain the same basic ethos. In addition to the striking maple tops and deluxe pearl inlays, the in-tune vibrato that Santana originally requested has become a cornerstone of PRS's proprietary hardware and appears on several other models. Of course, you need more than a resonant guitar and a pair of humbuckers to produce near-infinite sustain. Santana's tone is ably aided by a Mesa/Boogie MkI head (a model he has used since the early '70s) and a pair of Dumble Overdrive Reverbs, which are fed through a mixed set of speaker cabs with minimal effects processing. ✪

Carlos Santana hits a soulful note on his Paul Reed Smith Santana guitar. *Garry Clarke/Redferns/Getty Images*

THE GRETSCH 6120 BEARS ANOTHER star's name, but one could argue that no performer is more synonymous with the model than Brian Setzer. Sure, country virtuoso Chet Atkins established the model at Gretsch's bequest (and famously strayed from the template numerous times over the two decades following its introduction in 1955). But the 6120 Chet Atkins Hollow Body was always more a rockabilly roller than a country picker. Even though Setzer came along as part of a rockabilly revival (you could argue that his band, the Stray Cats, pioneered said revival in the early '80s) rather than amid the original wave of artists who popularized the style decades earlier, Setzer has arguably done more to bring the 6120 back to the masses than any other artist before or since.

Like many players who are enamored with a particular model of guitar, Setzer has owned and played several 6120s throughout his career, and he has often performed with recent Gretsch Brian Setzer Hot Rod and 6120 reissue models. The most iconic of all his Gretsches, however, is the very first one he ever acquired: a 1959 6120 Chet Atkins Hollow Body that stayed with him throughout his formative years with the Stray Cats in London in the early 1980s. The band's first three successive chart singles—"Runaway Boys," "Rock This Town," and "Stray Cat Strut"— absolutely define the tone of a late-'50s 6120 through a reverb-drenched amp . . . the tone that rang in Setzer's mind as something akin to that of Eddie Cochran, whose guitar he was on the prowl for before he even knew the name of it.

Facing page: Brian Setzer and his 1959 Gretsch Model 6120, Pine Knob Music Theater, Detroit, Michigan, July 1983. © *Robert Alford*

© *Robert Matheu*

Although the young Setzer purchased his 6120 because it was "just like Eddie's," his was actually a slightly different, later model with features that had evolved beyond the debut format of two DeArmond Dynasonic single-coil pickups, single pickup selector switch, and three-knobs-plus-master-control section. By mid-1957 Gretsch had added its own Filter'Tron humbucking pickups to the model (designed by Ray Butts at Chet Atkins's behest) and had also altered the guitar's electronics to employ a tone switch rather than a tone control. Whatever the specs, the '59 suited Setzer to a T and became the guitar with which he made a name for himself. And he gave it a workout in the process. When the two pickup volume control knobs fell off, he drilled holes in a pair of dice from a Monopoly game and glued them in place. When he decided that playing in tune would be a good idea, he pulled the guitar's failing original tuners and added a set of locking Sperzel machine heads. Along the way he removed the somewhat cumbersome tone switch from the upper bout too. In the course of taking on these minor modifications—plus the Lady Luck, hissing cat, and skull-and-crossbones stickers added for good measure—Setzer's 6120 became one of a kind while retaining its original Filter'Trons, Bigsby tailpiece, and all that played-in wood. ♣

Facing page: Brian Setzer surrounded by vintage and new Gretsch Model 6120s and Sparkle Jet guitars, all backed by his backline of Fender Bassman amps. *Robert Knight Archive/Redferns/Getty Images*

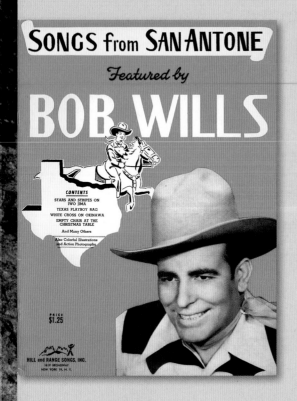

SONGS from SAN ANTONE

Featured by

BOB WILLS

CONTENTS

STARS AND STRIPES ON
IWO JIMA
TEXAS PLAYBOY RAG
WHITE CROSS ON OKINAWA
EMPTY CHAIR AT THE
CHRISTMAS TABLE
And Many Others

Also Colorful Illustrations
and Action Photographs

PRICE
$1.25

HILL and RANGE SONGS, INC.
1619 BROADWAY
NEW YORK 19, N. Y.

LEO FENDER WAS A COUNTRY MUSIC FAN through and through, so it's little surprise that one of the first Stratocasters presented to an artist was given to a country picker. And considering that Bob Wills and His Texas Playboys were about the hottest country band going circa 1954, it's also no surprise that Leo gave the guitar to Wills's hot player, Eldon Shamblin.

Whether he was picking his original Gibson archtop or the futuristic Strat, Shamblin became hugely influential in western swing, country, and jazz. He helped create Wills's sound; arranged many of his most famous songs, such as the band's trademark tunes "San Antonio Rose" and "Faded Love"; and even managed the big band for a time. Fellow Texas Playboy Joe Ferguson crowned Shamblin "The Chord Wizard." Years later, *Rolling Stone* named him "the world's greatest rhythm guitar player." Merle Haggard, with whom Shamblin played in later years, wrote in his 1981 autobiography *Sing Me Back Home*, "Eldon's guitar work is so great that he can just stop everybody in their tracks."

Bob Wills and His Texas Playboys, circa 1950, with Eldon Shamblin cradling his grand Gibson ES-5 archtop in the days before he switched to his Stratocaster. *Michael Oc Archives/Getty Images*

Eldon Shamblin's 1954 Gold Stratocaster, serial number 0569. *Ronny Proler (Anonymous Texas Collector); photo by Dirk Bakker, Artbook*

Shamblin was born in Weatherford, Oklahoma, on April 24, 1916. He taught himself to play as a teenager and was soon picking guitar in the Depression-era beer bars of Oklahoma City's skid row. "I got my basic training in the joint days, in 1933 and 1934," he said in a 1985 interview. "Those [were] low-life places, the worst joints in the country. But I had such a yen for music that I played wherever I could."

In 1934, he got a job picking on a regular thirty-minute program with an Oklahoma City radio station; his pay was two square meals per day. This exposure won him a seat with Dave Edwards's Alabama Boys, playing a lively, upbeat hybrid of country and jazz that became known as "western swing." Edwards's band with Shamblin picking his fluid, innovative guitar lines performed on KVOO radio station in Tulsa, where a cigar-chewing, hooting-and-hollering Texan fiddler named Bob Wills was also building his reputation. "I was the first one out of the Alabama Boys to join the Wills band," Shamblin remembered, "but they all gradually joined."

Wills's Texas Playboys was soon staffed by the best western swing players anywhere. The band began prolifically touring and recording, building Wills's reputation as the King of Western Swing. Shamblin co-wrote a number of the band's classics, including the bopping "Twin Guitar Special" with steel-guitar maestro Leon McAuliffe. Shamblin was a cornerstone of the band up until 1942, when he enlisted in the armed services during World War II. He re-upped with Wills in 1947 and played with him through 1957.

When Shamblin began with Wills, he was playing a radical Rickenbacker Electro B, the small semi-solidbody cousin to the firm's Frying Pan lap steel. As Shamblin told historian Rich Kienzle, Wills took him aside and said, "I like the sound of that thing, but hey, man, they don't know you're playin' a guitar." Shamblin soon bought a pair of massive Gibson Super 400 archtops that no one could mistake for anything but a guitar.

While Wills was antsy about Shamblin's first semi-solidbody, he didn't object to the newfangled Stratocaster. The 1954 Strat that Leo Fender presented to Shamblin was painted metallic gold, perhaps following the style of Gibson's Les Paul goldtop. Serial number 0569 wore a neck dated June 1954. But beyond the golden finish, the guitar was pretty much stock, not even having gold-plated hardware.

Shamblin remembered, "It was pretty beaten up when I got it; must have been some demonstrator." Or perhaps a test bed for Leo. Either way, Shamblin added many miles and many a show to its history, using the golden guitar the rest of his life. ✪

—Michael Dregni

KRIS DERRIG LES PAUL COPY

IT'S EASY TO FORGET that the popularity of Gibson's seminal Les Paul models was at a low ebb in the mid-1980s, when, on one side of the rock coin, heavier players were turning to Deans, B. C. Riches, Kramers, and a variety of "super Strats," and, on the other, indie and alternative players were championing Fender Telecasters and Jazzmasters and a variety of Rickenbacker and Gretsch models. Then along came Slash and his troubles with his own guitar of the moment. The Les Paul was born again as the ultimate rock icon, thanks—with no small bit of irony—to a Les Paul *copy* that saved the day.

While recording Guns N' Roses' seminal debut, *Appetite for Destruction*, in 1987, Slash (born Saul Hudson) was having trouble getting a satisfactory tone from the B. C. Rich and other guitars that had been his mainstays for some time. With the allotted studio sessions nearing their end, and nearly engulfed in panic at the prospect of blowing the band's big break, he picked up a reproduction of a late-'50s Les Paul 'burst that manager Alan Niven had acquired for him try out. The faux Paul nailed the tone that this hard-rocking riffmeister was seeking, and Slash laid down the bulk of the legendary lead work for the album in a flurry of overdubs at a small studio. "It became my main guitar for a really long time," Slash related in an interview for his website, slashsworld.com. "And because I couldn't afford a whole handful of that sort of thing, I took it out on the road for all of Guns' early touring." During one show, a careless moment of crowd surfing nearly lost the star his Derrig Les Paul, when a fan slipped it from him and made for the exit, only to be stopped by the band's security crew.

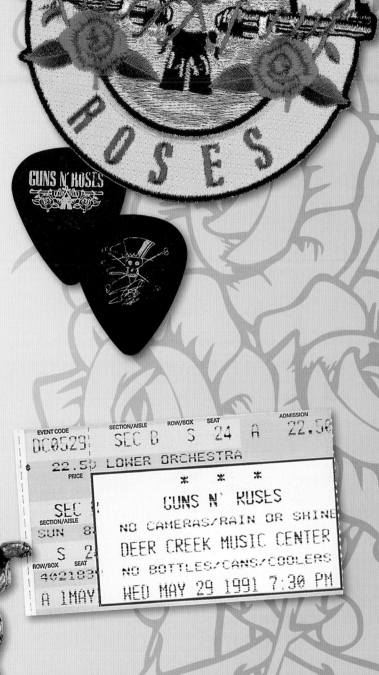

Facing page: Slash performing with Guns N' Roses in 1987. © *Christopher Lee Helton/Retna Ltd.*

Slash with his collection. The Kris Derrig replica is in the first row, to the immediate left of Slash. *Rick Gould*

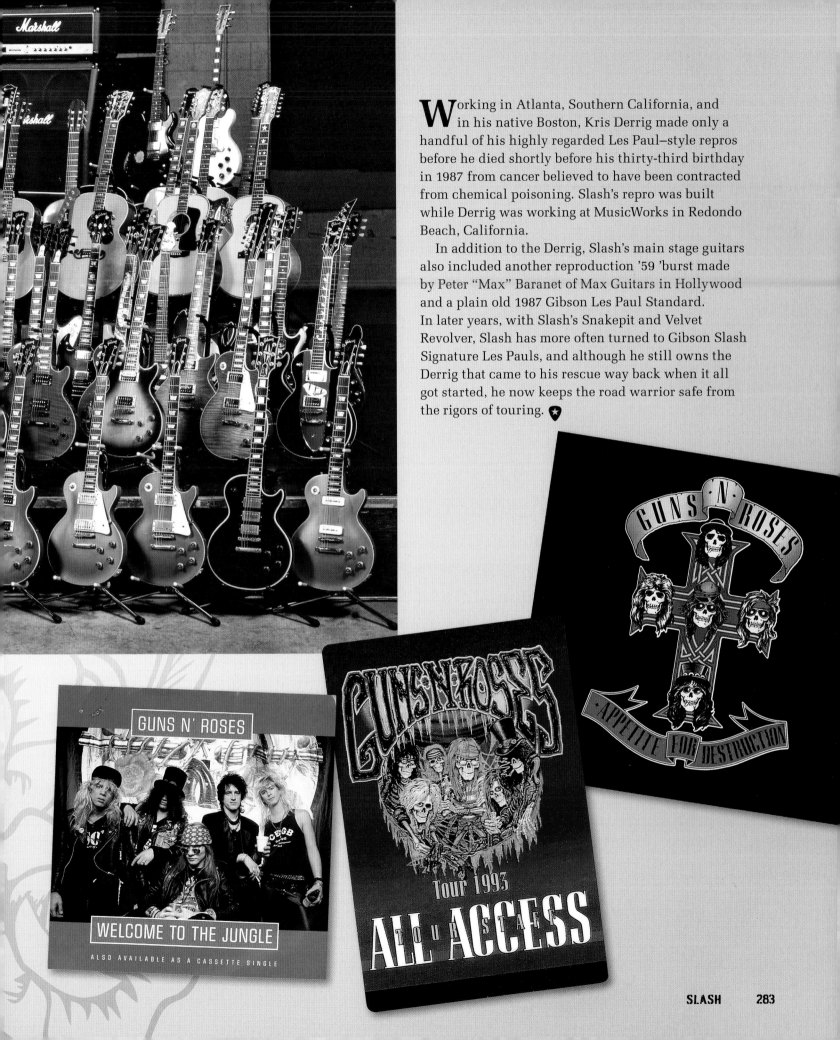

Working in Atlanta, Southern California, and in his native Boston, Kris Derrig made only a handful of his highly regarded Les Paul–style repros before he died shortly before his thirty-third birthday in 1987 from cancer believed to have been contracted from chemical poisoning. Slash's repro was built while Derrig was working at MusicWorks in Redondo Beach, California.

In addition to the Derrig, Slash's main stage guitars also included another reproduction '59 'burst made by Peter "Max" Baranet of Max Guitars in Hollywood and a plain old 1987 Gibson Les Paul Standard. In later years, with Slash's Snakepit and Velvet Revolver, Slash has more often turned to Gibson Slash Signature Les Pauls, and although he still owns the Derrig that came to his rescue way back when it all got started, he now keeps the road warrior safe from the rigors of touring. ★

BRUCE SPRINGSTEEN

1950s FENDER ESQUIRE

ONE OF THE MOST recognizable guitars in all of rock music, thanks largely to its appearance on the covers of the *Born to Run*, *Live 1975–85*, *Human Touch*, and *Greatest Hits* albums, Bruce Springsteen's Fender Esquire has often been sited by techs and The Boss himself as a 1953 or '54 model, and most fans have been happy to leave it at that. Closer examination of this hallowed instrument, however, shows that there might be a little more going on under the hood.

In live concert footage from the mid-'70s, Springsteen states that he purchased the guitar in the early '70s from New Jersey–based luthier Phil Petillo, who also cared for the instrument in the early days of Springsteen's ownership. Other reports indicate that Petillo purchased the Esquire at a liquidation sale for a New York recording studio and that the guitar was already somewhat modified when he acquired it, most notably having had a considerable amount of wood routed from beneath the pickguard to accommodate extra pickups, in addition to the previously unused factory route for the neck pickup (the star's Esquire outwardly has the look of a Telecaster anyway, thanks to the added pickup in the neck position). The instrument's heavily-worn Butterscotch Blonde finish and black pickguard uphold the 1953–1954 estimate, but the headstock wears a butterfly string guide for the B and E strings positioned roughly in line with the A string tuner post; the butterfly guide didn't replace the earlier round guide (which was more distant from the nut) until mid-1956, a change accompanied by a move of the logo decal to the far side of this guide. Myriad interviews also indicate that the neck has the soft *V* profile that came back into fashion at Fender in late '55 and remained largely through '57 (early '50–'51 necks were also *V*'d, or "boat necks," but were thicker overall). All of these indicators point to a neck made after 1954, and the possibility that the entire instrument is actually a 1956 or 1957 whiteguard Esquire with a swapped-in blackguard.

Other later modifications are beyond speculation. The Esquire already has replacement tuners in the *Born to Run* photo, although it still wears a three-saddle '50s bridge with a stamped-steel base plate. Sometime later, it received a titanium six-saddle bridge from Petillo, along with a set of the luthier's own patented Petillo Precision Frets, a fret wire with an inverted *V* crown for precise intonation. Not so easy to detect is the fact that Petillo also added hot rewound single-coil pickups, which the guitar retains to this day.

Ultimately, the fine points matter not. These were "Erector Set" guitars to begin with, and whatever kind of mutt of an instrument the thing had become by the time it landed in Springsteen's hands, it has been the driving force behind some of the most compelling rock anthems from the mid-1970s on. One listen to the searing solos from "Prove It All Night" or "Candy's Room" render the details moot. ✦

Facing page: Bruce Springsteen in 1980 with his working-man's guitar, his famed 1950s Fender Esquire. *Michael Ochs Archives/Getty Images*

Strummer and the Mescaleros, Shoreline Amphitheater, Mountain View, California, July 5, 2002. *Tim Mosenfelder/Getty Images*

THE PUNK ROCK MOVEMENT of the late
'70s embodied the ultimate anti-hero stance,
and the last thing any self-respecting punk
wanted to get caught doing was worshiping his
guitar. However much his band The Clash pushed
the boundaries of the genre, though—in sonics,
stance, and attitude—Joe Strummer couldn't help
but be enamored with his 1966 Fender Telecaster.
No, he never coddled the guitar—as evidenced by
his slipshod modifications and rough treatment of
the instrument—but he certainly *respected* it, and
he turned to this Tele far more than any other guitar
through the course of his entire career.

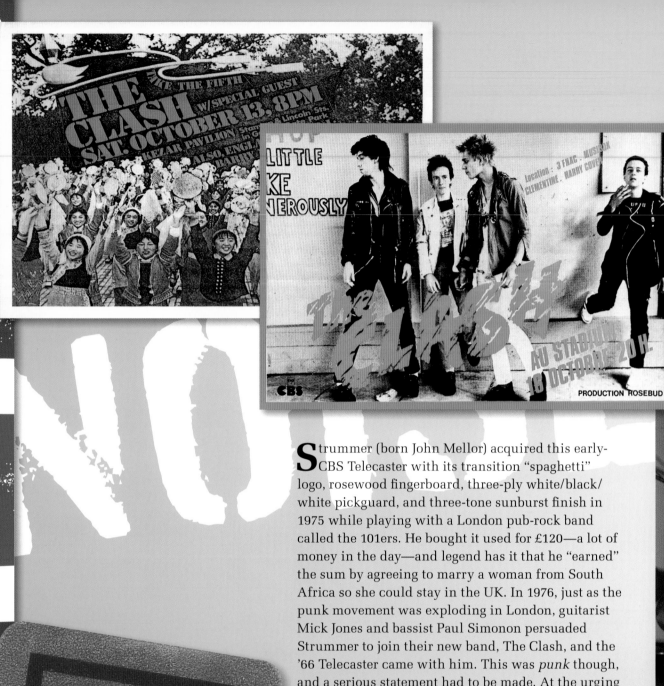

Strummer (born John Mellor) acquired this early-CBS Telecaster with its transition "spaghetti" logo, rosewood fingerboard, three-ply white/black/white pickguard, and three-tone sunburst finish in 1975 while playing with a London pub-rock band called the 101ers. He bought it used for £120—a lot of money in the day—and legend has it that he "earned" the sum by agreeing to marry a woman from South Africa so she could stay in the UK. In 1976, just as the punk movement was exploding in London, guitarist Mick Jones and bassist Paul Simonon persuaded Strummer to join their new band, The Clash, and the '66 Telecaster came with him. This was *punk* though, and a serious statement had to be made. At the urging of the band's manager, Strummer and company took a selection of gear to a friend's body shop, where the guitar's sunburst finish—a custom color option, now highly prized among collectors—was shot with a coat of gray primer and, finally, a thick coat of jet black paint. Strummer stenciled on the word "NOISE" in white and added the first of an evolving number of stickers to the front, this one reading "Ignore Alien Orders." With these overt statements of disrespect duly made, a punk legend was born.

Although he owned backup guitars, Strummer used the '66 Tele on the vast majority of his work with The Clash and on much of his solo work in the years that followed. The instrument is equally

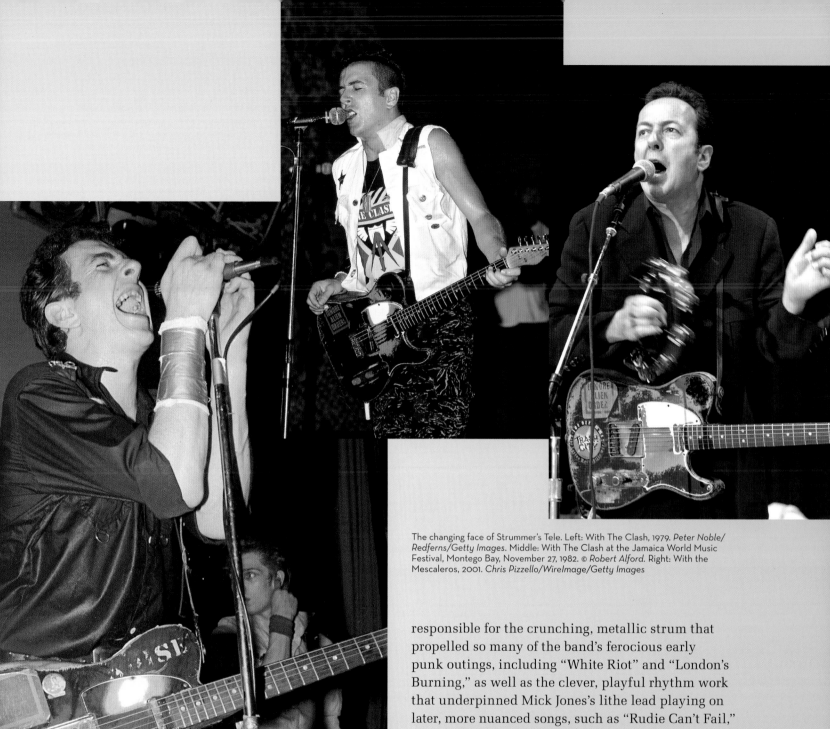

The changing face of Strummer's Tele. Left: With The Clash, 1979. *Peter Noble/ Redferns/Getty Images*. Middle: With The Clash at the Jamaica World Music Festival, Montego Bay, November 27, 1982. © *Robert Alford*. Right: With the Mescaleros, 2001. *Chris Pizzello/WireImage/Getty Images*

responsible for the crunching, metallic strum that propelled so many of the band's ferocious early punk outings, including "White Riot" and "London's Burning," as well as the clever, playful rhythm work that underpinned Mick Jones's lithe lead playing on later, more nuanced songs, such as "Rudie Can't Fail," "Spanish Bombs," and "Lost in the Supermarket." Strummer played the Telecaster so hard that much of the black overspray was worn down to the gray undercoat and even to glimpses of the original sunburst finish in places. Strummer took the faithful '66 Tele with him on the road again in late 2001 and 2002 before dying of a congenital heart defect in December of that year at the age of fifty. The guitar is believed to be in the possession of Strummer's family in England. In 2007, Fender released their Joe Strummer Telecaster, complete with worn gray/black finish and a selection of decals and stencils. ✪

OVER THE PAST FIFTY YEARS, the Chicago blues has evolved into something of a multinational brand propelling everything from radio hits to TV commercials. You can earn a college degree learning how to play it, and on any Saturday night find a corner bar in just about any town in America where some hot young gun is cranking out an entirely competent, if often overheated, approximation of "the sound." Amid all this emulation, the real deal could be heard in the playing of Hubert Sumlin, Howlin' Wolf's lead guitarist for twenty-five years.

The Howlin' Wolf Band in action at Sylvio's nightclub in Chicago, circa 1961. Hubert Sumlin intently comps on his Gibson Les Paul. *Raeburn Flerlage/Photofest*

Born in Greenwood, Mississipi, in 1931, and raised just across the Mississippi River in Hughes, Arkansas, Sumlin first saw Howlin' Wolf perform in West Memphis as a young boy of just eleven or twelve years. At fourteen, Sumlin left home to pursue his love of the guitar, played with his contemporary and future blues-harp legend James Cotton in West Memphis for a time, and in the early '50s moved to Chicago to become Wolf's guitarist and musical right-hand man until the great blues shouter's death in 1976.

Although he played other guitars on occasion, Sumlin was best associated with the Gibson Les Paul goldtop. Sumlin reported that Wolf gave him his first Les Paul, a goldtop with wraparound bridge and P-90 pickups, in the mid-'50s. After that one was stolen, Sumlin bought himself another, very likely the circa-1956 Les Paul goldtop with P-90s and Tune-O-Matic bridge that he is documented as having played later in his career.

As one of the great originators of Chicago blues, Sumlin was an influential force on the British blues-rock boom of the mid-1960s, but his playing, more so than the music of many other Chicago greats, revealed the Delta and rural blues roots of the Chicago blues. As a result, Sumlin's sound and technique were arguably more unique, and even more timeless.

Sumlin attributed one of the critical elements of his playing style, his frequent use of fingertips in place of a pick, to Howlin' Wolf himself. Legend has it that Wolf forbade Sumlin to use a pick for a time during the early years, because his playing was so nimble that the resultant guitar frenzy crashed all over the vocals (and a young man from Arkansas wasn't likely to argue with the formidable Wolf). Examine, as cases in point, the relentlessly snaky fills in "Goin' Down Slow"; the funky, syncopated riffs behind "Three Hundred Pounds of Joy"; the pinched, playful leads that punctuate "Shake for Me"; and, of course, the legendary licks behind seminal tunes like "Smokestack Lightning," "Wang Dang Doodle," and "Killing Floor," all of which brilliantly exhibit both Sumlin's own inimitable style and the thick, gritty bite of his P-90-equipped Les Paul. ✪

Hubert Sumlin in 2007—still playing a Gibson Les Paul goldtop—performing at the Guitar Center King of the Blues show. *Robert Knight Archive/ Redferns/Getty Images*

Andy Summers with the Police,
CNE Stadium, August 1983. © Robert Alford

THE POLICE

GIVEN HIS BACKGROUND IN JAZZ, fusion, classical, and psychedelia, Andy Summers might have seemed an odd choice as third man in a British "punk" trio that formed in 1977. He had already played with Eric Burdon and the New Animals, Soft Machine, Zoot Money and the Big Roll Band, Kevin Coyne, Kevin Ayers, and Tim Rose,

toured the US with major acts, and found time to earn a BA in music from California State University, Northridge, in the early '70s. But there was something about this outfit—bassist/vocalist Stewart "Sting" Sumner and drummer Stewart Copeland—that promised more than just the rudimentary power-chord romps that punk had embodied thus far, something that might just give Summers's eclectic, ethereal playing style room to breathe. Summers's hunch proved right, and the Police's blend of punk energy, psychedelic sonic explorations, and reggae-fusion rhythms proved not only the perfect foil for his diverse explorations, but extremely popular to the world at large, taking the guitarist to the top of his field in the process.

Through it all, Summers played a beaten vintage Telecaster that, seemingly against all odds, turned out to be the perfect guitar for this broad tonal palette. Summers bought the sunburst 1961 Telecaster Custom with maple neck from one of his guitar students for $200 in the early '70s while teaching in California to subsidize his studies. "There is a certain magic in life," he told Michael Molenda in *Guitar Player* in 2007. "It was destiny that brought that guitar to me. It was a great guitar to play, and it had a wide range of tonal colors—from a typical clean Tele sound to a thick and creamy humbucker tone . . . and it sparked something that really came together when I joined a band with these two other guys. That Tele was the main guitar for almost everything the Police did."

The guitar already had extensive modifications, including the addition of a Gibson PAF humbucker in the neck position (replaced by a Seymour Duncan after it failed on tour), a phase-reverse switch on the control plate, another switch above the control plate (and a volume control below it) that governed a preamp/overdrive unit mounted in the back of the guitar, and a brass replacement bridge with six individual saddles. The original single-coil bridge pickup was mounted into the ash body of the guitar rather than suspended from the bridge plate, and, perhaps the biggest alteration of all, the maple neck was clearly not original to the guitar, which would have been born with a "slab board" rosewood neck in '61. Bearing the "Telecaster" model name rather than the "Telecaster Custom" that the bound, sunburst body indicates, it was clearly taken from a '50s Tele

and updated with Schaller tuners and an extra string guide for the G and D strings.

In addition to the Telecaster, Summers's tones were supplemented by a wide range of effects units, which expanded from the famous Boss Chorus Ensemble–infused riff of "Message in a Bottle" to include a Maestro Echoplex, a Mutron III envelope filter, and several fuzz, overdrive, and phaser units, all controlled via a Pete Cornish pedal board in the original era of the Police, and a Bradshaw floor unit in recent years. ✪

FIRST PETER GREEN'S REPLACEMENT in John Mayall's Blues Breakers, then Brian Jones's replacement in the Rolling Stones, Mick Taylor was a gifted blues guitarist in his own right—in some ways more of a purist, in that regard, than the more famous guitarists in whose footsteps he followed—and was also another prime arbiter of classic Les Paul tone.

We have already visited Taylor's acquisition of the "Keith Burst" in Keith Richards's artist profile, but this is only one of the famous original 'bursts played by Taylor throughout his career. (Amid ongoing confusion over which of these guitars was which, given that Taylor and Richards later shared their Les Pauls somewhat indiscriminately in the studio and on tour during 1969–1972, I'm basing much of the detail on the assessment of the "Keith Burst" as a '59 by London guitar dealer Richard Henry, the last vintage-guitar authority to have examined the instrument closely before it passed into private hands.) Taylor took his own previous 'burst to the Mayall gig with him in 1966 at the tender age of seventeen, using it to record the Blues Breakers album *Crusade* before it was stolen. He replaced that guitar with the Les Paul purchased from Richards. Other genuine 'bursts would also grace the Taylor arsenal, although he has turned more to reissues and reproductions in later years, having sold off his original late-'50s Les Pauls.

Mick Taylor was born in Welwyn Garden City in central England and raised in Hatfield, a town in the county of Hertfordshire, just north of London. He became proficient on the guitar at an early age and was gigging with schoolmate bands while still in his mid-teens. A full year before joining the Blues Breakers as Peter Green's replacement, he sat in with Mayall's band for a full set at a show in Welwyn Garden City after seeing that Eric Clapton hadn't shown up for the gig and duly convincing the band's leader that he was up to the task. Thus began Taylor's career as premier journeyman guitarist, an adventure that would land him gigs with Jack Bruce, Mike Oldfield, Bob Dylan, and several others, in addition to his prolific solo work. He continues to be far and away best remembered, though, for his time as a Rolling Stone—the most enduring image of which is, perhaps, the young Taylor, still just twenty-one years old, striding out onto the stage with Les Paul in hand, blond locks flowing, before a crowd of a quarter of a million people in Hyde Park, London, just weeks after joining the band.

Taylor left the Stones in 1974, disgruntled over his treatment at the hands of Richards and the lack of credit given for his songwriting contributions. Many fans and critics say his departure marked the end of the most musically accomplished phase of the band's existence. ★

Above: In more recent years, Taylor has stepped out with reissues, having sold off his original late-'50s Les Pauls. In 2012 he sat in on select shows on the Stones' 50 & Counting Tour. Here, Woody and Keef seem to approve. *Kevin Mazur/WireImage/Getty Images*

Facing page: An early shot of Taylor (performing with Gods) and his Bigsby-equipped 'burst at the Starlight Ballroom, Sudbury, England, 1966. *Michael Putland/Getty Images*

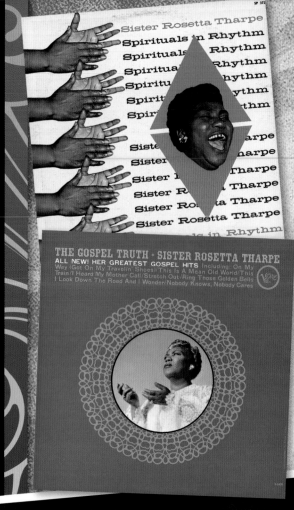

GOSPEL HAS A LONG HISTORY of influencing the blues, but rarely does it have such a direct connection as in the music of Sister Rosetta Tharpe. Blending a gospel diva's spirituality with a blues shouter's power and presence, Tharpe played a number of interesting guitars in her day—a single-cone National resonator, and a Gibson Super 400 and ES-330—but is most associated with an early-'60s Gibson Les Paul/ SG custom, a radical new design of its day (and a rock icon after) that is notable to many, as much as anything, for its seemingly odd juxtaposition in the hands of this good, churchgoing woman.

Just watch her turn loose on any of the several rockin' numbers captured for posterity on film, however, and the match makes perfect sense. Smashing all preconceptions to smithereens with the first licks to leap from her thumb pick, Tharpe rocks that radical, solid-body electric guitar without ever straying into the secular and offers a one-woman embodiment of diversity personified that it behooves every guitarist to dip into. Among many standout moments is an early-1960s TV performance of "Down by the Riverside." Tharpe's intentionally staccato, almost stilted instrumental introduction to the tune might lead the skeptical to snidely conclude she has strayed dangerously into actually playing her shiny white prop, but by the time she blows the roof off the chapel with a rousing solo midflight, peppered with frenetic rolls and driving bluesy double-stops, there can be few unbelievers left in the congregation.

Holding her Gibson Les Paul goldtop, Sister Rosetta Tharpe prays while she plays at a concert in Cardiff, Wales, during her 1957 tour of Great Britain. *Chris Ware/Keystone Features/Getty Images*

When Gibson transported the Les Paul Standard model name over to its pointy new double-cutaway guitar in 1961 (the instrument that would soon and forever after be known as the SG), it also gave the Les Paul Custom logo to the upgraded, three-pickup rendition of the same. Rather than stick with the "Black Beauty" vibe that single-cutaway Customs had maintained from their introduction in 1955 until their deletion at the end of 1960, however, Kalamazoo updated the model further with an eye-catching Arctic White finish, a look that stood out better on the black-and-white TV programs of the day. The 1961–1963 Les Paul Custom retained the ebony fingerboard, block position markers, and gold-plated hardware of the company's top-of-the-line solid-body, but also adopted the quirky "sideways" Vibrola unit that would soon be abandoned. With their thinner, solid mahogany bodies and ultra-slim necks, these "Les Pauls" have a little more snap than their predecessors but still have plenty of bite and grind thanks to the PAF humbucking pickups (or so-called "patent-number" humbuckers, toward the end of the run) that work their magic on the early-'60s Les Paul/SG Standards and Customs. Check out any of Sister Tharpe's work from the early '60s and you get a taste of the unadorned tone of these instruments, usually heard played straight through a matching Gibson tube combo of the same era. ★

Playing her Gibson L-5, Sister Rosetta Tharpe hits a joyful note at Cafe Society Downtown in New York City in December 1940. *Charles Peterson/Hulton Archive/Getty Images*

WHENEVER HE WAS ACCUSED of being a "punk originator," Johnny Thunders scoffed at the tag. Iggy was punk, the Ramones were punk, but Thunders (born John Anthony Genzale Jr.) was rock 'n' roll. That said, it's hard not to credit his band, the New York Dolls, and their unhinged early-'70s recordings and performances as pacesetters for a scene that was ultimately claimed more vociferously by the Sex Pistols and The Clash on the other side of the pond several years later. As for Thunders, he was just making the music the way he made it: hard, raw, driving, and four-to-the-floor. And there was no better guitar to make it on than a Gibson Les Paul Junior.

Loud as a mother . . . Thunders fronting the Heartbreakers, London, 1977.
Erica Echenberg/Redferns/Getty Images

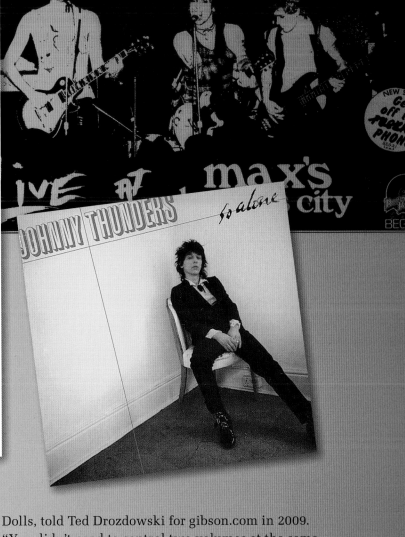

Thunders's Les Paul Junior beside his Country Gentleman on the stage of CBGB. *Roberta Bayley/Redferns/Getty Images*

Or, to be precise, a Les Paul TV Model. Those 1950s Les Paul Juniors or Specials with an off-white "limed mahogany" finish are often described as having a "TV finish," but the TV suffix actually denoted a specific model in itself—the Les Paul TV Model—that was, for all the world, a Junior, but with a light-blonde finish that showed up well on black-and-white TV sets. Introduced in 1955, it was a way to add a little glamour to the entry-level Les Paul Junior, which had arrived the year before in a basic sunburst finish. Both carried just a single P-90 pickup and volume and tone controls, and for years they languished as beginners' guitars and pawnshop prizes until rockers and, yes, punks of the '70s discovered the simple beauty of this solid, no-frills format (and the pocket-friendly price tags they could nab them for). "We called them 'automatic guitars,' like a car with an automatic transmission—easy to use," Sylvain Sylvain, Thunders's fellow guitarist in the New York

Dolls, told Ted Drozdowski for gibson.com in 2009. "You didn't need to control two volumes at the same time. It was the perfect guitar for the New York Dolls because it was stripped down—like the band was and like our songs were."

After a brief flirtation with a mid-'50s Les Paul Junior (two pickups!), Thunders adopted a TV Model with a double-cutaway body, an update applied in '58. He used the guitar through most of his work with the Dolls and, afterward, his own band the Heartbreakers, occasionally picking up other guitars for variety, notably a pair of Lucite-bodied Dan Armstrongs that he also owned.

Like too many rock 'n' roll legends, Thunders descended into drug and alcohol abuse, but he was believed to have been kicking his heroin habit with the help of methadone when he died in a New Orleans hotel room in 1991 amid suspicious circumstances. ◆

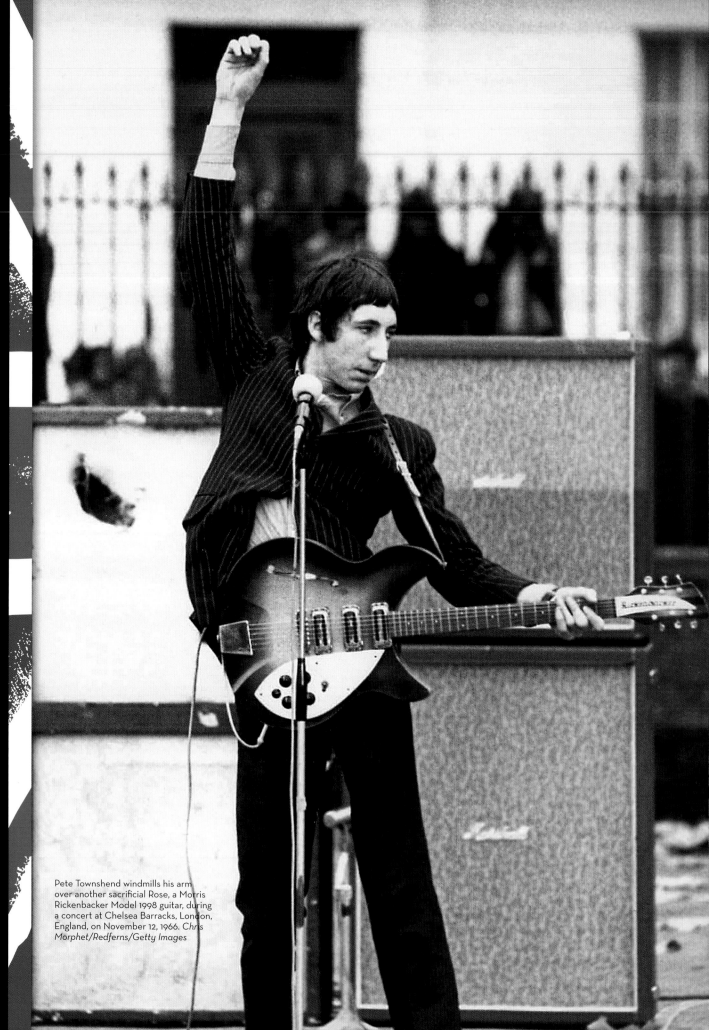

Pete Townshend windmills his arm over another sacrificial Rose, a Morris Rickenbacker Model 1998 guitar, during a concert at Chelsea Barracks, London, England, on November 12, 1966. *Chris Morphet/Redferns/Getty Images*

PETE TOWNSHEND HAS RUN THROUGH a succession of guitars in his days, but the windmilling Who-ster is best associated with the instruments he played—and smashed—so prominently during the band's rise to fame: Rickenbackers . . . a whole wall of Rickenbackers. Excluding a brief stint on an entirely worthy Epiphone Wilshire solid-body that he used with the Detours, a Rickenbacker was Townshend's first electric guitar of any real quality, and the instrument he had in his hands as the Detours evolved into The Who in 1964.

Rickenbacker had really gotten off the ground in the pop world when John Lennon picked up a short-scale 325 in Hamburg in 1960, and, of course, George Harrison embraced the 360/12 twelve-string the same year that Townshend first began using the company's six-strings, but it still seems like this American guitar maker had its export business bubbling along more smoothly and in a shorter period of time than one might have expected. Rickenbacker guitars exported to the UK in the '60s, where they were distributed by Rose-Morris & Company and were treated as entirely different models, with their own export numbers and specs; these are the guitars that Townshend played when he came into the Rick fold. He was primarily seen with dual-pickup 1997 and triple-pickup 1998 models, which were the export equivalents of the domestic 335 and 345, respectively, with a few cosmetic twists. At the request of Rose-Morris's Roy Morris, Rickenbacker made the larger, semi-hollow export versions of the 335, 345, 360, and similar

models with more traditional f-holes instead of the trademark "slash" or scimitar-shaped sound hole of the US models, largely because Morris thought these would have more appeal in the UK. The export Ricks were also given all-black control knobs in place of the silver-insert knobs, and they were more often seen with simple dot position markers rather than the triangular markers used for high-end US models. Most of the models Townshend purchased were supplied with vibrato tailpieces too, but he habitually removed these, preferring a muscular shake of the neck for any vibrato effects required. For all these minor details, the basic designs, woods, and, crucially, "toaster-top" pickups remained the same, and you can hear their characteristic Rickenbacker *clang* on great early Who hits like "My Generation," "I Can't Explain," and "Anyway, Anyhow, Anywhere" (including the use of a 360/12 Export Model twelve-string on the latter two).

Despite his reputation for destroying guitars, Townshend has stated that he only smashed about eight Ricks in total and that he was quite remorseful about the first, an accident: "I started to knock the guitar about a lot, hitting it on the amps to get banging noises and things like that and it had started to crack," he recalled in 2002's *The Who: The Day-By-Day Story*. "It banged against the ceiling and smashed a hole in the plaster. . . . When I brought it out the top of the neck was left behind. I couldn't believe what had happened. . . . So I just got really angry and got what was left of the guitar and smashed it to smithereens. . . . The next day I was miserable about having lost my guitar." ✪

NOT UNLIKE BOTH ERIC CLAPTON and Jeff Beck, British blues-rocker Robin Trower made the leap from playing a Les Paul with Procol Harum from 1967 to 1971 to being a Stratocaster fanatic in his own solo work from 1971 on. What he did with that Strat, though, was quite different from either Beck or Clapton and is perhaps more often associated with the playing and tone of Jimi Hendrix than with his British compatriots. In fact, Trower is a name that frequently came up alongside that of Hendrix in the boutique effects pedal world's Uni-Vibe renaissance of a few years back: if a Uni-Vibe cloner mentioned Hendrix's "Machine Gun" or "Star-Spangled Banner," they were going to name drop Robin Trower's "Bridge of Sighs" in the next breath. For all the Hendrix associations, however—and Trower himself has frequently said that he isn't copying Hendrix, as such, but trying to carry on in his footsteps—it wasn't his admiration for the deceased legend that prompted his switch to the Stratocaster but simply a "feel thing."

As Trower told Steve Rosen in *Guitar Player* magazine in 1974, he was struck by the Strat revelation upon arriving early for a sound check one day in 1971 while Procol Harum was on tour with Jethro Tull. He picked up Tull guitarist Martin Barre's Strat (a guitar that Barre had set up for slide), plugged it in, and yelled, "This is it!" Trower continues: "I then switched to Strat. Up to then, I had been playing Les Pauls. I always felt there was something missing on Les Pauls. They had a good fat sound, but they never had that 'musical' sound. When I played a Strat I realized it had that strident chord." As legendary as the PAF-loaded Les Paul has become, Trower's comments on the "musicality" of the Stratocaster echo the feelings of many other guitarists who have made it their choice through the years and reflect a recognition of the clarity and harmonic depth that Leo's pickups, wood choices, build technique, and the 25.5-inch scale length all bring to the table.

Trower first acquired a black Stratocaster that he would later deem "unplayable," which he demoted to backup status, making a white Strat from around 1973 or 1974—large headstock, bullet truss-rod adjustment, maple fingerboard—his main instrument through much of that decade. The artist dipped into the well-respected Squier JV series Stratocasters in the 1980s and has largely played contemporary Stratocasters since that time. Whichever Strat he straps on, though, he continues to prove that old truism that a true artist will sound like himself whatever gear he chooses to get the job done. That being said, a Fuzz Face, Uni-Vibe, and Vox or Tycobrahe wah-wah (or more recent Fulltone equivalents) all run through a pair of 100-watt Marshall heads might also be part of the equation. The Fender Custom Shop has issued a Robin Trower Stratocaster made to the specs of his favorite 1970s model. ✪

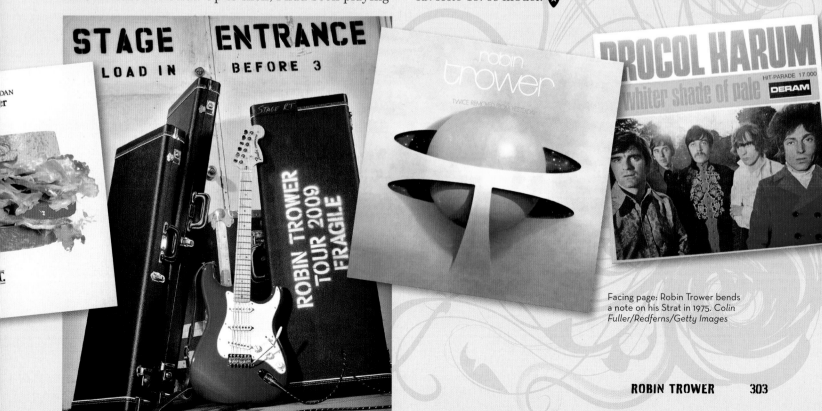

Facing page: Robin Trower bends a note on his Strat in 1975. *Colin Fuller/Redferns/Getty Images*

NIGEL TUFNEL.

NIGEL TUFNEL

ERNIE BALL/MUSIC MAN
"MR. HORSEPOWER"

304

THERE ARE SOME WEIRD and wild creations among the stars' guitars that have attained noteworthy status since the birth of rock 'n' roll, but there's none more rock than this hell-fired hot rod, the Ernie Ball/Music Man "Mr. Horsepower." Born from the twisted imagination of "guitar god" Nigel Tufnel (a.k.a. Christopher Guest, who plays Tufnel in the 1984 movie *This Is Spinal Tap*), this is an instrument with palpable sustain, tangible tone, and, more than anything else, as much satirical splendor as Rob Reiner's rock mockumentary itself. As Tufnel might say, "Don't touch it . . . don't even *look* at it!"

Guest didn't play Mr. Horsepower in the movie, but he devised it years later for Spinal Tap reunions and promotional appearances. The guitar's most prominent appearance was most likely its use at Spinal Tap's 1992 reunion concert at London's Royal Albert Hall, where Guest shreds on the custom creation in front of a red 20-foot Marshall stack (captured on DVD as *A Spinal Tap Reunion: The 25th Anniversary London Sell-Out*). In 2001 Ernie Ball/Music Man produced a limited run of twenty-five exact replicas of the original one-off, and these instruments—which sold for around $5,000 each at the time of their release—have attained collectible status alongside the limited-run and custom-shop signature models of many genuine guitar legends, now fetching upwards of $15,000 on the collector's market.

Housed in the slightly modernistic, offset body of Music Man's Albert Lee signature model,

Mr. Horsepower features eight fully functional pickup coils (an effect created by four humbuckers mounted side by side and sealed with the same continuous wrap of insulating tape); four independent pickup selector switches, each with its own indicator light; a Floyd Rose–style vibrato tailpiece with a rubber-booted four-on-the-floor vibrato arm capped with an eight-ball gearshift knob; quad exhaust pipes; a racer wheel volume knob; a maple neck with position markers that tell you what key you're in; and a fully working tachometer that actually gauges how fast you're playing. As outlandish as it all is, it's *Tap* through and through. In fact, the only real surprise is that the tach doesn't go to 11.

While hard rock and heavy metal were always rather easy targets for satire—often doing the job so well themselves that intervention from the other arts was unnecessary—*This Is Spinal Tap* captured something beyond mere spoof or mockery: a tone that all musicians recognize simultaneously as hilarious and really rather touching. In one fell swoop, in its own overtly self-aggrandizing manner, Mr. Horsepower embodies this same achievement: do we laugh, do we cry, or do we just strap it on and rock? ★

IKE TURNER WAS NOT ONE OF THE KINGS OF RHYTHM, as his longtime band was known. He *was* the king.

Rechristening the band "Jackie Brenston and His Delta Cats" for a session at the Memphis Sun Studios in 1951, he cut "Rocket 88," often tagged as one of the first rock 'n' roll songs. Ever. With Annie Mae Bullock—renamed for the stage as Tina Turner—he launched his Revue, shaking up the 1960s with a rafters-rattling blend of rock, R&B, and soul. Ike's career was often controversial, but throughout his life he made phenomenal music.

Ike was also one of the first—if not *the* first—bluesmen to take up the Strat. Photographs of the Kings of Rhythm dated circa 1955–1956 show Ike armed with an early sunburst Stratocaster. The guitar looks brand spanking new too: it still has the ashtray bridge cover in place and a nice, polished sheen to the body.

With Tina Turner fronting the Kings of Rhythm and Ike Turner playing what became his trademark Sonic Blue Strat, R&B would never be the same again. Here, they perform in Dallas, Texas, in 1962. *Michael Ochs Archives/Getty Images*

I LIKE IKE

From the early days of the Ike and Tina Turner Revue, Ike was toting the Strat that he made famous: a Sonic Blue guitar with rosewood fret board that was believed to date from 1961. He played that guitar and other Strats for the rest of his career.

Ike was born in 1931 in the heart of the Mississippi Delta in the county-seat town of Clarksdale. He was hardened early in life when he witnessed his Baptist minister father beaten and left for dead by a mob of white men. His mother remarried a violent alcoholic, who beat the young boy until Ike knocked him out with a piece of wood and ran away to Memphis. Ike began playing piano and guitar, forming the Kings of Rhythm in high school; he kept the name of the band throughout his career.

Along with playing across the South, Ike became a music scout. He brought B. B. King and Howlin' Wolf to the attention of Sam Phillips at Sun Records, who first recorded them and leased the sides to Bihari brothers' Modern Records in Los Angeles. Ike himself recorded in the 1950s and 1960s for Modern, Chess, Flair, and Mississippi's local label, Trumpet. With the Revue, he graduated to larger labels, including Sue, Blue Thumb, and eventually, United Artists. Together, he and Tina won two Grammys and were nominated for three others.

Ike's personality came through in his guitar sound: a biting tone and a driving sense of rhythm that propelled his band. Like James Brown, he was domineering and demanding of his Kings of Rhythm, not settling for less than music perfection and thrilling showmanship.

Interviewed by writer Dave Rubin in 2006, Ike explained that he started out on piano, learning boogie-woogie rhythms from his early idol, Pinetop Perkins, and always considered himself first and foremost a piano player: "B. B. King says I'm not a guitar player, and he's right. I just do tricks. I started playing because I couldn't get my guitar players to do what I wanted. Also, I can lead the band better when I'm not confined to the piano. I don't want to holler across the stage if somebody is out of tune. . . . I always had trouble with drummers, so I mostly played rhythm the way a drummer plays a high hat. That way I could hold the tempo down or pick it up."

Playing that Sonic Blue Strat, Ike would intermix chords, riffs, and bass lines, much like a piano player.

As Ike's then-guitarist in the Kings of Rhythm, Seth Blumberg, detailed, "His life is the rhythm—that's why his band is called the Kings of Rhythm. He plays with his left-hand thumb hooked over the neck laying down the rhythm, and he rarely plays upstrokes. A lot of the time, he doesn't even play chords; he's just shucking the rhythm on the muted strings. He has a great knack for what he calls 'marrying the rhythm,' where he'll decide how to accent the beat while the drummer is really driving… . Ike's all about energy, and he says, 'I don't wanna hear that mama-papa two and four. It makes me tired. You got to lay it down, man. Don't step around it—you got to step *in* it.'"
—*Michael Dregni* ✪

AMID THE VINTAGE SHOWPIECES and collector drool-fests that most top artists' instruments represent, the guitar with which Edward Van Halen launched himself to fame in the late '70s is a rare junkyard dog. Up close, the instrument looks almost unplayable, like something a kid cobbled together out of unwanted parts (which is essentially what it was), the kind of guitar that would get plenty of players laughed off stage. In Van Halen's hands, however, it sparked a revolution of stratospheric proportions.

Eddie Van Halen with his home-brewed Frankenstrat in its earliest black-and-white paint job, with Gibson PAF humbucker pickup, full pickguard, and repurposed Fender neck. *Jon Sievert/Michael Ochs Archives/Getty Images*

Facing page: Eddie Van Halen jumps with his tri-color modified Frankenstrat in 1982. *John Livzey/Redferns/Getty Images*

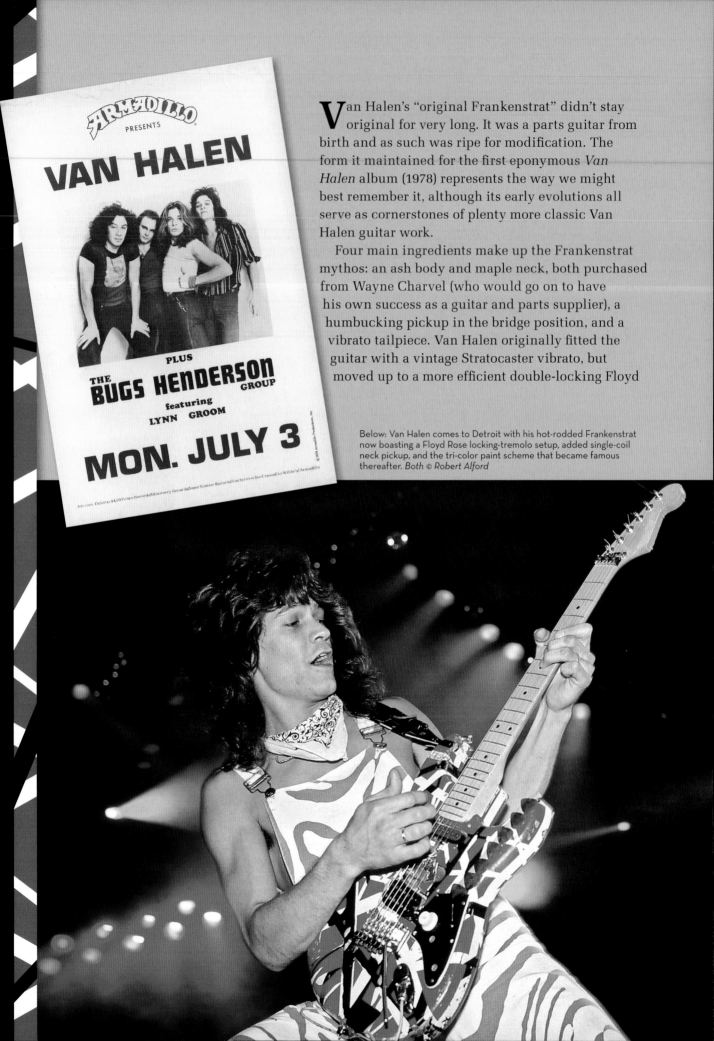

Van Halen's "original Frankenstrat" didn't stay original for very long. It was a parts guitar from birth and as such was ripe for modification. The form it maintained for the first eponymous *Van Halen* album (1978) represents the way we might best remember it, although its early evolutions all serve as cornerstones of plenty more classic Van Halen guitar work.

Four main ingredients make up the Frankenstrat mythos: an ash body and maple neck, both purchased from Wayne Charvel (who would go on to have his own success as a guitar and parts supplier), a humbucking pickup in the bridge position, and a vibrato tailpiece. Van Halen originally fitted the guitar with a vintage Stratocaster vibrato, but moved up to a more efficient double-locking Floyd

Below: Van Halen comes to Detroit with his hot-rodded Frankenstrat now boasting a Floyd Rose locking-tremolo setup, added single-coil neck pickup, and the tri-color paint scheme that became famous thereafter. *Both © Robert Alford*

Rose system shortly after they became available in 1977. This piece of hardware became a major part of his dramatic playing style. The pickup was an original Gibson PAF humbucker taken from a vintage ES-335 that purportedly had a short in one coil, so Van Halen—ever the DIY'er—proceeded to rewind it himself. (Some renditions of the Frankenstrat legend claim that Seymour Duncan rewound this pickup for Van Halen, while the artist has often stated that he did it himself.) Since he had no means of accurately counting the turns of wire around the coil, the pair came out unbalanced, a feature that is often credited with contributing to the bright, lively sound of this humbucker (which would have sounded brighter anyway in the 25.5-inch scale-length Strat-style guitar than in a 24.75-inch Gibson). Finally, Van Halen potted the pickup by dipping it in a paraffin bath to seal the coils and to fend off microphonic howl at high volumes.

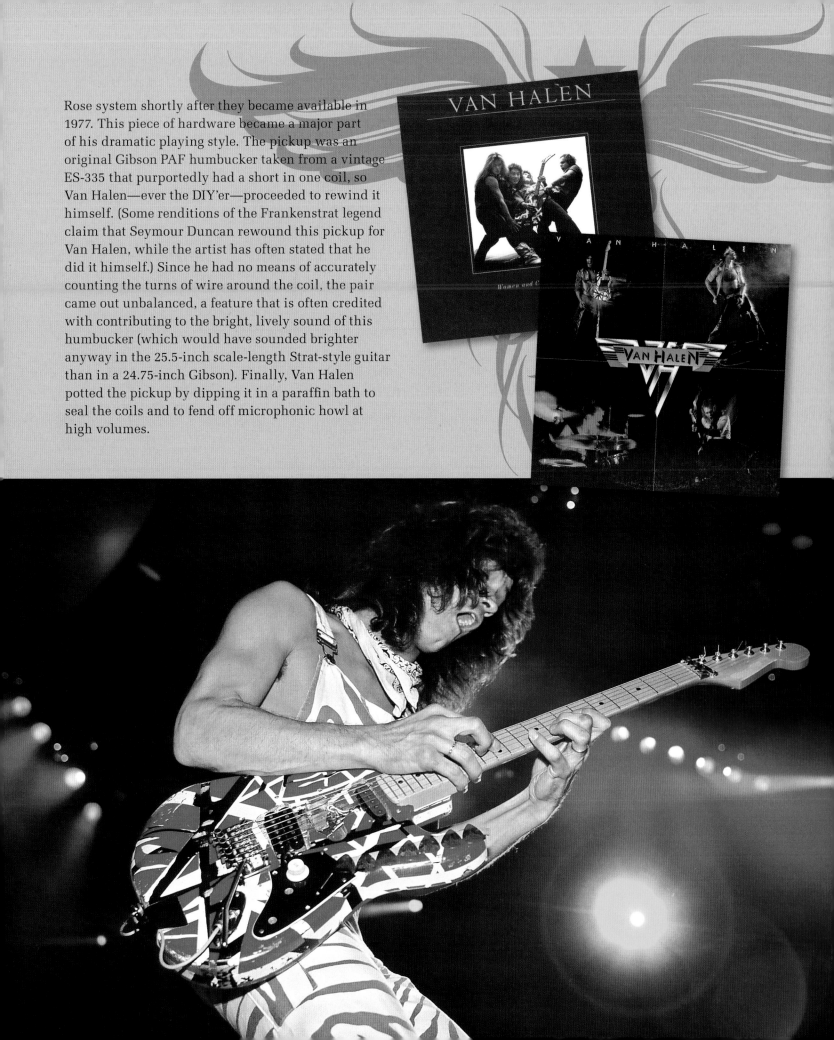

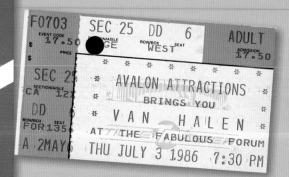

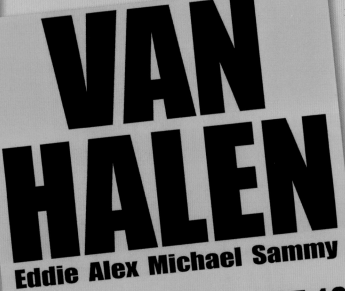

To the casual viewer, however, the Frankenstrat's most noticeable feature is its homespun striped paint job. The original white-with-black-stripes rendition was achieved by painting the entire guitar body black, then taping it up with semi-random pieces of masking tape and painting it again in white, creating a striped effect when the tape was removed. In 1979 Van Halen taped the body again in a different pattern and repainted it red, leaving the effect of black-and-white stripes on a red body.

As ramshackle as the instrument might have looked, it possessed an inversely glorious tone for powerful rock lead work, as evidenced by several cuts from the debut *Van Halen* album. The first single from this set, a bombastic cover of the Kinks' "You Really Got Me," thrust this new voice in rock upon a nationwide audience, and the follow-ups, "Runnin' with the Devil" and "Jamie's Cryin'," quickly cemented Van Halen's newfound guitar god status, although the short instrumental "Eruption" probably best shows off Edward's and Frankenstrat's capabilities. ♠

Eddie Van Halen in 1984 with the replica of his single-pickup Frankenstrat that he built in the Kramer factory and christened "5150." *John Livzey/Redferns/Getty Images*

HE REALLY WAS THE REASON WHY I started to play, watching him and seeing what could be done," so said Stevie Ray Vaughan of his big brother, Jimmie. What more really need be said?

Jimmie Lawrence Vaughan was born in March 1951 in Oak Cliff, Texas—T-Bone Walker's old stomping ground, on the edge of Dallas. As he himself relates, Vaughan "was weaned on classic Top 40 radio [which was invented in Dallas], vintage blues, early rock 'n' roll, and the deepest rhythm and blues and coolest jazz of the day, thanks to the sound of Dallas's AM radio powerhouse KNOX and border radio stations like XERB, where personalities like the legendary Wolfman Jack sparked a youth revolution. I never got over that stuff, and I never will."

Sidelined by a football injury when he was thirteen, a family friend gave Jimmie a guitar to occupy his time during his recuperation. From the moment his fingers touched the strings, he proved himself a natural talent. As his mother, Martha Vaughan remembered, "It was like he played it all his life."

Jimmie launched his first band, the Swinging Pendulums, at fifteen and was soon playing Dallas clubs several nights a week. A year later, he joined one of Dallas's top local bands, the Chessmen, which opened shows for Jimi Hendrix. Hearing Muddy

Left: Jimmie Vaughan Tex-Mex Olympic White Stratocaster. *Fender Musical Instruments Corporation*

Facing page: Vaughan and one of his well-used Strats at the New Orleans Jazz & Heritage Festival, May 1995. *Clayton Call/Redferns/Getty Images*

Waters and Freddie King play, Jimmie focused on the blues, founding the band Texas Storm in 1969.

In 1974, Jimmie formed the Fabulous Thunderbirds in Austin with singer and harpist Kim Wilson, drummer Mike Buck, and bassist Keith Ferguson. They released their debut album in 1979, *Girls Go Wild*, with a tough blues sound tempered by 1950s rock 'n' roll. With the 1986 *Tuff Enuff*, the title track single, and followup single "Wrap It Up," the Fab Thunderbirds found a widespread, national audience. The album became a Top 40 hit, peaking at No. 10 on the *Billboard* charts.

Shortly after, Jimmie left the 'Birds to play in a duet with his kid brother, which came to a halt following Stevie Ray's death in 1990. The duet album *Family Style* arrived shortly after. Ever since, Jimmie has remained a solo artist.

Jimmie is famed for taste. He's never needed a virtuosic volley of notes to make a statement, relied on effects to find his voice, or hidden behind razzle-dazzle. Instead, he often says his piece with the perfect double stop played with the perfect tone.

He's made music on many guitars, but his well-traveled, beat-up '62 Olympic White Strat has long been his trademark instrument. That Stratocaster has had much surgery with a maple-fretboard neck and plenty of other changes to keep it alive after all its years on the road.

The Jimmie Vaughan sound is a Strat through a Fender narrow-panel tweed Bassman. As Jimmie says, "You can get that sound through a Matchless and several different amps, but it's really basically all the same amp from my perspective—they all came from a Bassman. I mean there's always an exception, but for the most part, a Bassman it is. Tell me what's better than that? I don't know what is." ♦

—*Michael Dregni*

Family photo, 1990: brothers Jimmie and Stevie Ray Vaughan with "Number One."
Robert Knight Archive/Redferns/Getty Images

316

FEW PLAYERS HAVE DONE as much to establish the Fender Stratocaster as *the* American blues machine as Stevie Ray Vaughan. Vaughan was devoted to the Strat, and he owned and played several, but the name he gave his favorite of the bunch—"Number One"—really said it all. Vaughan spent more time on this heavily beaten early '60s Strat than on any of the others in his collection. Today, it's the guitar most associated with the late blues hero. Although Vaughan referred to the guitar as a '59 Strat, and it did have '59 pickups on it, the body and neck both carried date stamps from 1962, so it appears it originated from that year, although by the end of the star's ownership of the instrument it had really transmogrified into something of a Parts-O-Caster.

Stevie Ray Vaughan's ace guitar tech, René Martinez, repairs "Number One" in October 1989 in Columbus, Ohio. He was cleaning the bridge saddles with a Dremel Tool grinder and putting plastic sleeves on the strings to protect them from breaking at the saddles during Vaughan's aggressive picking attack. Famed guitar tech Dan Erlwine is in the photo at far right. *Brian Blauser/bandbstudios.com*

Stevie Ray Vaughan "plays" his 1962 Fender Stratocaster "Number One" at the Keystone Berkeley on August 19, 1983. *Clayton Call/Getty Images*

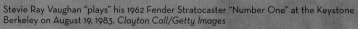

Vaughan bought his '62 Strat at Hennig's Heart of Texas Music Store in Austin, Texas, in the mid-1970s, and it possessed a certain magic for him right up until his death in a helicopter crash on August 26, 1990. Store proprietor Ray Hennig, who knew Vaughan as a regular customer, told music writers Joe Nick Patoski and Bill Crawford, "He lived for that guitar. He told me it was the only guitar he ever had that said what he wanted it to say." As much as Number One meant to him, Vaughan nevertheless set about modifying it to his specific requirements almost immediately. The most visible customizations included the reflective "Custom" and "SRV" stickers he added behind the vibrato bridge and on the replacement black pickguard, respectively, but several other alterations had more to do with the feel and playability of the instrument. The addition of a left-handed vibrato unit in the early '80s is accounted for by two stories, one being that it was the only replacement available in Texas when the original broke, the other that it helped the guitar mirror the upside-down, right-handed Strats of hero Jimi Hendrix (there's nothing stopping both from being true). Vaughan also had the original frets replaced with jumbo frets, and in fact the neck would be refretted several times over the years—to the extent that, toward 1990, it just couldn't take another refret and was replaced with the original neck from another '62 Strat known as "Red." Also in 1990, Number One was given a whole new set of gold-plated hardware.

Details aside, Number One is really best known for the huge tone Vaughan wrangled from it, which was aided, of course, by a set of pre-CBS pickups that seemed to have been wound slightly on the hot side and the artist's preference for heavy .013–.058 strings, but mostly by a muscular left hand and a ferocious right-hand attack. ♦

STEVIE RAY VAUGHAN AND DOUBLE TROUBLE

JEFF BECK WITH TERRY BOZZIO AND TONY HYMAS

THE FIRE MEETS THE FURY

SPECIAL LIMITED EDITION

1989 TOUR SAMPLER

ESK 1901 © 1989 CBS RECORDS INC.

JEFF BECK WITH TERRY BOZZIO AND TONY HYMAS

STEVIE RAY VAUGHAN AND DOUBLE TROUBLE

STRATOCASTER "LENNY"

Stevie Ray Vaughan's 1960s
Fender Stratocaster "Lenny."
*Collection Guitar Center/Photo
Robert Knight Archive/Redferns/
Getty Images*

IF HE WASN'T PLAYING NUMBER ONE, odds are Vaughan was playing "Lenny," a Stratocaster he first saw in an Austin pawn shop in 1980. He was unable to afford its $350 price tag at the time, but the guitar was later given to him as a birthday present by his wife Lenora and six other friends who all chipped in $50 each. Named in tribute of Lenora, Lenny was an early '60s Strat that carried its original rosewood fingerboard, pre-CBS pickups, and a three-ply white scratchplate—which is not to say the guitar hadn't been modified in other ways. The body had been stripped and stained a rich brown color, and a scrolled Victorian mandolin-style inlay had been added beneath the vibrato bridge, which itself was a contemporary replacement unit with diecast saddles. Vaughan further modified the guitar to suit his needs. First he added the customary reflective "SRV" stickers to the pickguard then later swapped the original neck for a modern all-maple unit given to him by Billy F Gibbons of ZZ Top. Vaughan pressed Lenny into service most notably on the songs "Lenny" from *Texas Flood* and "Riviera Paradise" from *In Step*. When performing the former tribute tune live, he would invariably put down Number One and strap on Lenny, a guitar to which he understandably felt a close bond.

Number One is now in the hands of Stevie's brother, Jimmie Vaughan, while Lenny was sold to Guitar Center for $623,500 in Eric Clapton's 2004 Crossroads Guitar Auction. ♦

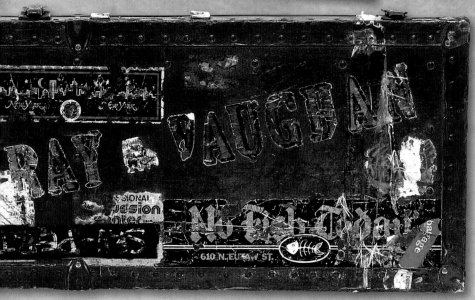

Redd Volkaert's 1951 Nocaster.
Courtesy Redd Volkaert

MAYBE IT'S SOME FORM OF ARTISTIC KARMA, the universe sending out the tools that our gifted music makers most need, but Redd Volkaert, like so many other great Telecaster players, virtually fell into his first Esquire through a rather poetic repayment of a debt owed. "The first one I got," he told the author, "was actually a '58 Esquire, and in fact I've still got it. My dad shot pool with a bunch of guys, and one of them owned a music store. I guess he must have cleaned him out; he didn't have any money left, but he said, 'I've got plenty of guitars to pay my debt.'" The instrument Volkaert Sr. took home to his twelve-year-old son that night in 1970 was a like-new Fender that had come in on trade to his debtor—but it wasn't a gift for young Redd. The boy would have to earn it. "He said, 'I've got this guitar that you're gonna' like, it's an Esquire, it looks like a Telecaster like Buck Owens and Merle Haggard use.' So I was like, 'Oh, cool, that's a cool sound.' And he said, 'Alright, I'll sell it to you. . . .' I had a couple of paper routes strapped together so I was making big bucks [boisterous laughter]. He gave me a deal where I could make payments on it, but I couldn't take it out of the house or show anybody or nothin', and I was mad as hell about that. He only let me play it twenty minutes on Sundays. But I got the guitar like that, and as soon as I started plunkin' on the thing I just fell over for it. From then on, I was a Tele hog big time."

Every inch the Texan both in speech and in attitude, Volkaert, who now calls Austin home, actually acquired his twang and drawl in rural Canada. Born in New Westminster, British Columbia, he left home at seventeen for Saskatoon, Saskatchewan, then various parts of Alberta before roving south to California, then Nashville, then Texas. Long before crossing the border, though, Volkaert was messing heavily with the guitar, and the music. Working on the latter, he forged his own breed of searing twang by melding his beloved country and the inevitable rock 'n' roll. On the former, he did what most kids did in the mid-'70s, and hacked some wood out of an otherwise pristine vintage instrument to wedge a fatter pickup into the neck position. "I ruined it early on," he confesses. "I wanted to be a rock god. . . . I took a screwdriver and a hammer, like a fourteen-year-old genius, and made a big old gaping hole under there." First in was a Gibson P-90, but after seeing Roy Nichols come through Edmonton playing with Merle Haggard, with a Charlie Christian pickup in the neck position of his own Telecaster, Volkaert ripped a Christian from an old lap steel and popped it into his Esquire, where it has remained ever since.

Aspiring rock god-dom gave way to the country music that was proving his true love, and in 1981 Volkaert joined traditional outfit the Prairie Fire Band, moving over to Danny Hopper and Country Spunk (featuring fiddle virtuoso Calvin Vollrath) a few years after that. Following the seemingly inevitable path south, Volkaert headed to California in 1986, where he landed some significant gigs but ultimately struggled to stay afloat financially, before drifting the way of all serious pickers to struggle even more, initially, in Nashville. Hard work and hot licks eventually paid the dues, though, and Volkaert landed a much-needed residency job with the Don Kelly Band at the Stage Coach Lounge, a gig that had proved a springboard for the likes of Sid Hudson, Brent Mason, Walter Garland, and other successful pickers. While the four-year run with Kelly would help to secure Vokaert's reputation, his own springboard to more significant success came in 1997, when a country music legend called to ask him to replace one of his own early heroes.

In his stint with Merle Haggard, Volkaert was often been praised as the most Ray Nichols–like of the Nichols replacements. And as such, he wowed audiences in parts faurther afield than he had ever traveled before. In 2000, tiring of the "bubble-gum" nature of Nashville's popular music scene, Volkaert—though still touring with Haggard—relocated to Austin, and has called it home ever since. "I always liked the live music scene in Austin," he relates. "The crowds in Austin seem to accept people for their musical ability more than their clothes or lack of, hair or lack of, hats or lack of. . . ." The Haggard gig aside, the intervening years have seen Volkaert take his solo career from strength to strength (with four solid releases since the move to Austin, after his 1998 solo debut *Telewacker*) while also landing him sit-ins with, perhaps, one of the longest lists of eminently droppable names in the business, including Al Cooper, Johnny Paycheck, Merle Travis, the Statler Brothers, Albert Lee, John Jorgenson, Marty Stewart, Eric Johnson, Billy Gibbons, Neko Case, Hank Williams III, Bobby Bare, Ray Price, Garth Hudson, and on, and on. In 2009 he also earned a Grammy Award for Best Country Instrumental Performance as one of the pickers on Brad Paisley's "Cluster Pluck."

Through the years, the hard road time and heavy twang have earned Volkaert the reputation of being a Tele player's Tele player, and he is still addicted to the instrument today. "There isn't a Fender on the planet that plays as good as a Gibson, I don't think," he opines, "but by the same token, to me, if it's too easy it's kind of harder for me to get something out of the guitar. Whereas if you're wrestling with something, you're going to milk and squeeze and twist and turn and bite your tongue and move your lip a certain way just to get it to work for you. When you do . . . it's kind of like puttin' your stamp on the sound a little bit more." ★

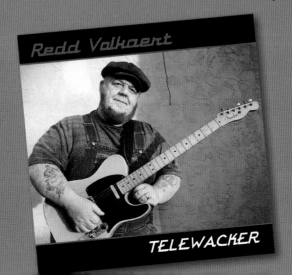

Redd Volkaert

TELEWACKER

SLIM, HANDSOME, immaculately tailored, and as flamboyant a showman as the music world has known, T-Bone Walker put the whole package together. Not only was he a consummate songwriter, bandleader, and all-round entertainer, but he served as a sort of midwife for electric blues in the process, forming a bridge from acoustic Delta blues to the electrified Chicago-based idiom that is most recognized as "blues" today. Born Aaron Thibeaux Walker to musician parents in Linden, Texas, in 1910, T-Bone—as he would come to be known—had a musical pedigree, and in his early teens he even worked for a time as an assistant to Blind Lemon Jefferson, leading the seminal bluesman from show to show around the streets of Dallas.

After turning professional, Walker was among the first notable players to go electric and even surrendered his post as guitarist in the Lawson Brooks Band to a young Charlie Christian upon departing for Los Angeles in 1934.

Although he played other Gibsons early on, Walker is best known for his use of a big, blonde Gibson ES-5N archtop electric, which he acquired around the time of its introduction to the market in 1949. The precursor to the ES-5 Switchmaster that replaced it in 1955, the original ES-5 had three P-90 pickups but no selector switch whatsoever, requiring the player to use the three individual volume controls to craft his desired tone (which could be tweaked with the single master tone control). Its successor, the Switchmaster, introduced the selector switch (by then old hat on other models) to improve the guitar's functionality. Nevertheless, the ES-5 had the distinction of being the first big-brand electric guitar with three pickups, and the excess clearly appealed to Walker. He made the guitar a major feature of his live show, holding it aloft, plucking the strings with his teeth, and playing it behind his head while doing the splits. Even in more somber moments his playing style was an odd one—he held the guitar in a horizontal manner that became his trademark.

While his playing was impressive for the day, Walker's intuitive use of the amplified instrument

Facing Page: Strollin' with the Bone: T-Bone Walker does the splits while playing his Gibson ES-5N behind his back. All in a day's work. *Michael Ochs Archives/Getty Images*

to craft his tone and performance was a big part of what got him noticed, and he was arguably the first player to understand the electric guitar as an entirely new instrument rather than just as a loud extension of the acoustic guitar. As such, Walker most clearly expressed what an amplified guitar was all about in the first place: getting the guitarist out of the rhythm section and up into the spotlight, playing single-note solo lines right alongside the featured horn players. This he achieved, and then some, and his six-string descendants have never looked back. ★

T-BONE JUMPS AGAIN
(Walker)

BLACK & WHITE

INSTRUMENTAL
T-BONE WALKER
and HIS GUITAR
LLOYD C. GLENN, Piano
HUBERT M. MYERS, Tenor Sax
ARTHUR W. EDWARDS, Bass
JOHN E. BUCKNER, Trumpet
OSCAR LEE BRADLEY, Drums

125 B
(BW 636)

DIG THE WORK OF ANY TRULY GREAT PLAYER through the course of their career and you soon learn that they have the ability to stamp their tonal signature on their performances no matter what gear they use. Blues great Muddy Waters was no exception. From guitar, to vocals, to songwriting, he embodied a sound that was all his own and which has become associated with a timeless breed of electric blues.

Early in his career, Waters played a range of acoustic and semi-acoustic electric guitars, including models by Gretsch, Stella, and Harmony. He was famously photographed in the early 1950s with a Gibson Les Paul goldtop with P-90 pickups, and he was filmed playing a blonde maple-neck Fender Telecaster at the Newport Jazz Festival in 1960. He is far and away most associated, however, with the red Telecaster that became his mainstay from the late 1950s until his death in 1983, a guitar that was distinguished by its black plastic Fender amp knobs but was otherwise largely stock.

Muddy Waters slides on his red, road-worn Fender Telecaster during a gig in 1970. *Jan Persson/Redferns/Getty Images*

QUEEN CITY RAINBOW
TUESDAY, MAY 1st

9:00 P.M.   Admission: Advance, $1.75

"THAT HOOTCHIE COOTCHIE MAN"

MUDDY
WATERS
AND HIS
ORCHEST

Famous for "I'm Ready" and "

CHESS
RECORD CORP

ARC MUSIC
8393
GOT MY MOJO WORKING
(M. Morganfield)
MUDDY WATERS
1652

Muddy Waters' custom-color
Fender Telecaster from his final tour.
Collection Steven Seagal/Photograph
Rick Gould

Generally thought of today as more of a country or bare-bones rock 'n' roll instrument, the basic, slab-bodied Tele isn't associated with the blues as much as its sibling the Fender Stratocaster, or Gibson's ES-335 and Les Paul, but in the hands of Muddy Waters this simple, two-pickup, bolt-neck guitar, with its alder body finished in candy apple red and its maple neck with a slab rosewood fingerboard, epitomized the raw, wiry, and emotive voice of this artist's instrumental side. The real magic in the Tele sound occurs at the bridge pickup, where a fat but bright-sounding single-coil pickup is suspended in a thin, stamped-steel bridge plate to which three two-string saddles are mounted. This entire bridge assembly becomes a resonating, honking, microphonic tone machine—for better or worse—which gives the Tele a blend of sizzle and twang, and the kind of strident yet beefy highs that really can't be achieved by any other electric guitar. This is the definitive country lead guitar sound, but played aggressively with the raw, unique style of a master such as Muddy Waters, it also yields an unforgettable blues tone, which, from the mid-'60s onward, he preferred to broadcast to the world through a Fender Super Reverb amplifier.

As with any great artist, there's far more to Waters's tone than just the guitar-and-amp combination. Waters had an unusual playing style that has become a benchmark for a particular genre of electric blues. He picked the bass notes on the lower three strings with a thumb pick, while strumming upwards with bare fingers on the three treble strings for his melody and lead lines, which he frequently executed with a small steel pinky slide. Waters strung his Tele with heavy .012–.056 gauge strings, but he often played in open-G tuning, taking a little tension off the strings, and frequently used a capo too. To hear the best of Muddy Waters's fluid yet frenetic electric style, seek out live recordings of his great tunes such as "Mannish Boy," "Rollin' and Tumblin'," "Hoochie Coochie Man," and "Rock Me." ◆

Walsh cradles his 1960-issue Les Paul Standard at an Eagles show in Rotterdam, The Netherlands, May 1977. *Rob Verhorst/Redferns/Getty Images*

WITH SO MANY EARLY PROPONENTS of the Les Paul being either blues-rockers, Brit-rockers, or both, Joe Walsh stands out as a good-old stateside rock 'n' roller of the late '60s who went on to great heights of fame on the instrument. He played a lot of slide, sure, and his hot, vocal tone might have had plenty in common with that of the blues-influence LP gods of the day, but his style and attitude were more good-time party-rock right from that start, and that stance has continued

to hold him apart from the crowd throughout an impressive career.

Walsh also seems time and again to pop up as one of rock's great "tone enablers." Whether it was delivering Jimmy Page's "Number One" Les Paul to the Zep guitarist in San Francisco in 1969, or presenting Pete Townshend with the gift of a Gretsch 6120 and tweed Fender Bandmaster amplifier in 1970 (a rig that recorded some of The Who's most seminal tones on *Who's Next* and *Quadrophenia*, even if they were replaced by other ingredients onstage), Walsh seems always not only to have cared deeply about his own tone, but also to have been extremely generous in considering the tone of others.

After attending Kent State University in Ohio in the mid-'60s, Walsh settled in nearby Cleveland, where he played in a number of popular local bands before being tapped to join the James Gang as a replacement for guitarist Glen Schwartz. Walsh's thick, driving, and occasionally squawky tone became a signature of the band, and was something he carried over to his work with the band Barnstorm in 1972. This move signaled the start of an on-again, off-again solo career, with the release in 1973 of *The Smoker You Drink, the Player You Get* (technically the second Barnstorm album, but billed as a Joe Walsh record). A single from that set, "Rocky Mountain Way," was marked by his creative use of a talk-box and brought him his first significant commercial success.

Following another well-received but not massive-selling (and this time official) solo outing in 1974's *So What*, Walsh ascended to the stratosphere of commercial-rock success as replacement for Bearnie Leadon in the Eagles. In addition to tracking—behind Don Felder's original part—the harmony to the twin-guitar solo in the massive hit "Hotel California," Walsh co-wrote "Life in the Fast Lane" with Don Henley and Glenn Frey, and is generally credited with bringing a harder-edged rock sound to the Eagles' erstwhile laid-back California country-rock. His favored Les Paul throughout these years, and the one he *didn't* sell to Jimmy Page, was a slim-necked '60 'burst, reproduced by Gibson Custom as the Joe Walsh Les Paul Standard. ★

The Joe Walsh 1960 Les Paul model. *Gibson Musical Instruments*

FEW ALTERNATIVE-ROCK GUITARISTS since
Kurt Cobain have blown as much life into nasty,
minimalistic rock guitar tones almost overnight
as Jack White of the White Stripes. And none,
we can safely say, has *ever* done so with such an
assemblage of oddball gear. At the center of it all was
White's red 1964 Res-O-Glas model electric guitar
from cataloger Montgomery Ward's Airline range
of guitars and amplifiers. Long considered a C-list
vintage guitar, and available for pretty easy money
should you have stumbled upon one at a pawnshop or
backstreet guitar store, the fiberglass Airline became
exponentially more desireable with White's use,
while smashing all preconceptions
of what this unusual contraption
might sound like.

For a little taste, take a listen to
the White Stripes' "Fell in Love
with a Girl," "Seven Nation Army,"
or "Icky Thump," for example,
and you'll quickly get the idea.
Of course, recording artists will
grab whatever's on hand, guitar
or otherwise, to help a track
stand out, and White has played
a number of other guitars both
live and in the studio, but the red
Airline was his clear favorite with
the stripes and is purported to
have been used on a broad swath

of the band's second studio album, *De Stijl* (2000). On
the other hand, ram anything through White's array of
overdrive and fuzz pedals (an Electro-Harmonix Big
Muff among them) and into an old 100-watt Silvertone
with 6×10-inch speaker cab, a Fender Twin, or a
vintage Selmer tube amp (all on "10" naturally), and
it's likely to come out sounding pretty mean.

The Airline Res-O-Glas, also famously used by
Chicago bluesman J. B. Hutto in the 1950s and '60s,
has become perhaps more beloved for its retro-modern
looks than for its sound. The guitars were made in
Chicago by Valco from around 1962 until shortly
before the company's demise in 1967. Valco supplied
guitars and amplifiers to a range
of major department stores and
catalog companies in addition
to Montgomery Ward, and it
produced similarly equipped
but differently shaped hollow
fiberglass models—marketed
both as Res-O-Glas and "Hollow-
Glas"—that were sold under the
National and Supro brand names.
Outwardly, its pickups might
appear to be humbuckers in the
style of the Gibson PAF, but they
are in fact single-coil units and
are known for their bold, brash,
lively tone. Whatever the thing
sounds like, it sure looks radical
in the process. ★

Chicago bluesman J. B. Hutto plays
an Airline at the 1969 Ann Arbor
Blues Festival in Michigan. *Courtesy
Bob Frank (www.bluelunch.com)*

Facing page: White with his White Stripes
accomplice, Meg White, and the Airline
Res-O-Glas, 2003. © *Simon Clemenger/
Camera Press/Retna Ltd.*

THE WHITE STRIPES   07.25.07   WITH DAN SARTAIN

appearing at the Chevrolet Theatre in Wallingford, Connecticut

Artist: Rob Jones (www.animalrummy.com)

THE WHITE STRIPES

THE BIG
THREE
KILLED
MY BABY

Concert
JOHNNY WINTER
COLUMBIA RECORDS

S P O R T S   A R E N A
310 Chester Ave., S. E. — ATLANTA, GA.

SUNDAY, APRIL 12, 1970

4:00 P. M.

N⁰ 21432

Admission $3.00

General Admission Only

AMBOO PRODUCTIONS Presents
JOHNNY WINTER

DAYTON HARA ARENA & EXH. CENTER
DAYTON, OHIO

FRIDAY EVENING AT 8:00 P.M.

GENERAL ADMISSION

ADVANCE $6.00

Prem.-Sc. Tkt. Co. Cin., O. NO REFUNDS-NO EXCHANGES

N⁰ 3607

WHILE PLENTY OF ARTISTS bend their guitars to performances that work against type, Johnny Winter's sound has always epitomized exactly what Gibson was seeking from his instrument of choice. Bright, sharp, metallic, and eviscerating, the tone from Winter's 1963 Firebird V exemplifies a Gibson doing Fender-flavored tricks and working up a Texas dust storm worth of momentum in the process.

The Firebird was one of the most radical guitars the world had ever seen when it hit the market in 1963, and that was a very conscious move on Gibson's part. Chasing a hip new look that would help it rival Fender's sleek offerings in the competitive solid-body scene of the early '60s, Gibson went right to the source of marketing style and hired automotive designer Ray Dietrich—who had done design work for Duesenberg, among others—to take the standard vision of the instrument back to the drawing board. The result was a guitar clearly ahead of its time. The new Firebird had a body that appeared to be the reverse image of Fender's newfangled Jazzmaster and Jaguar, an upside-down six-in-line headstock with "banjo" tuners to avoid spoiling the lines of the phoenix-head profile, and a solid integral neck/body section (known as a "through neck") with glued-on wings, a rarity in guitar manufacture at that time.

Beyond merely seeking a different look, Gibson wanted a different *sound* too. Known for its thick, gritty P-90 and fat, warm humbucker, the company found itself losing ground to Fender in an age when bright, cutting tones ruled the rock 'n' roll stages. Gibson's own quest for twang and jangle came via an entirely new pickup design that looked something like the mini-humbuckers Gibson had inherited from Epiphone, but it was actually made entirely differently underneath the cover. Rather than using steel pole pieces in two narrow coils with a magnet mounted underneath, the Firebird humbucker used coils that were wound directly around each of two alnico bar magnets, a process that gave it a bright, cutting sound. Check out any of Winter's best work on the '63 Firebird, and you can hear the sharply defined snap and sizzle that this pickup produces, with outstanding clarity and a slightly glassy, metallic edge, even through a raging stack of cranked amps. Few other guitars can spit out that gnarly, slinky, electric Texas slide blues like a Firebird with mini-humbuckers—and few artists can play it quite like Mr. Winter. ★

Winter's 1963 Firebird V.
Rick Gould

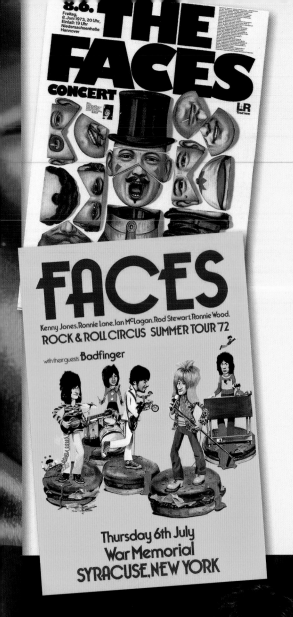

FACES
Kenny Jones, Ronnie Lane, Ian McLagan, Rod Stewart, Ronnie Wood.
ROCK & ROLL CIRCUS SUMMER TOUR '72
with their guests Badfinger

Thursday 6th July
War Memorial
SYRACUSE, NEW YORK

SO OFTEN REFERRED TO AS "that Les Paul with the metal top on it," the unique instrument that Ronnie Wood played first with the Faces and later with the Rolling Stones is one of the earliest solid-body electric guitars made by A. C. "Tony" Zemaitis and a piece of rock history. Born in England to Lithuanian parents, Zemaitis first got serious about guitar-making in the 1960s, when he crafted a handful of finely wrought acoustics, one of which ended up in the hands of Jimi Hendrix. He got the idea for covering the front of an electric guitar with metal sheeting from the metal shield that was mounted under the pickguard of '60s Fender Stratocasters to cut down on electrical interference, and he made his first metal-fronted electric for Tony McPhee of the English band the Groundhougs in 1971. Wood's metal-fronted Zemaitis is purported to be either the second or the third such solid-body produced by the luthier, also in 1971 (some accounts put Marc Bolan's guitar before it, some after).

Wood's first Zemaitis, engraved, like many others, by shotgun engraver Danny O'Brien, gained national attention in the UK when he played it with the Faces on the popular TV music show *Top of the Pops* soon after receiving it, alongside bandmate Ronnie Lane's Zemaitis bass. Soon musicians all over the country were clamoring for Zemaitis's creations, but due to the custom nature of the instruments and their high price tags, relatively few made it

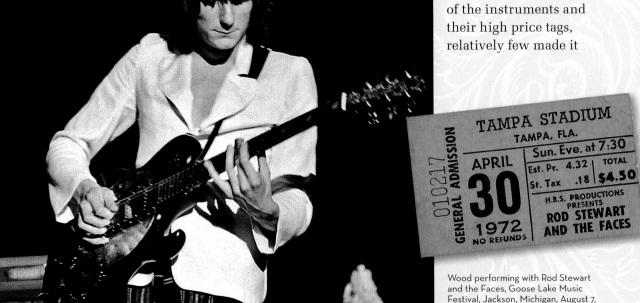

Wood performing with Rod Stewart and the Faces, Goose Lake Music Festival, Jackson, Michigan, August 7, 1970. © *Robert Matheu*

into circulation. Most estimates indicate Zemaitis only built six to ten guitars per year, and all remain highly sought-after collector's items.

Wood commissioned a second Zemaitis in 1972, a black-bodied guitar with a round metal plate and three pickups that he refers to as his "Stay with Me" guitar, after its use on the Faces' song of the same name, and which he has continued to use for open-tuning slide work with the Stones. After this, he ordered two more, which have mainly been used as backups. Wood no longer takes his first Zemaitis on the road with the Stones, and he is more likely to be seen playing either a 1954 or 1955 Fender Stratocaster, which he uses for the majority of standard-tuning guitars.

More than just Les Paul–styled guitars with metal tops, Zemaitis electrics were original creations from the ground up. In addition to crafting each body and neck individually and joining them with a longer tenon than those used in most set-neck guitars, Zemaitis machined his own bridges, tailpieces, and pickup rings, and he gave many guitars individual headstock designs and unique fingerboard inlays. Several guitars were also given mother-of-pearl mosaic tops in place of metal tops. In addition to the guitars made for Wood, Bolan, Lane, and McPhee, Zemaitis also made electric and acoustic guitars for Keith Richards, Eric Clapton, Bob Dylan, David Gilmour, Paul McCartney, George Harrison, Donovan, Greg Lake, Bobby Womack, Francis Rossi, and James Honeyman Scott. Several other notable artists have acquired them on the vintage market in later years.

Tony Zemaitis retired in 2000 and died in 2002. Ron Wood's Zemaitises, however, and several others, keep on rockin'. ★

Wood and the Rolling Stones performing in Germany, June 1995.
© Bernhard Kuhmstedt/Retna Ltd.

IN ADDITION TO BEING one of the most straight-talkin' figures in rock 'n' roll—and one whose musical palette makes it impossible to pigeonhole him—Black Label Society frontman and longtime Ozzy Osbourne guitarist Zakk Wylde is also owner of perhaps the most instantly recognizable Les Paul in the world. And it all came about quite by accident.

Wylde, of course, is the infamous guitar-slinger behind "the Grail," that famous Alpine White Custom sprayed with black concentric circles. And like any star guitar worth its salt, this '81 model comes with a story that nearly rivals all the great music that's been played on it. Wylde, the story goes, received the Les Paul as a high school graduation present. Shortly afterward, he was hired by Ozzy Osbourne to replace Jake E. Lee, who had himself replaced Wylde's idol, the late Randy Rhoads, five years earlier. Hoping to differentiate his guitar from Rhoads's own crème-colored Custom (see pages 262–263), Wylde was inspired by a cable TV commercial for the Alfred Hitchcock film

Vertigo to bring his Les Paul to a friend in L.A. and have the movie poster's iconic Spirograph-like rings painted on it. When he returned to retrieve the guitar, however, he was somewhat bummed to find his prized "fiddle" painted with the now-famous bull's-eye design.

Fast-forward a few years when Wylde was on tour in Texas and a roadie forgot to latch the gear trailer. As the guitarist later told *Vintage Guitar* editor Ward Meeker in 2005, "God forbid we would've f***in' killed anybody—we've got SVT cabinets in the back of that thing. . . . Then [the tour manager] told me that a couple of the guitars fell out. . ."

One of those guitars was—you guessed it—the Grail. But in one of those rare twists of a guitar being reunited with its owner (e.g., Joe Perry, pages 242–243), a fan stumbled upon a bull's-eye bedecked Les Paul in a Texas pawnshop. Assuming it was a reissue, he plopped down $250, brought it home, began to puzzle over the authentic "relic'ing," and pulled out a pickup to find Wylde's initials etched on it. He contacted Wylde's website, and player and guitar were soon reunited.

Wylde, incidentally, has had several guitars painted with the bull's-eye theme. And in 2012, Gibson issued the Wylde signature *Vertigo* model, which more closely cops the Master of Suspense's famous film poster. ♦
—*Dennis Pernu*

PLENTY OF GUITARISTS have sounded filthier, and certainly others have sounded hotter, but you'd be hard pressed to find many who have sounded as out-and-out huge as AC/DC's Young brothers, Angus and Malcolm. The Aussie duo offered the one-two punch that defined rock rhythm and lead guitar playing for nearly forty years, while also establishing two of the most admired tones in the business.

Think "heavy rock," and most of us imagine a dirty, high-gain guitar tone with a scooped EQ curve that runs from heavy crunch to sizzling, saturated overdrive. Revisit any of AC/DC's standout recordings, however, and as often as not you hear size, punch, and presence far more than sheer distortion. In rock terms, their rhythm tone is right on the edge of being clean—while ramping up into searing, eviscerating overdrive for leads, of course—but it carries bone-crushing weight and makes a huge impact on the listener. As Angus told Jas Obrecht in *Guitar Player* in 1984, "Most people hear distortion and they think it's loud. We keep it as clean as possible. The cleaner you do it, the louder it will sound when they do the cutting of [the record]." The gruesome twosome famously achieved their dual assault on a pair of guitars to which they remained faithful throughout their careers: for Angus, a Gibson SG Standard; for Malcolm, a Gretsch Jet Firebird.

Facing page: Cleveland Municipal Stadium, Cleveland, Ohio, July 28, 1979. © *Robert Alford*

Roseland Ballroom, New York City, March 11, 2003.
George De Sota/Getty Images

1963 GRETSCH JET FIREBIRD   MALCOLM YOUNG

Angus's number-one SG is a 1968 model that he acquired secondhand in 1970 after, legend has it, falling in love with its double-horned image in a friend's catalog. It has remained his go-to guitar from the time of the band's formation in 1973 until the present day, although it has occasionally been laid up for live use and/or repair, given its value and age. The AC/DC lead man has often declared his love of this particular SG's ultra-thin neck, found to be slimmer than other SGs from the era when examined by the Gibson factory in the late '70s or early '80s. His guitar's neck also has a 1⅝-inch width at the nut, a narrower width adopted by Gibson for a few years in the late '60s, which better suits Angus's small hands and short reach. His 1968 was originally equipped with the Maestro "lyre" vibrato tailpiece that many SGs featured in the '60s, but Angus removed this and replaced it with a standard stop-bar stud tailpiece to accompany the Tune-O-Matic bridge. Other than this, his favorite guitar was and remains largely original, down to its original Gibson "T-top" humbucking pickups.

© Rock 'N' Roll Comics No. 22, Revolutionary Comics, 1990. Courtesy Jay Allen Sanford

1968 GIBSON SG STANDARD AND 1963 GRETSCH JET FIREBIRD

ANGUS & MALCOLM YOUNG

Malcolm and his Gretsch before it was stripped of its red paint (and a couple of pickups), Albert Studios, Sydney, 1976. © Philip Morris

Older brother Malcolm's Gretsch was a double-cutaway 1963 Gretsch Jet Firebird given to him by Harry Vanda, one of his brother George's bandmates in the Easybeats, a popular Australian rock 'n' roll band of the '60s. In addition to a red finish, the guitar would have left the factory with a Burns vibrato tailpiece, a floating bridge, and two Filter'Tron humbucking pickups, but over the years Young modified the guitar to suit his austere tastes. At first Malcolm "upgraded" the Jet Firebird with the addition of a Gibson humbucking pickup in the middle position, hence its appearance as a three-pickup guitar (the Jet Firebird was only ever made with two pickups), but by the mid-'70s he had removed this and the Filter'Tron in the neck position, giving his Gretsch the single-pickup status that it maintained ever since. The now-irrelevant switches and controls came out too, and he replaced the vibrato with a stationary Badass wraparound bridge, and, finally, stripped the red finish. Malcolm reinstated the Burns vibrato around 2000. Sadly, he retired in 2014 due to the onset of dementia. Between them, they are two very different guitars. But blend the Gretsch's clean and the Gibson's mean, and the Young brothers pack a punch as big as the Outback. ✪

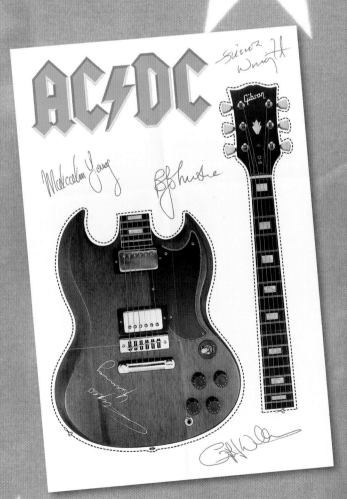

A make-your-own-SG poster included in vinyl copies of *Who Made Who*, 1986.

Facing page: Is it warm in here? Angus's '68 SG appeared without its tailpiece and vibrato for AC/DC's legendary US club gig at the Whisky A Go Go, Los Angeles, August 29, 1977. © Jenny Lens/Cache Agency

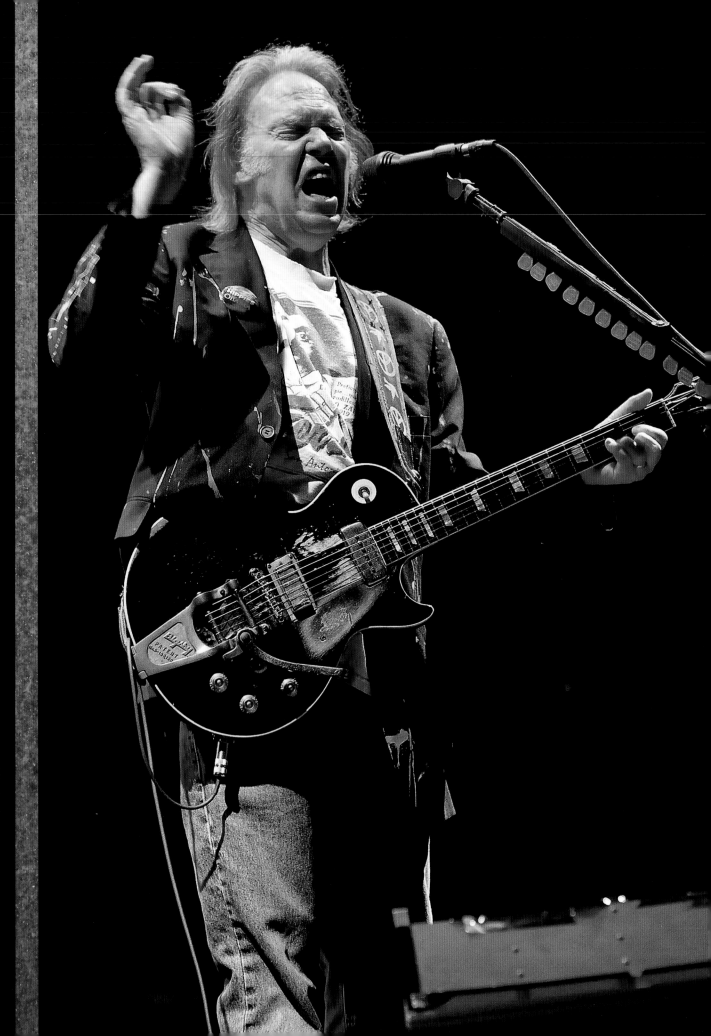

NEIL YOUNG

1953 GIBSON LES PAUL "OLD BLACK"

A MUSIC FAN IN 1968 WOULD HAVE found Neil Young an odd candidate to be credited as a founder of the heavy-rock movement. Up to this point, his work with Buffalo Springfield and his self-titled solo debut (1968) all worked toward crafting his image as a country-rock originator and a moving force in the burgeoning singer/songwriter scene. With the release of his second solo album, *Everybody Knows This Is Nowhere* (1969), extended electric guitar workouts in songs like "Cinnamon Girl," "Down by the River," and "Cowgirl in the Sand" hinted at a more unhinged musical fury. Young's stinging, slightly venomous musical persona—both sonic and thematic—continued to boil to the surface, first with a few tracks on the mostly folk- and country-informed *After the Gold Rush* (1970) and *Harvest* (1972), and more so on later releases like *Zuma* (1975), *Rust Never Sleeps* (1979), and *Ragged Glory* (1990). Though Young has long been associated with acoustic-flavored country-rock, this is an artist who likes to *rock*—and when he does, he more often than not does so on a modified 1953 Gibson Les Paul known as "Old Black," one of the quirkiest and most colorful star guitars out there.

Young acquired Old Black from former Buffalo Springfield bandmate Jim Messina in 1969 (some accounts credit the former owner as Stephen Stills), by which time the Les Paul had already been thoroughly modified. Born with a classic early-1950s Gibson "goldtop" finish, it had been painted black by a previous owner. The original "wraparound" combined bridge and tailpiece had also been replaced by a Bigsby B7 vibrato/Gibson Tune-O-Matic bridge combination. Apparently the guitar's original neck or headstock were replaced as well sometime in the '60s, as evidenced by the SG/ES-335-style "crown" inlay found where the "Les Paul Model" logo would normally be seen. Other cosmetic alterations include pinstriping tape added to the back of the neck and body and the aluminum pickguard that has replaced the original cream-colored plastic guard. More pertinent to its signature tone, however, is the addition of a Gibson Firebird mini-humbucking pickup in the bridge position, while the neck pickup is still the original P-90, though this has been updated with a metal cover over the years. An exceedingly lively pickup, this Firebird 'bucker, which Young's longtime guitar tech Larry Cragg describes as microphonic, plays a big part in Young's characteristic feedback-laden soloing assault. An additional toggle switch acts as a bypass, sending the Firebird pickup directly to Young's amplifier.

Facing page: Madison Square Garden, December 15, 2008.
Joe Kohen/WireImage/Getty Images

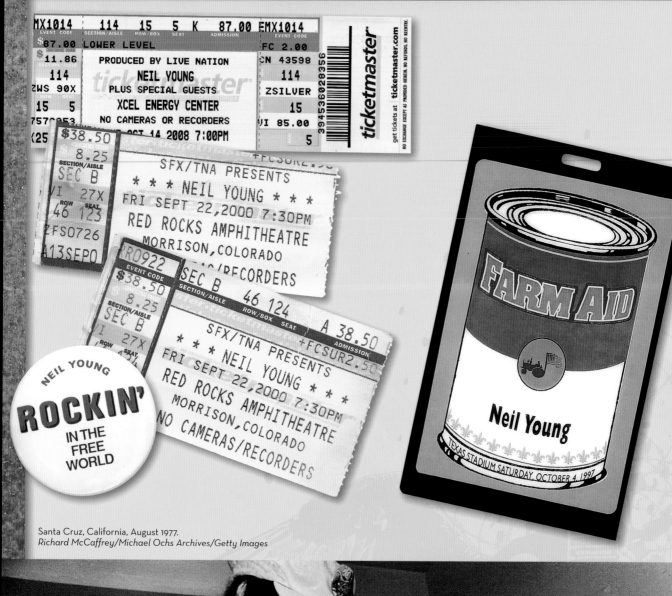

MX1014   114   15   5 K   87.00 EMX1014
EVENT CODE SECTION/AISLE ROW/BOX SEAT ADMISSION EVENT CODE
$87.00 LOWER LEVEL   FC 2.00
$ 11.86
SECTION/AISLE   CN 43598
114   PRODUCED BY LIVE NATION   114
          NEIL YOUNG
ZWS 90X   PLUS SPECIAL GUESTS   ZSILVER
15   5   XCEL ENERGY CENTER   15   5
757C053   NO CAMERAS OR RECORDERS   UI 85.00
(25   OCT 14 2008 7:00PM   5

ticketmaster
get tickets at ticketmaster.com
NO EXCHANGE EXCEPT AS PROVIDED HEREIN. NO REFUND. NO REENTRY.
3945636028356

$38.50
$ 8.25
SECTION/AISLE
SEC B
VI   27X
ROW   SEAT
46   123
ZFS0726
A13SEP0

SFX/TNA PRESENTS
* * * NEIL YOUNG * * *
FRI SEPT 22,2000 7:30PM
RED ROCKS AMPHITHEATRE
MORRISON,COLORADO
.../RECORDERS
SEC B
SECTION/AISLE
46   124
ROW/BOX   SEAT
A 38.50
ADMISSION
+FCSUR2.50

EVENT CODE
$38.50
$ 8.25
SECTION/AISLE
SEC B
VI   27X
ROW   SEAT
PR0922

SFX/TNA PRESENTS
* * * NEIL YOUNG * * *
FRI SEPT 22,2000 7:30PM
RED ROCKS AMPHITHEATRE
MORRISON,COLORADO
NO CAMERAS/RECORDERS

NEIL YOUNG
ROCKIN'
IN THE
FREE
WORLD

FARM AID
Neil Young
TEXAS STADIUM SATURDAY, OCTOBER 4, 1997

Santa Cruz, California, August 1977.
Richard McCaffrey/Michael Ochs Archives/Getty Images

"OLD BLACK"

Of course some of the credit for Young's distinct sound is owed to that amplifier: a modified 1959 tweed Fender Deluxe that has long been Young's number-one amp. Young's legendary, super-saturated overdrive sound is derived from Old Black injected straight into the Deluxe—other pedals are used for different effects, but none for added gain or distortion. Unprecedented control over the simple Deluxe's three-knob control panel is afforded by a gizmo named "The Whizzer," an automated unit built by Young's late amp tech Sal Trentino in the late 1970s. The Whizzer can rotate volume and tone controls to four preset configurations with the stomp of a footswitch, to elicit subtle—and sometimes radical—changes in the amp's performance. Add it up, and it's a fierce assault enabled by relatively basic (and ancient) gear. And, as witnessed on albums and performances from 1969 to present, the rig proves more than enough to earn Young his "Godfather of Grunge" tag. ★

Young with Crazy Horse, Los Angeles, April 26, 1991. © Robert Matheu

349

INDEX